# Principles of Operations Management

## Mike Harrison

Head of Division of Operations and Information Management,
Business School Staffordshire University

**FINANCIAL TIMES**
PITMAN PUBLISHING

**FINANCIAL TIMES**
# MANAGEMENT

LONDON · SAN FRANCISCO
KUALA LUMPUR · JOHANNESBURG

*Financial Times Management delivers the knowledge,
skills and understanding that enable students,
managers and organisations to achieve their ambitions,
whatever their needs, wherever they are.*

London Office:
128 Long Acre, London WC2E 9AN
Tel: +44 (0)171 447 2000
Fax: +44 (0)171 240 5771
Website: www.ftmanagement.com

*A Division of Financial Times Professional Limited*

———————————

First published in Great Britain in 1996

© Mike Harrison 1996

The right of Mike Harrison to be identified as Author
of this work has been asserted by him in accordance
with the Copyright, Designs and Patents Act 1988.

ISBN 0 273 61450 9

*British Library Cataloguing in Publication Data*
A CIP catalogue record for this book can be obtained from the British Library

10 9 8 7 6 5 4 3

Typeset by Pantek Arts, Maidstone, Kent
Printed and bound in Great Britain by Clays Ltd, St. Ives plc

*The Publishers' policy is to use paper manufactured from sustainable forests.*

# CONTENTS

# INTRODUCTION

This book introduces the key ideas in Operations Management. It provides a first step in the study of Operations Management for students following courses in Business and Management. It is also relevant to non-business specialists who require an introduction to the principles and language underlying this most practical area of organisational work.

This book is suitable for undergraduates from the first level onwards provided that it is used over two semesters (around 24 weeks). For more advanced undergraduate and post-graduate students it may be used for a one-semester module (12 weeks), provided that other modules in management (for example, management accounting, organisational behaviour and marketing) have been studied in previous semesters or are followed in parallel with operations.

Students using this text do not require previous practical experience of operations or any other facet of management. The examples and exercises included here have been chosen because they are relevant to everyday experiences (particularly in service operations) or because they are easy to visualise. Students with practical management experience should, however, have no difficulty in relating the text to their work and they may find that they can use the text independently of other management courses.

A brief description of chapter contents and their possible relationships with taught modules are given in Table 1 (see p. vii). The general reader may, however, simply wish to read the text through in the order presented.

## OBJECTIVES

The objectives of the book are to:

- introduce the subject of Operations Management and to show how an understanding of its principles are of value to any manager
- show why operations and its effective management are important to all organisations
- relate operations to other management disciplines and functions
- introduce the language and concepts of Operations Management, providing a guide to how the concepts are inter-related
- provide a balanced treatment of manufacturing and service operations and show their relationship with office operations
- give examples of the application of operational concepts to typical management situations
- show a number of standard techniques and approaches, and explain how and why such techniques were developed
- encourage innovative approaches to operations problems through an understanding of basic principles.

## STRUCTURE OF THE BOOK

The book consists of 12 chapters which are summarised below:

**Chapter 1** provides an introduction to the language of operations, some examples of operational situations and a discussion of the key issue of process choice in manufacturing, service and office situations. It also includes a simple profit model in order to show how operational decisions relate directly to financial performance. This chapter is quite long but is a pre-requisite for most of the later work. It may therefore, require two weeks' study (assuming a 12-week module) and the compression of later chapters.

**Chapter 2** provides a broad introduction to the central issue of quality management, a subject which may itself constitute a full module in the later stages of a management course.

**Chapter 3** begins with a fundamental examination of the idea of a control system. Though apparently more theoretical than much of the factual and practical detail in this book, this material should not be ignored as it provides a language for describing and analysing many management problems, especially in quality control. This chapter continues with a description of some standard ways to improve operational processes. Chapters 2 and 3 may be seen as complementary and should be studied together even if the text as a whole is not being used in sequence.

**Chapter 4** is concerned with the central role of human resource management in operations. It is, however, only indicative of key issues rather than comprehensive in its treatment of this area of work as it is assumed that the reader will also undertake at least one full module on human issues in management. This chapter is therefore intended to provide links rather than a complete discussion. Some details of Japanese management practices are included, reflecting the influence of the Japanese on manufacturing operations.

**Chapter 5** introduces some of the ideas in the use of technology in operations, with an obvious central place for information technology. It includes some comments on the financial appraisal of technology, an area which can cause problems due to the scale of expenditure and the risks involved. This chapter also includes some notes on the maintenance of technological systems.

Chapters 4 and 5 are similar in that they describe areas of professional concern to other managers, specifically personnel, engineering and information systems staff. The material presented therefore is mainly descriptive and may be included at any stage of the module. The principle concern is that it should be related to operational decisions and re-considered when examining issues raised in other chapters. For example, how do technology and human resource management affect (and are affected by) the implementation of Just-in-Time flow control as described in Chapter 11.

**Chapters 6 and 7** are concerned with the management of projects and should be studied in sequence. Chapter 6 concentrates on the principles of project management, including organisational issues whilst Chapter 7 is more concerned with the techniques of project management. Thus, Chapter 7 is the first occasion in the book where a chapter is mainly devoted to quantitative methods applied to the solution of operational problems. Chapters 8 to 10 also have substantial quantitative content.

**Chapters 8 to 11** are all concerned with matching supply and demand over a variety of timescales. Chapter 8 sets out general principles and deals with forecasting and with capacity and aggregate planning in a manufacturing context. Chapter 9 deals with inventory decision making and is relatively self-contained. Chapter 10 is concerned with the tactics of managing capacity and flows in service operations and includes a number of approaches to the management of queues of customers. Chapter 11 is devoted to manufacturing situations and the contrast between Just-in-Time management and centralised computer based approaches.

Finally, **Chapter 12** introduces a number of issues in operations strategy and in the newer area of environmental operations. This provides a link with further study, for instance in the final stages of undergraduate degrees or MBAs which traditionally take a more strategic and holistic view of organisations.

**Table 1**

| Chapter | Plan A | Plan B | | Plan C |
| --- | --- | --- | --- | --- |
| | | Module 1 | Module 2 | Minimum pre-requisites |
| 1 | ** | * | | None |
| 2 | ** | * | | Chapter 1 |
| 3 | ** | * | | Chapter 2 |
| 4 | * | * | | None |
| 5 | * | * | | Chapter 1 |
| 6 | ** | | * | Chapter 1 |
| 7 | * | | * | Chapter 6 |
| 8 | ** | | * | Chapter 1 |
| 9 | * | | * | None |
| 10 | ** | | * | Chapter 8 |
| 11 | ** | | * | Chapter 8 |
| 12 | * | | * | Chapter 1 |

In Table 1 we show alternative ways in which the chapters of the book may be linked with lecture plans, assuming a 12-week semester (that is, around 24 hours tutor contact time or 80 hours study time in total). In Plan A, typical of a post-graduate or post-experience course, we assume that all the material will be delivered in one module. The double-starred chapters form the essential core of lecture and tutorial sessions with the possibility of single-starred chapters being read as background by the student.

Plan B relates to a two module delivery pattern (24 weeks) with every chapter receiving lecture and tutorial attention. This would be typical of a first level undergraduate course or a slower paced post-experience group. The possibility of a 'pick and mix' approach is addressed in Plan C which shows the minimum essential prerequisites for each Chapter. Thus Chapter 4 may be read in isolation but Chapter 5 requires at least a quick prior reading of Chapter 1 (in this case to relate process choice and the level of fixed cost investment to technological decision making).

## Chapter structure

Each chapter begins with a brief introduction describing its contents, approach and links to other chapters. At the end of each chapter is a 'Further reading' section which points to sources of further information. In order to maintain a continuous flow, the main text includes few references and therefore the Further reading material provides some essential link with the large body of literature on Operations Management.

All the cases given in this text are case exercises derived from a general knowledge of a range of operational circumstances. They are tailored to illustrate specific points relative to the main text. As knowledge and confidence in using operational concepts and techniques grows, there is much to be gained from the study of real cases relating to identifiable organisations. References to such cases are contained in the further reading and lecturing staff will no doubt be able to extend the range of examples of operational problem situations.

Most chapters contain a number of 'Tasks'. These are an essential part of the development of operational themes and should be attempted at the relevant point, either individually or working in small groups. Similarly, the quantitative examples illustrate specific points in Operations Management and should be worked through in detail. Further quantitative examples can be found in full texts on Operations Management and in specialist texts on quantitative methods.

A short glossary at the end of the book provides a quick reference survival kit to the terminology used in the book. One of the challenges of studying any new subject is becoming familiar and confident with the language specific to that subject. The reader is strongly encouraged to use the language of Operations Management in describing work based on everyday operational situations. As your confidence grows, you should also be willing to challenge the fashions and jargon typical of all management writing. For example, it is a considerable achievement to be able to state clearly what JIT actually is, where it can be properly applied and what its limitations are in a given situation!

## THEMES AND LINKS

Like all areas of management, operations is subject to fashions and miracle cures. For some peculiar reason these are often given three letter acronyms and the reader may like to explore the book for examples, in addition to TQM, JIT, MRP, SPC, BPR, CIM! You should not imagine, however, that such approaches are worthless. The ones listed above have been extensively researched and shown to be of considerable value if appropriately applied. As so often in practical management, ideas cannot easily be divided into good ones and bad ones. Most can be put to some use given the appropriate situation and effective implementation.

This book therefore concentrates on basic principles and uses the fashionable approaches as examples of what might be of value. There are three basic roles for the Operations Manager to address:

- managing actual transformations (or processes), such as, serving customers, making products
- planning how operational capacity should be used
- designing and continually improving transformational and planning systems.

In order to do this, the Operational Manager must consider the following points.

1. Relationships with other functions:
    - marketing (particularly in service delivery)
    - human resource management
    - engineering
    - information technology staff
    - designers
    - finance and accounting staff
    - top management.

(In many countries, experience in Operations Management is considered an important developmental stage for top management.)

2. Relationships with other disciplines and areas of knowledge:
    - general management
    - other functions (see above)
    - strategic management
    - organisational behaviour and the social sciences
    - computer science and IT systems
    - production engineering
    - quantitative techniques
    - economics.

(Most business and management courses have modules relating to many of the above, as do engineering, design and a variety of modern, imaginative courses.)

3. Potential value of 'hard systems' approaches based on measurement, management accounting, information systems and operational research

4. The potential value of 'soft systems' approaches viewing the organisation essentially as a social system.

This text assumes that both of the latter two approaches are essential and complementary. Indeed any practical approach which produces results in line with an organisation's legitimate objectives is of value but one should not forget that an approach which worked in the past may not work in the future.

Operations generate substantial revenue and incur large expenditure for many organisations. Unfortunately, the gap between revenue and expenditure may be wafer thin and subject to continual competitive pressure. In addition the quality of operational delivery (in the broadest sense) of products and services has an impact, to a great extent, on all of us. Operations Managers can make a real impact on the quality of life of employees and the general public.

# CHAPTER 1

# Introduction to Operations Management

In this first chapter we introduce some of the concepts and language of operations management, including relevant examples of operational systems. We are particularly concerned with differences between manufacturing, service and office contexts and also, through the concept of 'process choice', to show how operations may have a very different form between organisations within a given industrial sector and perhaps even between differing parts of the same organisation. Finally, we provide a basic link with management accounting through the use of a simple method of analysing some of the financial characteristics of an operational system.

## OBJECTIVES

This chapter:

- introduces Operations Management as an organisational function
- gives a range of examples of operational situations relating to manufacturing and service provision
- explores the concept of 'process choice' in manufacturing, service and office operations
- shows some ways in which operational decisions have an impact on profitability by using a numerical example.

## WHAT IS OPERATIONS MANAGEMENT?

In an organisational context, we define 'operations' as the processes by which a range of inputs are converted into the products and services required by the customers of the organisation.

If we are referring to manufacturing or production operations, then the most obvious inputs are materials. We see in Figure 1.1 how the input of materials becomes the output of a physical product. The conversion process, however, also requires people who sometimes act directly on materials to effect changes, provide management support, and play a whole range of indirect roles in planning and controlling the conversion process.

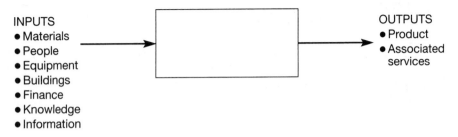

**Fig. 1.1 Manufacturing operations**

We then require equipment and buildings. The former may directly convert materials (through heating, cutting, bending, assembling ...) or may take measurements to check the quality of materials at various stages of production. Equipment also plays a part in moving materials (conveyors, fork-lift trucks and similar equipment inside a factory or road transport between sites) and in planning and controlling such movement (computer systems). This leads us on to the information technology systems which exist within the organisation and, indeed, to all the other equipment (central heating, for instance) which are part of the building infrastructure supporting the direct operations.

Money is also an input to the system, whether in the form of long-term capital (to buy buildings and equipment as well as to pay for strategic developments such as research into new production processes) or as cash and working capital to maintain the day-to-day working. One interesting way to view some monetary flows are as the reverse of other resource flows. This is illustrated in Figure 1.2 with revenue from the customers matching the flow of products, and expenditure on inputs matching resource flows. The figure also shows the need for long-term funding, or capital, to set up and improve the system in advance of customer revenues being received. Such funding must be paid for through shareholders' dividends, interest on long-term loans and the eventual repayment of the capital unless the providers of the capital are satisfied that continuing growth and improvement is being achieved.

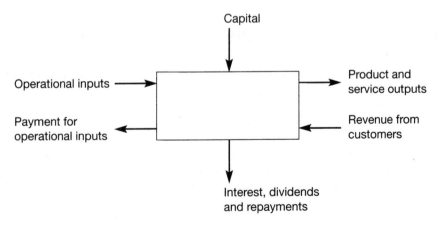

**Fig. 1.2 Physical and financial cash flows**

Even at this early stage, we should note the importance of two complementary financial aspects of operations. The first is that operations must add value and be profitable. This is not the place to explore the complexities of financial performance measurement so we use a simple notion of profit as revenue minus costs within some relevant time period. We return to this idea at the end of this chapter. The second point we must consider is the timing of cash flows. Not only do we require substantial investment to set up our operational systems in advance of receiving customer revenues but, even in the short term, the timing of receipts and payments are unlikely to match. We may have to pay for raw materials at an early stage, to hold them or finished goods in stock and then have to wait some time to receive payment from the customer. These delays can ruin an otherwise profitable enterprise.

Interestingly, operational systems can be designed to reduce this problem through paying close attention to the flow of materials. Japanese industrialists discovered this in the early 1960s when a shortage of materials and funds forced them to make things 'just-in-time' for the customer. This management of time is perhaps best seen in mass retailing which has the additional advantage of receiving customer revenue immediately (payment for goods in shops) rather than having to wait months for payment as is typical in industrial situations. Indeed, if you can manage your operations with great care you may be able to receive sufficient revenue in advance of your own expenditures that you can drastically reduce your capital requirements.

The final class of input we will mention at this stage is knowledge and information. To be able to run our operations effectively we require knowledge of many things, including:

- the needs of our customers
- technical capabilities of our processes and future available processes
- the law regarding safety at work, environmental impacts of processes and so forth
- the availability of resources
- trends in the economic, social and political environment.

This basic introductory discussion of manufacturing operations as an input–output conversion process should have shown you that:

- operations is central to the organisation
- it is of some concern to all employees and the major preoccupation of many of them
- it draws on a number of disciplines (engineering, finance, Information Technology, management of people ...)
- it requires careful management if it is to be profitable.

## Introducing the 'Tasks'

At various points in the text you will see the heading 'Task(s)'. These activities are mainly exercises designed to encourage you to think creatively about operations by suggesting situations and problems for you to analyse. Depending on the context in which you are studying operations, you should work through the tasks either in groups or individually. The emphasis is often on brainstorming and drawing on common sense and everyday experience as well as work experience to help you form a richer mental picture of operational situations. There are usually no final 'right answers' but further reading of the text will draw your attention to points you may have missed and therefore it is useful to return later to previously attempted tasks.

**TASKS**

1. In the context of a factory, try to list the jobs that people might do:
   - as labour, acting directly on materials to convert them into something different
   - operating equipment to convert materials
   - other jobs directly dealing with materials
   - directly managing shopfloor activities
   - providing immediate support to shopfloor activities
   - other jobs in an organisation which are essential in supporting shopfloor activities.

2. In the context of transportation – moving materials and finished products between factories, warehouses and shops – list the operational tasks involved.

Our discussion so far has dealt with production or manufacturing operations, that is situations where materials are converted into products for a customer (which may be another industrial firm). We will often begin by discussing manufacturing situations as they can be simple to visualise, even if hard to manage. Though operations management has its origins in production management, as great an emphasis is now placed on the management of service situations and on the effective management of the information flows which accompany production and service operations.

The key characteristic which defines service operations is the necessary presence of the customer. The operational delivery of education, health care, consultancy, advice, travel, entertainment and so forth involve the customer as a more or less active participant. The economic effectiveness of a food supermarket depends on the customer doing much of the work and many services are designed to make full use of technology and the customer in order to reduce labour costs. Other services necessarily require expert delivery – we are still some way from the robot-delivered haircut!

Strictly speaking, we have here been describing the 'front office' aspects of service delivery. In the front office, the customer is both an input and an output. Supporting the front office is the 'back room' where much of the service value is actually added (see Figure 1.3). A particularly clear example of this is a bank where part of the service involves direct contact with the customer and part involves transactions in the absence of a particular customer. This is shown in the traditional layout of a bank with a customer service area clearly separated by a screen from an office. It is interesting to think how this conceptual framework translates into more modern and open layouts involving desks, computer screens and cashpoint machines and finally into telebanking

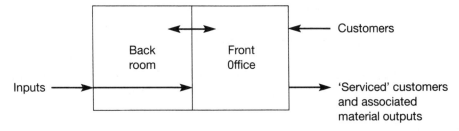

**Fig. 1.3  Service operations**

where contact with the customer is not face to face but involves other communication devices, such as telephones, fax machines and computer networks.

Having mentioned some of the variety of operational concerns, we now look at a small number of examples of operational situations to provide some further contexts. We then move on to a more structured discussion of the terminology of operations management.

## EXAMPLES OF OPERATIONS

As an introduction to some of the major areas in Operations Management we will first examine a number of situations which illustrate the range of issues which will concern us in this book.

When reading the following it is useful to bear in mind one of the major preoccupations of management theorists, that is, whether the situations we are managing are recurring or unique. Recurring situations are ones which are repeated many times in basically similar form and require, what is sometimes termed, regular management. Truly unique situations are unusual as most situations have some similarity with the past. Many situations which require management, however, have a sufficient number of unique features to necessitate individual attention. In such cases we may refer to the 'Management of Change' or 'Project Management'.

Read through the following situation descriptions and then examine them again whilst attempting to answer the short set of questions at the end.

### Company A

Company A is a manufacturer of domestic appliances such as fridges, freezers and cookers. Goods are made to standard specifications (based on customer needs, safety and cost) using standard production methods for high volume, low cost manufacture with modest levels of product variety (different sizes, performance, colour and so forth). By manufacturing in this way for a number of years, the production engineers and managers in this company have been able to refine and adjust the materials and methods used in manufacture continually so as to ensure quality at an acceptable level as well as to reduce costs, and hence prices, for the customers. Considerable attention is paid to technology, as it is incorporated in the product itself as well as in the production and production control. Much of the factory and office work in the company is routine and potentially boring.

In addition to the regular activities of this company, there is a need to develop new products (an intelligent dishwasher, perhaps) and to modify existing ones substantially as customer needs, technology and competitors' products change. A radically new design can involve risks in terms of development cost, time and market acceptability. A total redesign is a challenging project involving staff from most areas of the company.

There is always a need to refine manufacturing processes continually. This in itself is a further process which involves training, work and materials analysis, and the implementation of change whilst continuing production. In addition there is an occasional need to change manufacturing in more radical ways, for instance by installing new machines, reorganising the factory layout and working methods or by implementing new computer based production planning and control systems. Drastic change, involving management and working practices, is often the hardest to implement effectively.

## Company B

Company B is a travel agency and runs a large number of high street shops. Though each customer has different needs, staff in the shops attempt to match these either by choosing from the large range of packaged holidays on offer or by tailoring travel and accommodation schedules. Computer based information technology is used extensively to facilitate the above processes and the customer contact involved can make the work interesting and challenging. Long hours of work are, however, necessary. Working at weekends and evenings, and the uneven arrival pattern of customers in shops, can give rise to a mixture of boring periods with no customers alternating with periods of frantic activity and stress. Opportunities for alternative patterns of work, including travel abroad, exist within the company.

Company B regularly opens new shops and occasionally closes less successful outlets as patterns of customer demand change. In some ways the opening of a new shop is a regular and routine event which has occurred many times in the past and is governed by standard procedures. A new site and new staff will, however, create new challenges and operational problems which will in turn lead to quality and cost problems if managers are not alert and attentive.

## Company C

Company C is an engineering consultancy which offers a complete design and construction management service to its clients. Though the company has standard operating procedures, the requirements of each customer are substantially different and involve both services (advice, knowledge of engineering solutions, management) and physical artefacts (a new factory building fully equipped with production machines and infrastructure). Most of the employees are professionally trained, highly paid and must be capable of managing their own activities in a profitable manner.

## Organisation D

Organisation D is a large general hospital. You are invited to construct your own profile in the manner of those given above.

**TASKS**

Having read through the above, now attempt to answer the following questions for each company:

1. Who is the direct customer?

2. Does the customer require and receive individual attention? Is the customer involved in the operational process?

3. How will operational performance affect the customer? In what circumstances will they return or, alternatively, go elsewhere when they require a similar product or service again?

4. How regular or unique are the processes described?

5. How is technology used?

6. What features of the management of the people providing the product or service are of key importance?

## Organisation E

Organisation E is your own employer, college or some other body for which you have worked in the past. Can you answer the above questions for some operational situation of which you have experience as a provider or a customer?

The remainder of this book is concerned with providing some guidance in answering the above questions but you must expect the whole of your working life to consist of further explorations in this area! In order to begin our classification of operational issues, however, the following are obviously relevant:

- the characteristics of the customer and their needs
- how do we know their needs so that we can match our provision to them?

- the scale and the uniqueness or regularity of the process
- whether the process is based in a factory, shop or office
- how the product or service is produced and how this process is designed, planned and controlled
- how the people producing the goods or delivering the service are managed
- the role of technology.

(Note: The Glossary at the end of the book provides further details of the terms used in describing Operational Management situations.)

## KEY ROLES OF THE OPERATIONS MANAGER

The following classification is widely accepted and is useful to describe the primary responsibilities of the Operational Manager:

- process design
- work planning
- implementation.

Process design is concerned not only with the physical context of production or service provision (buildings and machines) but also with the design of the workplace from a worker's point of view. It includes appropriate information technology, indeed, it may be based around formal computer systems analysis methodologies. It must take into account intended interactions with infrastructures and the environment. In particular there is an obvious link, particularly in manufacturing, with product design through CADCAM and Computer Integrated Manufacturing.

Work planning includes all the procedures, from aggregate planning (linked to business and strategic planning) through to detailed work scheduling, which set out the organisation's future plans. These plans will be concerned with output that is intended over various future time periods and how resources are to be employed in achieving such outputs. This is a major concern in the second half of this book.

Implementation is concerned with ensuring that intentions are actually carried out, with monitoring and controlling progress and with reviewing operational effectiveness and profitability.

One danger with this three-way separation of design, planning and implementation is that they can be viewed as separate issues and responsibilities. This can lead to a number of severe problems if plans are not feasible or designs appropriate. Unfortunately the folklore of Operations Management (and management in general) provides all too many examples of such occurrences. One of the apparent strengths of Japanese management is the avoidance of such problems through extensive consultation and discussion prior to decisions being finalised. As a general rule, it is better to remove barriers between those who design, those who plan and those who implement. Perhaps if the same individuals or groups do all three tasks then some problems may be avoided, though this may not fit well with the functional hierarchies still present in so many organisations.

# PROCESS CHOICE IN MANUFACTURING

All manufacturing plants are different. Not only are the locations, the people involved, and the machinery different but also the products made and the systems which control the work. If we can only see differences, however, it becomes hard to make general statements about how manufacturing operations should be managed. Therefore, it may be more constructive to ask 'In what ways are factories the same?'

To some extent the terminology of Operations Management (see Glossary) relates to similarities. All production, for example, takes input from the environment (materials, people, finance, knowledge and so forth) and transforms it into material outputs. A given company or factory might, of course, contain a diversity of methods which transform materials. Is it possible, then, to arrive at classifications of production situations which will help us understand how to manage production?

Consider these different manufacturing situations: Company X makes standard food cartons by the million; Company Y manufactures batches of printed circuit boards which are then used as standard parts in a range of control devices designed for different customers; Company Z makes items of clothing by hand for special occasions. Each of these three situations involve a material transformation but the differences are considerable.

We might attempt to characterise the differences by asking the following questions and relating them to each of the three companies.

**1.** *Should we use standard machines designed specifically for one job or general purpose machines which could fulfil a number of functions?*

*Company X* It might be economical to develop a particular machine to do the job in a highly efficient manner, or alternatively to adapt standard production equipment for the task in hand. It makes sense to invest in the right equipment in order to keep down running costs and ensure regular quality. The most extreme examples of this are such things as chemical processing plants where large amounts of money and effort are spent in setting up a plant which will then be used for many years to make the same basic products.

*Company Y* Here we require some flexibility of operation as each batch will require some differences in manufacturing methods. It is also important that it doesn't take too long to change a machine from making one batch to making the next (the 'set-up' time for the machine). Many engineering machines have been designed with this form of work in mind. As a simple example, a drilling machine can be adjusted to use different sizes of drill and work on different shapes of material up to designed size limitations. Each changeover of drill bit and fixtures, however, takes time and incurs expenditure.

*Company Z* We are now likely to require very flexible, multi-purpose tools (possibly with some specialist equipment) in order to cope with the varying range of customer needs.

**2**. *How do we organise, control and motivate the workforce?*

*Company X* We may not require continuous human effort with an automated process or if the process is (in part) manual then the work may be boring and repetitive. High levels of technical skill may, however, be required to set up the process and care will be needed to keep it operating in an efficient and economical manner.

*Company Y* The actual work may be machine based or manual with similar problems to those mentioned above. The major problem may, however, lie in coping with the variety of batches at different stages of completion in the factory. This will require organisational skills and attention to detail with an emphasis on communication.

*Company Z* The success of the enterprise may well depend on the skills and inventiveness of all the staff involved. Motivation may be less of a problem than maintaining communication with the customers and coping with the pressures of their varied needs whilst working to tight schedules.

**3**. *How do we control the quality of output?*

*Company X* We should know exactly what is required (detailed product specifications) and know exactly how we intend to make it (detailed process specifications) and hence the control of quality may appear simple. It is likely, however, that in order to obtain the work we have had to quote a low price and hence cost control is important. Similarly we will often have to work to tight schedules and guarantee to produce large volumes of output at regular intervals. In addition, mistakes can be very expensive, even if detected early. Thus, quality control in mass production can be very demanding!

*Company Y* Once again, the above comments apply to some extent but the problems are worsened by the variety of outputs and the quality problems which can occur when machines and people change over from making one batch to another with differing specifications.

*Company Z* Here we should have the advantage of human attention to detail but we may now be less clear about what the customer wants and how it should be made. This type of work requires continual problem solving.

These questions are only a sample of the management issues raised by differing forms of manufacture. We should, however, now have a flavour of the way in which a classification of transformational process can be helpful. The actual classification used below is widely known and usually (if confusingly) referred to as 'manufacturing process choice'. In this context 'process' has a more general meaning than the actual machines used and relates to the underlying logic and economic rationale of the situation. The three manufacturing situations above are examples of:

- line (or mass) production (Company X)
- batch production (Company Y)
- job-shop (or jobbing) production (Company Z).

These categories are often extended to include project management (as an extension of jobbing) and continuous process (as an extension of mass production). In Chapters 6 and 7 of this book we discuss project management as a separate topic although the related issues of management decision making and control are present. The continuous process industries have been briefly mentioned above (for example, chemical processes, power generation and so forth) but will not be developed further here as their operational management requires a good knowledge of the particular engineering technologies involved.

The basic trio of jobbing, batch and line are often represented on a graph as shown in Figure 1.4. Here the horizontal axis represents the volume of manufacture (roughly speaking the number of similar items made in a given time period) and the vertical axis represents the variety of manufacture (the range of items made). Therefore the job shop represents high variety and low volumes of each item (possibly down to only a single item made to one design) whilst line production gives high volumes with low variety. Batch manufacturing relates to medium volume and variety and, in fact, covers an enormous range of manufacturing activity.

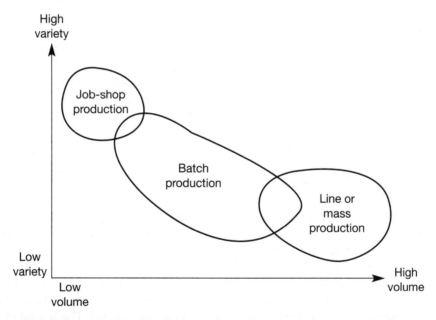

**Fig. 1.4 Manufacturing process choice**

To summarise, high volume is associated with a standardised product, often at a mature stage in its product life cycle, which is produced at low cost so as to offer competitive pricing in the market. This low cost is often achieved through investment to give economies of scale in production and also through the operation of the learning curve, whereby long experience in manufacturing an item teaches us new ways in which to produce it more economically (for example, through the use of cheaper materials, different production methods and so forth).

In contrast, low volume is associated with product variety, whether to individual customer designs or based on a large 'catalogue' but also usually involving frequent new product launches. Each of these approaches, and various compromises, may be present in the same factory as a company targets differing market segments with differing needs. This can lead to considerable confusion and it is often argued that differing process forms should be separated in order to simplify operational management and concentrate effort on each process's differing needs.

One obvious point from the graph of volume and variety (Figure 1.4) is the apparent trade-off which occurs. Whilst few would want low volume and variety (unless a standard product happens to be very hard to make and hence commands a high price for each unit made) it would seem highly desirable to be able to produce in high volumes with high variety, thus satisfying individual customer needs at low cost. If this can be achieved economically, it then gives a company a great market advantage and many engineering developments (flexible manufacturing systems and so forth) have this aim in mind. Experience shows that the managerial control of such an enterprise may be very demanding but it is obviously an ideal to aim for. In practice, many organisations have difficulty in achieving far more modest goals!

Thus, categorising manufacturing process choice is very useful in helping us to classify and relate issues of manufacturing operations. It helps us to see the 'wood' rather than the 'trees' in terms of operations and also shows us how operational issues relate to market strategy, economics and engineering technology. It also gives us a direction for the future – how can we break away from the volume–variety trade-off?

## SERVICE PROCESS CHOICE

Having explored a very useful classification of manufacturing operations we now move on to ask whether something similar can be done for service operations. In practice this is far from easy. The manufacturing classification has been known as a standard for some time but the service operations literature has been far more fragmented. This is due to some extent to the highly varied nature of 'service' industries and an apparent unwillingness to see comparisons between them.

One approach is to adopt the manufacturing classification in a slightly different form. In order to do this, however, it is important to explore the mechanics of service delivery in more detail. The following questions are suggested as appropriate to classify services (Silvestro et al. 1992):

- *To what extent is the service delivered by equipment or people?*
- *How much customer contact time is there per transaction?*
- *What degree of customisation is there? (Is the service adapted for the individual customer or do they choose from a list of standard options?)*
- *To what degree is the customer involved in service delivery? (What is the extent of self-service?)*
- *Can the direct service provider vary the service?*

- *Is value added in the front office (through direct customer contact) or in the back room?*
- *Is there a product focus (what the customer buys) or a process focus (how the service is delivered)?*

Once again let us explore these classifications by considering some examples, remembering that the answer to one of the above questions may be a compromise rather than one of the extremes suggested.

## Example 1: Visit to a GP complaining of back pains

We expect the service to be delivered by a person, though a subsequent visit to a hospital for an x-ray is more dependent on equipment. In the future, conversation with a medical practitioner may be preceded by a session with a computer to gather details of background and symptoms and to relate these to your case history.

Contact time is likely to be relatively short and you may have to wait some time for an appointment and before being seen when you attend. This reflects the economics of providing a general medical service to a large population.

One would expect the diagnosis to be specific to your back but the remedies offered are likely to be standard. Your co-operation will, of course, be required and subsequent treatment involving, say, exercising may be dependent on your own efforts.

The matching of problem and solution is typical of the skills required in many professional services. We would expect the doctor (unless being supervised under training) to be able to respond without seeking management approval. Consider how this could change with greater demand on medical services and the need for tighter resource control.

The value added is mainly through direct contact, though if blood samples are taken for test then this 'back room' skill may be of great importance.

The patient is probably most interested in 'what is bought' in this instance (that is a treatment for back pain) though few would deny that the manner in which the service is delivered is of some importance here and may become very important in other medical consultations.

## Example 2: Visit to a cinema

Here the delivery (projection of a film) is automated, though some minimal delivery by humans of ancillary services is likely.

Customer contact time is a couple of hours in the context of a tight schedule, although many customers are processed at once. The service 'product' is highly standardised and there is no discretion on the part of the deliverer. Customer interaction in service delivery is possibly not desirable in this context.

Value is mainly added in the back room, that is in the making of the film, and customer satisfaction is primarily related to this product assuming that a minimal level of other services (for example, cleanliness of the cinema) have been achieved.

These two examples have been chosen to show a very strong contrast and it is suggested that you now work through the following (if possible through group discussion – it's more fun!) in order to add more variety to the responses.

**TASK**

Discuss the dimensions of service delivery in the following contexts.

1. A journey by plane to Hong Kong, with reference to the services delivered:
   - on a visit to a travel agent when booking the ticket
   - at the airport on departure
   - on the plane.

2. A visit to a restaurant:
   - the fast food variety
   - in an expensive hotel.

3. A financial services consultant discussing family investments (long-term savings and pensions).

4. A weekly visit to a supermarket for food and other household consumables.

Completion of the above should have shown the large range of types of service delivered to the general public. It should of course be remembered that many services are internal to organisations or of a professional nature between organisational staff and hence our exploration is only partial. Some grouping of responses should, however, have been noted. This suggests that, as with manufacturing, some classic forms of service process could be derived and the following have been suggested as one possibility:

## Mass services

Mass services are based on equipment for delivery of a standard product with value added in the back office and a product focus. Many customers are processed within a short time period, possibly through the use of self-service. The totality is comparable with line manufacturing with its emphasis on high volumes, low variety and low unit cost. Typical industries are transport, mass entertainment and mass retailing.

## Service shop

This is a mixed response to each of the factors, and covers a very wide range of situations where some trade-off is attempted between handling a number of clients whilst achieving some adaptation to their individual needs. Examples include hotels, some restaurants and shops as well as many industrial services.

## Professional services

In professional services the emphasis is on meeting the specific needs of the customer, often at high cost. These are labour intensive with a lot of front office time devoted to the client. The high cost means that such services either relate to organisational needs or to crisis points, for instance the need for urgent medical care by an individual.

**TASK**

With reference to the three forms of service process described above, find appropriate examples from the following service contexts:

- college education
- personal banking
- selling industrial products (one company to another).

We have spent some considerable time establishing the context for classifying service delivery but why is this important for the Operational Manager? Unless we can associate operational issues, problems and solutions with the above dimensions and classification then we are no further forward, except perhaps in developing helpful ways of thinking about services.

In fact much of the specialist service operations literature does relate to the above, or similar, classifications. Two examples are given below but the interested reader is encouraged to refer to the list of readings at the end of this (and each subsequent) chapter for details of the source of these ideas and ways in which they may be followed up.

## Use of people or equipment to deliver the service

**Challenges of high labour intensity:**

- recruitment, training and welfare of staff
- development of standard working procedures to contribute towards quality and cost effective working
- scheduling of the workforce in the context of variable customer demand
- control of staff in differing locations
- managing growth and decline.

(Example: management of staff in a very busy, high street store.)

**Challenges of machine based service delivery:**

- effective investment, particularly as technology may be changing rapidly
- matching fixed investment in delivery capacity with variable customer demand

● control of the delivery process (including safety of equipment and customer).

(Examples: use of vending machines, cash machines, transport systems.)

### Degree of customisation of the service

#### Challenges due to high customisation:

● maintaining quality at an acceptable cost
● managing the often autonomous service deliverers (for example, professionally trained staff may identify more with client needs than the organisation which employs them).

(Examples: some forms of health care, education, social services.)

#### Challenges due to low customisation:

● making a standard service (possibly machine delivered) attractive to the customer and in suitable physical surroundings
● maintaining quality at low cost.

(Examples: fast food outlet, cash machine, mass transport.)

## OFFICE PROCESS CHOICE

Having described manufacturing and service process choice, a natural question to ask is whether office operations can similarly be characterised. Office transformations involve data and information and are an important adjunct to service operations as they are the primary basis of the back room. Similarly manufacturing involves a great deal of information transfer, in particular for the control of the flow of materials. Both service and manufacturing activities must have links with commercial systems such as order taking and accounting, the latter being typical of office activities.

Aside from the links with service and manufacturing systems, the management of data and information flow is, in itself, an important concern. Prior to the widespread use of computer based systems, the large offices of major organisations could in a sense be characterised as production units. Whilst work study techniques were developed to improve manufacturing effectiveness, Organisation and Methods (O&M) has a similar role to play in the office using similar methods with similar ends in mind, that is, the effective design and control of the workplace.

The early introduction of computer based systems resulted in the automation of some office activities. Indeed the term 'batch processing' is typical of such systems where activity was concentrated on batches of work in order to make efficient use of the scarce resource of computing time. As the economics of computer hardware have changed dramatically, systems have become more distributed with the widespread use of real-time processing and hence computing technology, in conjunction with communications technology, has facilitated new forms of office working.

In practice, manufacturing process choice provides a useful framework for office operations if the latter are remote from the external customer. If direct contact with the customer is necessary then we are properly in the area of service operations. If contacts with the customer are more occasional, or if the computer system is supporting the direct service provider, then structured systems analysis methods should be used to provide a balance between service support and the effective use of computing capacity. In each case the concepts are not new but must be imaginatively applied in the context of rapidly changing technology.

The rapidly developing area of Business Process Re-engineering (BPR) addresses this area and rightly draws attention to the strategic implications of changing information systems as well as the opportunities for rethinking organisational structures and boundaries. By referring to informational transformations as 'office operations' we might inadvertently give the impression that such activities take place in a traditional physical office setting. In practice such activities take place at a variety of locations, in particular at the point of service delivery and of production. BPR draws attention to the need to see processes in an integrated fashion throughout an organisation and between organisations.

An interesting example of this is in the area of supply chain management. This might in the past have been seen to be mainly concerned with the physical movement and storage of materials. Key issues would therefore be the choice of mode of transportation, location of warehousing, purchasing procedures and so forth. Whilst these are still of great importance, the flow of information which accompanies the flow of materials is now seen as critical. Attention has, therefore, been focused on electronic mail and on communication technologies as well as the systems, procedures and relationships that define how organisations work together.

This strategic importance is reflected in the tendency to speak of the 'Business Re-engineering' which should precede BPR. Unfortunately this has at times been confused with another piece of current jargon, 'downsizing', and has led to the conclusion that BPR leads to staff redundancies. The picture is far more complex. If classifications of manufacturing have been with us for many years and those of service operations developed in the 1980s then appropriate theories of information, organisation and operations are still in the melting pot.

## REVENUE, COST AND PROFIT

As we mentioned earlier in this chapter, the operational manager must always view decisions with an eye to their financial implications. This may relate to the amount and the timing of cash flows, both of which may be dramatically affected by the design and running of operational systems.

Courses in cost and management accounting explore such issues in detail from the financial point of view. For our purposes, it is useful to take a very simple model of a company in order to illustrate points which can then be further amplified in more advanced courses. In order to explore the relationship between revenue, cost and profit in a variety of operational settings, we ignore issues of timing (assuming that cash flows all take place within a chosen time period) and look at what is often called the 'Break-Even' graph.

For the examples below we choose a year as the period of time under consideration and assume that no material stocks were held at the beginning and end of this period, all goods were paid for and all revenue received from our customers. The independent variable in our model (shown as the horizontal axis on our graph) is the volume of work carried out in the period. As we have no initial and final stock holding, this must be equal to the quantity of goods sold. Figure 1.5 shows a graph of this model with further details added as we will describe below.

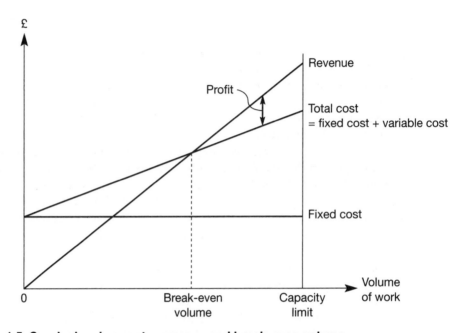

**Fig. 1.5 Graph showing costs, revenue and break-even volume**

First of all, however, a word on the nature of models and the process of systems modelling. All models involve explicit simplifications and therefore are only partial representations of reality. A good model will, however, illustrate essential features of reality and allow us to draw inferences which will still be valid in a more comprehensive model. It will also suggest actions in the real world which will help us achieve our objectives. It is perhaps better not to think of models as being true or false but to consider whether or not they are useful in a given circumstance.

The basis of the model we are describing here is the idea of showing cost, revenue and profit as a function of volume (of production and sales). Volume is assumed to be the decision variable, that is to a greater or lesser extent we will decide on the volume and the graph shows us the profit which we will receive as a result. Of course in a complex world, price and cost rates will be related to volume and this may be shown through a more detailed analysis.

An example of this basic relationship, showing the algebra and arithmetic, is given below in the context of the 'Milon' case. The graph in Figure 1.5 gives a visual impression with the following features:

- There is a limit on the total volume of work which can be carried out in the time period (the capacity).
- Fixed costs are independent of volume (by definition).
- Variable costs rise with volume. Variable costs are shown here as additional to fixed costs thus giving a line representing total cost. For simplicity we have chosen a constant rate of variable cost and therefore the total cost function is shown by a straight line.
- A fixed selling price has been assumed and therefore the revenue function is also a straight line.
- Profit is defined as revenue minus cost and is not shown as a separate line on the graph. The amount of profit can be seen as the difference between the revenue and the total cost lines.
- The 'break-even' point occurs at the volume where revenue is equal to total cost. To the left of this point we are making a loss and to the right we are profitable.

A graph such as Figure 1.5 is useful for carrying out 'thought experiments' (to borrow a phrase from the physical sciences). By looking at the graph, can you see the effect on the break-even point of the following (each occurring separately):

- an increase in fixed cost
- a decrease in the rate of variable cost
- an increase in the selling price.

A particular problem occurs if the break-even point moves to the right to the extent of meeting the capacity limit. In this case profitability is not possible. What would have to happen to the various cost and price factors (taken separately) for this to occur?

Different process forms tend to lead to different graphs. For instance in line manufacturing, the capital cost of equipment can lead to a very high fixed cost with highly efficient operations and a low variable cost, thus giving the relationships seen in Figure 1.6a. In this case profits and losses increase rapidly as one moves away from the break-even point. By contrast Figure 1.6b shows the situation where low fixed costs are present (for instance with an organisation which relies heavily on sub-contracting) but where the contribution rate (that is, the difference between the selling price and variable cost rate) is also quite low. In this type of situation, even with a low break-even point, there is less profit potential for sales far in excess of the break-even point.

The operational significance of these models is that the factors we have been discussing above are key operational decisions, that is we have been exploring the direct relationship between how we set up operations and the range of profits we might achieve. Similarly we could explore the relationship between these factors and operational control. If quality yield is poor or if cost control is inadequate, what will be the effect on profits in differing process choice situations?

These models can be adapted to service situations and can also throw some light on non-profit making situations where revenues must still cover costs. It must be emphasised that this is only the first step in producing financial models of operational situations. In particular, if we now add considerations of stock holding and the timing

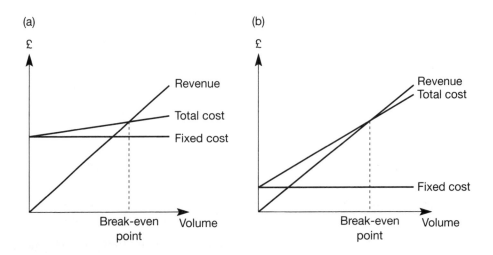

**Fig. 1.6 Break-even graphs with differing levels of fixed cost**

of cash flows to these models we will be able to explore far more fully the financial implications of operational decisions. In real competitive industries, the difference between profit and loss may well depend on getting a whole range of operational details right and continually adjusting them as environmental factors change.

## The 'Milon' Case

'Milon' is a worked case example which continues over several chapters in this book. It covers a variety of issues in operations management through the use of a quantitative example involving financial and production data. It should be seen as complementary to the discussions of principles and issues found in other parts of the book. It is strongly recommended that you work through the arithmetic details of this example in order to appreciate the underlying argument fully. Some very basic knowledge of management accounting is assumed in addition to earlier comments in this section (for instance the difference between fixed and variable costs and the use of a 'break-even' graph) but if you have not yet covered this material in other modules its use here is self-evident from the context.

THE MILON MANUFACTURING COMPANY

Milon are a small company making standard units of high quality shelving for domestic use. The demand for this well-designed product is growing strongly but the company is anticipating considerable problems in managing its operations profitably in the future.

In the year which has just ended (1995), Milon had the capacity to make at most 400 000 units of standard product. (Note: Though Milon make a range of products, production is expressed in terms of 'standard' units of product, the most popular product line to which other lines can be related.)

## Part 1
## Current profitability

In 1995 the following characteristics were noted for the standard product:

| | £ per unit | £ per year |
|---|---|---|
| Selling price (to wholesalers) | = £10.50 per unit | |
| Material cost | = £2.00 per unit | |
| Variable labour cost | = £3.20 per unit | |
| Fixed cost | | = £1 400 000 per year |
| Sales in 1995 | = 320 000 units | |

(Assume at this stage that production and sales are the same and that no stock is held.)

---

**TASKS**

On this basis (for 1995):

1. What is the profit function for Milon?

2. Draw a profit–volume–cost graph

3. What profit did Milon actually make?

4. What was its break-even point?

---

Worked solutions

*1. What is the profit function for Milon?*

As standard notation for the Milon case we use the following abbreviations:

R   = Revenue per unit sold
P   = Annual Production
S   = Annual Sales
VC = Variable cost per unit
FC = Fixed cost per year

Therefore we have:

Profit = Total Revenue – Total Cost

  = Revenue per unit × Annual Sales – (Variable cost per unit × Annual Production + Fixed Costs)

Now if we assume that Annual Sales = Annual Production, then using the notation given we have:

Profit = R.P – (VC.P + FC)

  = (R – VC)P – FC

where R – VC is the contribution per unit to meeting fixed costs and earning profits.

2. *Draw a profit–volume–cost graph*

See Figure 1.7, which also identifies the break-even point.

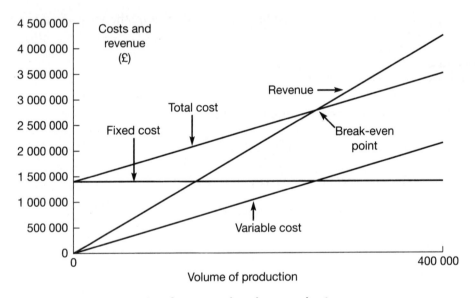

**Fig. 1.7 Milon Manufacturing Company: break-even chart**

3. *What profit did Milon actually make?*

In this instance:

  R   = £10.50 per unit

  P   = S = 320 000 units in the year

  VC = £2.00 + £3.20 = £5.20 per unit

  FC  = £1 400 000 in the year

Hence Profit = (10.50 – 5.20) × 320 000 – 1 400 000 = £296 000

4. *What was its break-even point?*

The break-even point (BEP) is the production or sales volume for which there is no profit, that is total contribution and fixed costs exactly balance out.

Therefore: Profit $= 0 = (10.50 - 5.20) \times$ BEP $- 1\,400\,000$

and by simple algebra: BEP $= \dfrac{1\,400\,000}{5.30} = 264\,151$ units per year

As actual sales and production were 320 000 units then Milon is comfortably in the region of profitability.

An interesting further statistic is the profit which could have been made if 400 000 units had been made and sold. This is the maximum possible profit for Milon and is easily found to be £720 000.

Part 2
Quality problems in 1996

In planning production for 1996, Milon are considering using a different raw material supplier. This would reduce material costs to £1.70 per unit but the product would now be harder to make and it is estimated that a yield of only 88 per cent would be achieved (in 1995 we had a 100 per cent yield). This means that 12 per cent of production would have to be scrapped. Therefore in order to meet sales of 320 000 units we would have to make $\dfrac{320\,000}{0.88} = 363\,636$ units. (To check this, subtract 12 per cent scrap from 363 636.)

**TASK**

Assuming that other factors remain the same, what would be the effect on Milon in 1996 if this new material were used?

Worked solution

To summarise for 1996:

| | Unit | £ per unit | £ per year |
|---|---|---|---|
| Selling price (to wholesalers) | | £10.50 | |
| Material cost | | £1.70 | |
| Variable labour cost | | £3.20 | |
| Fixed cost | | | £1 400 000 |
| Sales target in 1996 | 320 000 | | |
| Production | 363 636 | | |

$$\text{Profit} = \text{Total Revenue} - \text{Total Cost}$$

$$= \text{Revenue per unit} \times \text{Annual Sales} - (\text{Variable cost per unit} \times \text{Annual Production} + \text{Fixed Costs})$$

$$= \text{R.S.} - (\text{VC.P} + \text{FC})$$

$$= 10.50 \times 320\,000 - (4.90 \times 363\,636 + 1\,400\,000)$$

$$= £178\,184$$

This is a considerable profit reduction relative to 1995. We now analyse exactly how this reduction has come about:

We save $(2.00 - 1.70) \times 320\,000 = £96\,000$ in material cost of sales.

We lose $1.70 \times 363\,636 \times 0.12 = £74\,182$ in the material cost of scrapped production.

We lose $3.20 \times 363\,636 \times 0.12 = £139\,636$ in the labour cost of scrapped production.

Thus the net loss of profit is £117 818 as the scrap costs far exceed the materials savings.

In addition to this the profit potential has now been reduced as follows. If production is a maximum at 400 000, then sales are $400\,000 \times 0.88 = 352\,000$. Hence potential profit = £336 000 which is less than half the potential profit in 1995. Using this new supplier is obviously not a good idea.

It is interesting to note how this reduction in potential profit comes about (note that the calculation is slightly different from the earlier unconstrained case). With a production level of 400 000 and a yield of 88 per cent:

We save $(2.00 - 1.70) \times 352\,000 = £105\,600$ in material cost of sales.

We lose $1.70 \times 400\,000 \times 0.12 = £81\,600$ in the material cost of scrapped production.

We lose $3.20 \times 400\,000 \times 0.12 = £153\,600$ in the labour cost of scrapped production.

We lose $(10.50 - 5.20) \times 400\,000 \times 0.12 = £254\,400$ in lost contribution.

Scrap costs and material gains produce a net loss of £129 600 but this is far outweighed by the loss of contribution of £254 400.

Thus we see that when a quality control problem occurs and the system is near to capacity then the effect is considerably greater due to a potential loss of revenue.

## FURTHER READING

The emphasis on process choice in manufacturing is particularly evident in Hill (1985) and the model for process choice in service is derived from Silvestro et al. (1992). Further details are available in general texts on Operations Management (for instance Slack et al. (1995)).

Issues of process choice in service contexts underlie most texts on service operations, for instance see Fitzsimmons et al. (1994), Jones (1989) or the early work in Voss et al. (1985).

Business Process Re-engineering is addressed in Johansson et al. (1993), though new texts are continually becoming available in this area.

A number of real case examples of operational situations are contained in Johnston et al. (1993).

Fitzsimmons, J. A. and Fitzsimmons, M. J. (1994), *Service Management for Competitive Advantage*, McGraw Hill, New York.

Hill, T. (1985), *Manufacturing Strategy*, Macmillan, London.

Johansson, H. J., McHugh, P., Pendlebury, A. J., Wheeler, W. A. (1993), *Business Process Re-engineering*, Wiley, Chichester.

Johnston, R., Chambers, S., Harland, C., Harrison, A. and Slack, N. (1993), *Cases in Operations Management*, Pitman, London.

Jones, P. (ed.) (1989), *Management in Service Industries*, Pitman, London.

Silvestro, R., Fitzgerald, L., Johnston, R. and Voss, C. (1992), *Towards a Classification of Service Processes in International Journal of Service Industry Management*, Vol.3, No.3, 62–75.

Slack, N., Chambers, S., Harland, C., Harrison, A. and Johnston, R. (1995), *Operations Management*, Pitman, London.

Voss, C., Armistead, C., Johnston, B., Morris, B. (1985), *Operations Management in Service Industries and the Public Sector*, Wiley, Chichester.

# CHAPTER 2

# The Management of Quality

**The concept of quality is central to operations management thinking. The primary objective of this chapter is to explore some uses of the word 'quality' and relate them to operational management practice in manufacturing and services contexts.**

## OBJECTIVES

**This chapter:**

- **introduces a customer-centred view of quality**
- **shows how this relates to product manufacture**
- **introduces the concepts of Total Quality Management and the Supply Chain**
- **briefly describes some techniques of quality management**
- **introduces the basic ideas of service quality.**

## INTRODUCTION

In this chapter we begin our consideration of one of the most important issues in Operational Management: how can we ensure that customers receive the product and service quality to which they are entitled. Indeed, as current thinking on the management of quality is truly integrative, it might be more appropriate to place this area of work in the context of general management. Certainly the management of quality is now thought of as an important issue in strategic management.

This situation is in sharp contrast to that which prevailed some 30 years ago when Western companies considered quality control as a minor technical function, the domain of awkward inspectors and a few statisticians. By contrast, the managers in large Japanese companies had developed concepts and techniques to improve product quality and were beginning to exploit the real commercial potential of increasingly reliable mass manufacture.

Now the texts on 'Total Quality Management' are highly visible on bookshelves, with contents ranging over a large number of organisational issues. Service quality is extensively researched and the benchmarking of public sector services is a major political issue. The writers, whether consultants or academics, who helped to bring this about are referred to as the gurus of quality and organisations invest heavily in quality training. Whether the latter is a genuine attempt at organisational transformation or a public relations exercise is not always clear but we will 'optimistically' assume the former.

The recipe for the effective management of quality is, therefore, a diverse mixture of techniques, procedures and organisational concerns. It is by no means straightforward even to provide a coherent general outline of this area of work. Thus in this chapter and the next we raise a number of issues, emphasise the specifically operational points and provide some links to the extensive literature which will support future study. It must be emphasised, however, that the management of quality is an essentially practical concern. Whether we are concerned with customer rights or commercial revenue maximisation, we have to recognise that the 'quality' of the product or service that the customer actually receives (however defined) will have a real effect on organisational performance.

## QUALITY AND THE CUSTOMER

Having made some general comments on the importance of quality, we now consider a specific type of situation. This is where a consumer buys a standard manufactured product, typical of millions of transactions which occur every day. This situation is chosen as product quality is in many ways conceptually more straightforward than service quality. Later in the chapter we will look briefly at the latter along with public sector quality. In Chapter 6 we also introduce some of the ideas surrounding quality in a project management context, that is, where quality outcomes are directly negotiated with the client and an individual performance specification produced.

A useful and natural starting point is to recognise that customers have needs and choose to buy products which best promise to meet those needs. We may separate out a number of key dimensions of need, in particular:

- product attributes
- product performance
- service characteristics
- warranty
- delivery availability
- total price.

A concrete example may help. Perhaps we wish to buy a computer to support our studies and amuse the family (in that order, of course). Then the following might summarise our needs:

**Product attributes:**

- desk top hardware (not too large) including printer
- standard office software, including good word processor and spreadsheet
- multimedia and internet connection capability.

**Product performance:**

- fast processor (perhaps we have sufficient technical knowledge to specify speed, RAM, hard disc storage capacity and so forth)

**Service characteristics:**

- help-line in case of difficulties in initial use
- training software included.

**Warranty:**

- inherently reliable product
- one year warranty at least
- possibility of cheap servicing if things go wrong after the first year.

**Delivery availability:**

- now!

**Total price:**

- competitive
- below £1000
- pay over one year with low interest.

After contacting a range of suppliers, we finally choose our machine. Perhaps some compromises were necessary in matching our needs with available products, but at the end of the selection process we should have a clear idea of the way in which our needs should be met by the chosen product. We will refer to this as a statement of our requirements.

We must be very clear on this point. It is unreasonable to expect any provider of goods or services simply to 'meet our needs'. Needs may be overly ambitious and may change radically over time. They may also be modified, even increased, as our knowledge of the market improves. A purchase decision will, however, be based on some assumed set of requirements and the promise that these will be met. Some of the requirements will be implicit (for instance, that a product is electrically safe), some will be based on product literature and some will be discussed and agreed. In an industrial situation, the statement of requirements will be in the form of specifications and contracts.

Following this line of argument, quality is now seen as the extent to which the customers' requirements are actually met in practice. It is concerned with actual performance relative to promised performance. This is usually termed the 'conformance' view of quality, that is quality is measured by the extent to which a product or service conforms to the stated requirements.

In the example given above, the customer will judge the computer system bought by whether it does the intended job. It may fail to do so because it simply doesn't work or parts of the system which were promised are not delivered. Such problems are easily remedied but at cost to both parties. A more problematic situation arises when the system meets the requirements as stated but the customer now realises that needs exceeded these requirements. The supplier may now not be legally at fault but the customer will go elsewhere in the future. This is still a 'quality problem' for an organisation with an eye to its long-term future.

This points to a problem with the 'conformance' view. A product may conform to agreed (or implicit) requirements but the customer may not be satisfied. One cannot avoid this by saying the product must 'fully satisfy needs' – the supplier may not know them and their fulfilment may be uneconomic. Similarly, the problem is not avoided by stating that quality is 'fitness for use'. Thus we are drawn to consider product design and communication with the customer as key parts of a 'quality delivery system'. We can also see why some writers have concentrated on a 'value for money' style of quality definition.

**TASK**

Think of some item which you regularly buy and list your requirements. Divide these into essential features (without which you would not buy the item) and desirable ones (on which basis you will choose between alternative competitive offerings).

(For example, you might wish to buy a breakfast cereal. Perhaps the essential feature is that it is a specific brand and type of cereal and you then might shop around for the lowest price. Of course, a supermarket will try to persuade you that another brand will give you the same satisfaction at a lower price, or that an alternative cereal is worth the extra money. Much of the art of selling is changing the customer's ideas on what constitutes 'quality'!)

## PRODUCT QUALITY AND OPERATIONS MANAGEMENT

The above discussion places quality management in the context of the general management of an organisation. It is appropriate at this point, however, to consider the more sharply focused question, 'How can operations contribute to delivering a quality product?'

There are two ways in which this can be answered. One is based on traditional relationships between operations and other management functions. Thus if we accept that:

- 'sales' deals directly with the customer
- 'marketing' decides on the product mix, channels of distribution, advertising and product promotion
- 'design' sets the product specification
- 'engineering' decides how the product is to be made technically

then 'operations' is concerned with deciding on the most suitable production process through job design, production planning and control, obtaining resources for production and with quality control in the sense of ensuring that products leaving the workplace conform to specifications. We assume that specifications exist which adequately reflect customer requirements.

Although, following this line of argument, we have separated the 'production trans-formation' from other organisational activities, we should not now separate 'quality control' from other operational activities. The full set of production decisions impact on conformance quality. For instance if we pay inadequate attention to job design we may inhibit production operatives from making things to within specification or may motivate them (for instance through ill considered bonus systems) to produce in volume with less attention to conformance quality.

In addition we should remember that the customer requires more than conformance quality. Referring back to our computer purchase example, the customer wanted:

- *product attributes and performance* – presumably covered by the specification and the classic area of quality control
- *service characteristics* – an operational process in themselves
- *warranty* – which assumes continuing availability of spare parts and a repair or replacement facility, a major concern for production and inventory planning and control
- *delivery availability* – addressed by production planning systems
- *suitable price* – which entails cost control and productivity.

Thus however broadly or narrowly we wish to define quality control, the customer has a broad set of requirements which are addressed by production operations man-agement as a whole.

The traditional literature emphasises the trade-offs which may exist between pro-ductivity and quality. This is quite contrary to modern thinking where it is asserted that high quality is completely consistent with high volumes of production and with cost effective production. The latter certainly appears to be the case in electronic assembly, for instance, but some production processes appear to be less controllable. The point we are making, however, is valid whether trade-offs exist or whether 'zero-defect' and 'right-first-time' production is possible. Decision making in production must simultaneously consider a range of issues – quality decisions are not separable from the totality of operational decision making.

---

**TASK**    Consider once again a regularly purchased item. What must operations in the supply-ing firm (or the supply chain as a whole) get right in order to satisfy the customer's quality requirements?

---

This leads us to the second organisational approach. If operational decisions should be viewed as a totality, then why should they arbitrarily be separated from designing, selling and other associated areas of work. The simple answer is that the full process is immensely complicated and some form of division of work is necessary. Whilst true, it is also the case that the boundaries between different areas of functional responsibility are the scene of endless quality management problems. Might it be simpler to reject functional boundaries and concentrate on building teams focused on satisfying the needs of specific customer groups? In many instances this is possible, particularly in small production units where the people who make things can talk to the customers about their needs but it fits uneasily with the economics of traditional mass production where job specialisation is seen to be important for productivity and cost reduction.

A partial answer to this problem is technological in that communications technology can reinforce supplier–producer–customer links (for example, through the use of electronic mail), process technology can cost-effectively produce high quality goods and information systems can aid production planning and control. An organisational answer is provided by the supply chain concept and Total Quality Management.

## SUPPLY CHAINS AND TQM

Rather than viewing an organisation as functional blocks, it is useful to consider it as a set of processes linked together to form a chain of supply. This chain may encompass many organisations and is therefore a flexible concept, not radically affected by organisational boundaries. This is an important point as operational activity becomes more based on small, autonomous units with extensive sub-contracting. Thus rather than concentrating on one producer and customer relationship we have a chain of supply with many supplier–customer links. In particular we use the concept of the 'internal customer' within an organisation to refer to any individual (or process) receiving goods, services or information from another individual (or process). Note that this relationship may apply between automated processes, though some human intervention is initially required in setting the parameters of the relationship.

One advantage of this disaggregated, though linked, view of process inter-relationships is that we can readily use the language of quality management to describe the relationship and this is a key idea behind Total Quality Management (TQM).

TQM is based on the individual processes and their relationship to other parts of the chain. It emphasises, at every link in the chain, the need to arrive at agreement on performance requirements, supplier capability, timing, cost and the monitoring of changing needs. Every process is both a supplier to other 'downstream' processes and a customer to 'upstream' processes. It shows the value of being close to your customer and of maintaining good communications.

The underlying philosophy of such an approach is one of decentralised planning and control with active management of the boundaries between processes. This may well include the assumption of a market relationship between the processes, for instance a production process may obtain its raw materials from another department in the same organisation or may go outside if it can get a better deal. It is an approach which fosters flexibility and the management of changing relationships but can also result in high levels of uncertainty and should be applied judiciously to key processes and areas of innovation and long-term investment.

Indeed a point of warning is appropriate here. One of the main recurring issues in this book is whether centralised or decentralised planning and control are most appropriate. For instance in Chapters 9 and 11 we consider this issue in the context of stock control and production planning. It is recognised from systems theory that optimising the behaviour of sub-systems does not necessarily lead to optimal results for the system as a whole. An overall framework of aims, objectives and procedures is necessary to preserve the fundamental strategies and core processes of a business and to satisfy the customers' long-term needs. Of course this raises a number of thorny issues in the area of strategic planning and organisational design which are beyond the scope of this book. It should not be imagined, however, that any easy answers are available for the solution of fundamental organisational problems.

Thus, we have argued that whether quality management is based on traditional or supply-chain lines, it is a central issue in operations management. We now turn from matters of principle to those of practice – how do we actually manage quality?

## PRACTICAL ISSUES IN PRODUCT QUALITY MANAGEMENT

We concentrate now on outlining some basic techniques of quality management in production situations before considering service quality. We return to the general principles of quality control and improvement in Chapter 3.

### Yield management

It is necessary from the start to separate two distinct, though connected, issues. We should be fully aware from the discussion above that, given a product specification, we want all items delivered to the customer to conform to that specification. It is commercially very valuable if we can guarantee 'zero defects' to the customer (along with correct numbers of items and time of delivery), not least because it removes the need for customer goods–inwards inspection and facilitates Just-in-Time control (see Chapter 11). If defects are possible, then inspection, selection, return, rectification and a variety of other non-value-adding activities become necessary.

Customer 'zero defects' can be obtained in two different ways. We may have manufacturing processes which are so well controlled that no defects are contained in the output. We refer to this as 'right first time' manufacture (a concept that dates back to the 1950s at least) or we can apply a selection procedure to a less than perfect output to remove defectives (we are assuming, somewhat optimistically, that the selection method is 100 per cent reliable).

The first issue therefore is the conformance quality of goods delivered to the customer. A highly desirable goal is zero defects at this point in the supply chain.

The second issue is the conformance quality of items produced by each stage of our manufacturing process, including receipt from suppliers. We refer to this as the yield from each process and can readily see that a 100 per cent yield is economically desirable though it may be technologically infeasible.

If our processes can produce 100 per cent good items, then we can promise zero defects to the client, assuming we can ensure that no damage occurs in transit. If our yield is less than 100 per cent then a highly efficient selection process involving all production will be necessary to ensure zero defects to the client.

Thus we can readily see the importance of yield management in ensuring good quality goods as well as avoiding expensive selection processes. In addition, yield management is important in preserving capacity (see 'Milon' case, Part 2, in Chapter 1) and allowing effective production planning and scheduling.

A particular difficulty obviously arises if the yield is not only less than 100 per cent but also fluctuates over time. This can cause massive problems for all areas of operational control and be highly uneconomic. It is not surprising that Deming, one of the original quality gurus, makes 'variability' the key problem in quality management. One of the major techniques for reducing production variability is Statistical Process Control (see below and Chapter 3).

## Inspection, selection and acceptance sampling

For a number of years, statistically based sampling procedures have had a place in the tool-kit of the quality manager. In particular, if testing the performance of an item involves its destruction (for example strength tests of materials) then only a sample can be tested.

Statistical Quality Control (SQC) was evolved to handle such situations as well as situations where the economics of testing makes 100 per cent inspection infeasible. Even when high levels of quality or thorough inspection and selection are in place, SQC is useful for designing auditing procedures which are usually based on samples.

Acceptance sampling, based on a range of published sampling plans, was developed half a century ago. It assumes that a batch of product (or raw material) will either be accepted for use or rejected and sent back for selection and rectification and that this decision will be made on the basis of samples taken from the batch.

Sampling procedures involve a risk, even if competently carried out, that too many or too few of the defects in the batch will be found. In particular a few defectives scattered in a large batch are unlikely to be found unless a very large sample is taken. Thus acceptance sampling may result in the wrong decision being made (sending a poor batch to the customer or rejecting a reasonable batch) and can never guarantee zero defects in the batch. These risks are summarised by the 'operating characteristic curve' (OC) of the sampling plan (see specialist SQC texts for details).

It should also be noted that the use of such methods assumes that production comes together in (large) batches, that the test procedures are reliable, that sampling is unbiased and that systems exist to handle all eventualities (for example, rectifying rejected batches and mollifying unhappy customers). If this account seems somewhat cynical it should be noted that SQC is far superior to the casual, unstructured methods where the risks are not even quantified and proper procedures put in place. It does, however, show the value of reliable, high quality production methods if good customer quality is truly sought.

## Statistical Process Control (SPC)

For many, SPC is the foundation of technical approaches to quality control. It is based on the idea of sampling the output of all work processes not just to spot defects but to note trends in the process outputs which, though not currently unacceptable, point to problems which may occur in the future. Thus actions may be taken to head off trouble before it occurs. To put it bluntly, prevention is better than cure.

Once again the emphasis is on the management of risks. You may be unlucky in your sampling, check only very good items of output and a problem develops unnoticed. Similarly your samples may pick up the few slightly dubious items of output and you overhaul the machine (or upset a human producer) unnecessarily. A well developed SPC system will, however, enable you to control the risks you are taking. Naturally this technique is of far greater application than controlling production. It can be applied to many aspects of service and information processing situations, often by the process operator. Furthermore it can be linked to a variety of diagnostic techniques to form a package to control current operations and suggest ways to improve things in the future.

## Taguchi methods

It is possible to go somewhat further than SPC through the consideration of issues of manufacturability and product design. Manufacturability, as the name suggests, is concerned with whether an intended product can in fact be reliably made in suitable quantities at an economic cost.

Part of SPC is a consideration of process capability and the inherent variability in the output of a process. If this variability is large, control may be difficult, or even impossible, and it seems natural to employ technical knowledge in an attempt to reduce variability wherever possible. This approach is emphasised by Deming, along with the idea that variability may result from human resource and systems problems.

Genichi Taguchi developed an alternative called the robust design methodology. This assumes that some levels of process variability may be unavoidable and therefore seeks to design products in such a way that their performance is less sensitive to process variability. The statistical methods involved in this approach are quite complex and the interested reader is referred to the advice for further study given at the end of this chapter. The existence of such methods, however, should be known by all Operations Managers and the fundamental idea of designing products (and services) so that they are less sensitive to the inherent variability in their delivery processes is of great importance.

## Quality function deployment

Having raised the issue of the links between design and production it is appropriate to mention that structured methodologies do exist for the design process. Modern product design is often highly complex and technologically sophisticated. Competitive pressures, however, require that design time is reduced and that the overall result is fully aligned to customer needs at a reasonable cost as well as being manufacturable. Product design is usually carried out by teams of specialists who need to communicate with one another and with other individuals. There is therefore a need for a common language and a systematic approach.

Quality Function Deployment (QFD) is an example of one such methodology. It is described fully in the specialist TQM texts (see Further Reading) and, once again, shows the need for an integrated, organisation-wide approach to quality management.

## Monitoring quality costs

Taguchi has a definition of quality as '... the loss imparted by the product to society from the time the product is shipped'. By placing the emphasis on 'society' and the total life-span of a product this is interesting as a 'green' concept of quality. However, making practical use of such a definition would present problems. The emphasis on discussing quality through its costs is, however, perfectly well accepted. Indeed, the costs of quality are an essential basis for decision making.

What are the costs of quality? The most obvious costs are, not surprisingly, the ones which are easiest to measure:

- internal costs of scrap and rework
- external warranty costs and replacement of faulty goods
- costs of inspection and testing procedures and all administrative costs.

Even then it is by no means easy to measure the above adequately. For instance, the internal cost of rework must include not only the variable cost of such activity (labour, materials, etc.) but also the loss of capacity due to such work in the production system. If we are more ambitious in our measurement, it will quickly occur to us that this can be extended to include further systems costs:

- capacity loss
- long lead times due to rework delays
- overtime payments to reduce demand backlog
- extra stock as buffer against yield variability.

Moreover, if we now look outside the walls of our factory we discover:

- loss of goodwill and sales due to a poor reputation for quality.

Shocked by this catalogue we decide to take action to improve quality, thus further incurring costs in:

- training
- development of quality management systems.

Effective quality management is costly and the quantification of such costs is essential. Only then can we know how best to divert our expenditure from cure to prevention, and in the long run to have satisfied customers at minimal cost of quality.

## Benchmarking

On several occasions we have emphasised the competitive dimension of quality. One obvious need, therefore, is to obtain information on the quality of product and service provided by our rivals (or by similar public services if appropriate). This form of benchmarking, often involving extensive market research and examination of competitors' actual offerings, has been well known and widely practised for some time.

An interesting, recent development has been the extension of this approach to all aspects of operational processes. For example a company will identify a specific operation and search around for data (times, costs, methods, results, etc.) on similar operations in other organisations or departments in the same company. This may involve no direct competition or secrecy. Indeed, non-competing organisations may form clubs in order to pool such information for mutual benefit. The overall objective is to identify best practice and seek to emulate it and perhaps even improve on it. This idea is an important component of the 'continuous improvement' (Kaizen) approach to be discussed in Chapter 3.

## Quality management standards – BS EN ISO 9001:1994

The majority of managers at all levels of organisations will, in the past few years, have heard of BS5750. This British Standard gives an organisation the opportunity to seek external recognition for its quality management systems. Companies who gain this form of 'systems accreditation' quite naturally exploit it for its public relations and marketing value. For many years, major industrial and retail organisations have set standards for their suppliers which cover both the goods being supplied and the quality control systems of the supplier. A national standard has the advantage of providing a common framework, though each organisation seeking accreditation must develop their own appropriate systems within this framework.

From an operational point of view, this approach at least provides a checklist of the components of quality planning and control systems. The latest version (the BS EN ISO 9000 series, a European Standard) includes management responsibilities, contracts and the control of design, purchasing and processing. It deals with inspection and testing, packaging, training – in fact, it covers all aspects of quality for which routine procedures can be set down.

It must be said that, at worst, such procedures are only a matter of concern when external auditing takes place. Many companies, however, now take a more enlightened view and understand that such systems can have a positive value in co-ordinating actions involving a wide variety of staff to ensure that quality standards are consistently maintained. In many ways this is the crux of the problem with quality management. Most organisations know how high quality goods and services could be delivered. Great things can often be achieved during a 'quality campaign' or under the scrutiny of external auditors and fiercely quality-conscious customers. Motivating organisations and their staff to maintain such standards consistently presents a very considerable challenge.

## SERVICE QUALITY

Having devoted a long section to the quality problems of product manufacture, it may seem something of an afterthought to now mention service and office operations.

Nothing could be further from the truth for the following reasons.

- Service and office operations often require accompanying products and material supplies so the issues of product quality management apply directly.
- The concepts of product quality management can easily be adapted to many service and information provision situations. For instance, Deming's ideas of variability reduction are equally applicable to the provision of consistently good mass services.
- TQM concepts are as applicable to service situations as to product ones. Similarly the supply chain concept is relevant to industrial service and office situations in an obvious way. Its application to consumer services (for example, banking and health care) is through the chain of support for the direct service provider.
- The presence of the customer in service situations necessitates the development of new concepts and models to reflect provider–client interactions.
- Public sector services, in particular, raise important ethical issues of rights and duties (for instance in the Health Service) and is a major area of research.
- Quality in information systems is becoming a critical issue as such systems become larger and more widespread in their use with the number of safety-critical situations increasing.

The key issue we will explore here, however, is the effect of the customer being present during operational delivery. This has a number of beneficial effects, depending on the form of service:

- The customer can choose directly from a number of offerings available (for example, at a cinema complex).
- The customer can help tailor the service by making requests (for example, in a hotel or restaurant).
- The customer can help provide the service (for example, in a supermarket).
- The service provider can directly question the customer to clarify their needs (for example, in an estate agency).
- An in-depth personal service can be provided (for example, a consultancy).
- The customer can be directly changed by the service provider (for example, in a hospital).
- The presence of the customer can provide direct motivation and feedback for the service provider, indeed many professional service delivery roles are highly regarded and satisfying.

The presence of the customer can also cause some fundamental operational problems.

- Variability in customer arrival and processing time causes problems for scheduling and hence affects service quality for other customers.
- Perceptions of quality, expected and received, can fluctuate throughout the service encounter.
- The service environment must be designed to accommodate customers with a wide range of characteristics.

- Customers can cause damage to the operational environment, possibly through misuse and ignorance, and may be abusive to service providers.

Thus, as with all service situations, universal rules are hard to find but some models and concepts of service quality have found fairly wide acceptance. The simplest of these, though one of the most useful, is presented in Figure 2.1. It is an everyday observation that the balance between knowledge, behaviour and systems may be imperfect to the detriment of the total service experience.

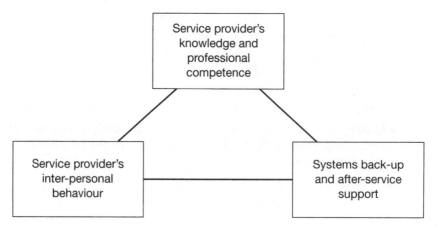

**Fig. 2.1 Determinants of service quality**

**TASK**

Consider some service encounters of which you have recent experience (for example, in a shop, leisure facility, etc.). Can you identify occasions when:

- the service was pleasantly, but incompetently, delivered?
- the server was obviously knowledgeable but unhelpful?
- the direct service was satisfactory in terms of behaviour and knowledge, but either the server was badly supported (for instance by poor computer systems or the unavailability of materials) or the follow-up to the service encounter was poor?

For one of the occasions identified above, what improvements would you suggest be carried out to produce an excellent and balanced service?

## Determinants of service quality and gap analysis

The presence of the customer potentially brings into play a number of factors which need not be considered in product quality situations. These are summarised in one of the most widely known service quality models, SERVQUAL. The list below suggests a range of determinants of service quality, some of which will be of key importance in particular service situations and all of which should at least be considered:

- *reliability* – providing the right service, every time
- *responsiveness* – providing prompt and willing service
- *competence* – skills and knowledge of the server
- *access* – contact is as easy as possible
- *courtesy* – polite and respectful
- *communication* – service is well explained
- *credibility* – trustworthy and believable (the server and their organisation)
- *security* – free from danger; confidential
- *understanding* – server takes care to learn the customer's specific needs
- *tangibles* – facilities, materials.

**TASKS**

1. With reference to the everyday service situations you described above in the context of the 'service triangle model' (see previous task), examine them now in terms of the SERVQUAL model in order to identify further problem areas. Once again, what could be done to improve operations?

2. Can you identify service situations which score badly for particular dimensions of the SERVQUAL model, in particular for specific client groups (for instance, access might be poor for wheelchair users; language problems might inhibit servers from appreciating real client needs ...)? What could you *realistically* do to improve the service?

(Note: Before attempting this task, you might re-read the discussion of service process choice in Chapter 1.)

One of the most quoted laws of service quality tells us quite simply that:

**Satisfaction = Perception – Expectation**

Our degree of satisfaction at the service we received is the difference between what we thought we actually got and what we thought we were going to get!

This draws our attention to the importance of communication, whether before, during or after the service encounter. It also reminds us that expectations change over time. This gives rise to the idea of service gap analysis and the notion of service quality dynamics, as illustrated in Figure 2.2. This material is as much the concern of the marketing specialist as the operations service delivery manager and shows once again the importance of quality concepts as 'organisational glue'.

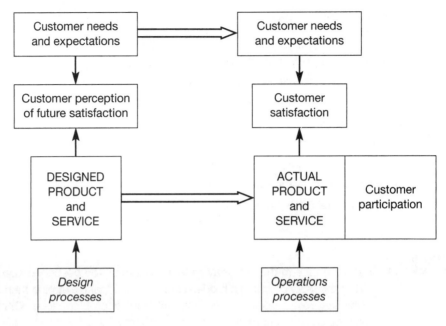

**Fig. 2.2 Service quality dynamics**

**TASKS**

1. Using your examples of service situations developed above, describe how customer expectations change over time in one or more contexts (if in doubt, perhaps service received in a bank or in a college might provide examples).

2. To provide a contrast, consider a situation involving the delivery of a complex professional service in a commercial context, for instance a management consultancy or an architect advising a client on a building project. Use appropriate parts of the above models to explore such a situation, noting that the discussion in Chapter 6 on client relationships in project management is relevant here.

## Public sector service context

Though it is somewhat difficult at times to know what is meant by the 'public sector', the quality of service we receive from, for example, health, education, transport and the police continues to be newsworthy and also to be the subject of considerable research.

Here we have some similarity with commercial service delivery overlaid with expectations and values which add considerably to the complexity of any definition of quality. Customers consider themselves to have traditional rights beyond those typical of commercial service encounters. Service delivery staff are often highly trained professionals with strong views on the meaning of 'quality' in their areas of work.

Work in such organisations is made even more demanding by the changing expectations of customers and other stakeholders, such as the government, representing both public opinion and financial feasibility. The above models can be adapted to throw some light on these types of service encounters and the literature mentioned at the end of this chapter should be consulted for further ideas and information.

# CONCLUSION

If the above brief introduction to quality management themes seems exhausting then one should realise that each section and each technique mentioned are, in themselves, the subject of a range of books and articles. It is therefore hard to summarise what is, in itself, a summary. The following three questions might, however, help in putting forward the broad issues:

1. *How do I know what quality means in a given context?*

   - Start with identifying the customer (external or internal).
   - What does the customer want (needs)?
   - What should I promise to provide (requirements)?
   - How can I ensure that I do in fact provide what I promised (systems for conformance)?

2. *What are the building blocks for the provision of good quality?*

   - communication
   - design
   - capability
   - control
   - training
   - quality culture
   - systems and procedures
   - continuous improvement.

3. *If an organisation has 'quality problems' what might be going wrong?*

Your turn to answer some questions! Try the above, remembering that the answers need not be subtle or complex. Keep it simple!

## FURTHER READING

The management of quality is one of the most extensively written about themes in management today. Any full text on operations management will give additional information, particularly on the details of techniques. The following give specific guidance on issues raised in this chapter:

Definitions of quality:

> Garvin, D. A. (1988), *Managing Quality*, Free Press, New York.

Total Quality Management (TQM):

> Bank, J. (1992), *The Essence of Total Quality Management*, Prentice Hall, New York.

TQM, comparisons between the gurus and techniques of quality management:

> Logothetis, N. (1992), *Managing for Total Quality*, Prentice Hall, New York.

Service and public sector issues:

> Fitzsimmons, J. A. and Fitzsimmons, M. J. (1994), *Service Management for Competitive Advantage*, McGraw Hill, New York.
>
> Morgan, C. and Murgatroyd, S. (1994), *Total Quality Management in the Public Sector*, Open University Press, Buckingham.
>
> Rust, R. T. and Oliver, R. L. (eds) (1994), *Service Quality*, Sage, London.

The words of a 'guru':

> Deming, W. E. (1982), *Out of the Crisis*, Cambridge University Press, Cambridge.

# CHAPTER 3

# Controlling and Improving Work

Continuing the general theme of Chapter 2, this chapter considers how the performance of work systems may be controlled and improved. Performance may, of course, relate to the quality of output but also to the cost-effectiveness of the operational system.

**OBJECTIVES**

**This chapter:**

- **describes the basic structure of a closed-loop control system**
- **contrasts differing strategies for improvement in manufacturing, service and office operations**
- **outlines some techniques for systems control and improvement in the context of a case exercise.**

## INTRODUCTION

In Chapter 1 we emphasised the need for good product and process design. In particular a manufacturing company must ensure that a product is designed for manufacturability at a competitive cost in the desired volumes. Similarly a service should be designed for effective delivery, as for instance fast food restaurants demonstrate.

This is not the end of the story for the Operations Manager. The product manufacturing and service delivery processes must be controlled so that high levels of productivity and cost effectiveness are continually achieved. Moreover, in a competitive environment, it is usually necessary to improve the processes as well as the product and service offerings to keep up with the market.

In this chapter we consider some of the very practical issues in managing product manufacture and service delivery, not forgetting the role of information systems. A feature of modern Operations Management is the considerable and creative attention given to such matters, to some extent inspired by the practices and experiences of Japanese companies. We are principally concerned with the managerial techniques of process control (as opposed to the engineering issues) and the methods which may be used to promote process improvement. This in turn leads us to a consideration of the need for appropriate policies and strategies and to the human relations issues underlying operational practice (see Chapter 4).

A word of warning is appropriate here. Good practitioners have always understood that good operational performance depends on a wide range of interrelated systems features. Unfortunately, managerial and shop floor practice has often not reflected this. It is all too easy in a busy firm to assume that the training officer is handling training, engineers look after the machines and product design is the concern of individuals that shop floor workers will never meet in the course of an entire working life. Why worry about such matters – they are Someone Else's Problem.

A similar attitude can be seen in service delivery where, in spite of direct contact with the customer, casual and disinterested attitudes may be evident. In the delivery of professional services (teaching, health and so forth) a different problem can become evident where the direct service provider, quite naturally, identifies strongly with the client but sees organisation wide systems and management as both unhelpful and unchangeable.

The management of a modern organisation, working in a competitive environment, should work very hard to counter these damaging effects. One key to this will be well thought out policies for process control and improvement.

We will begin, therefore, by considering the essential nature of control processes. Subsequent sections will deal with styles of improvement (Kaizen contrasted with BPR), the differences between manufacturing, service and office contexts and give a brief introduction to the standard techniques developed to control and improve operations.

## THE NATURE OF CONTROL

The argument in this chapter depends on precisely what is meant by 'control' in the context of operational processes. One point, however, should be clear at the start; measuring and reporting are not the same as control! All too often, managerial 'control systems' (particularly regarding cost control) put a great effort into reporting variances and blithely assume that the manager receiving the reports will take some appropriate action. Control involves a suitable information system allied to action.

Engineers and systems theorists have studied control systems extensively with particular reference to the automatic control of machines. The resulting models are often highly mathematical and may be capable of precise predictions of systems behaviour. Managerial and social uses of the word 'control' are more varied, on occasions with unpleasant overtones for the individuals being controlled. The limited operational literature includes elements from both approaches, although the interested reader should consult the writings of Stafford Beer for a sophisticated use of biological control systems as an analogy with organisational control (see Further Reading at end of this chapter).

The basic form of a 'negative feedback single control loop' is shown in Figure 3.1. It consists of the elements listed in Table 3.1. The definitions given in this Table are very general and it is best to consider them in the light of a few concrete examples:

**Table 3.1 Features of a control system**

| | |
|---|---|
| Process | the part of the system whose behaviour we are attempting to control over time |
| Output | any result of the process (which may or may not be intended for customer use) which may be used as a basis for control |
| Measurement | the collection of appropriate data based on the output, usually at regular intervals of time |
| Statistics | information based on the output data collected (perhaps from a number of past time periods) in a suitable form for comparison with standards |
| Standards | reflect our expectations regarding the output from the process; may be based on designed features of the output (for instance product tolerances) or expected features of a process which is 'in control' |
| Comparison | consideration of differences between statistics (reflecting actual performance) and standards (reflecting desired performance) as a basis for action |
| Decision maker | takes in the results of the comparison (and other information as appropriate) and manages the input in such a way as to achieve performance which is within standards |
| Input | the full range of inputs (material, human, informational, financial) which are required by the process and whose characteristics determine the performance of the process. |

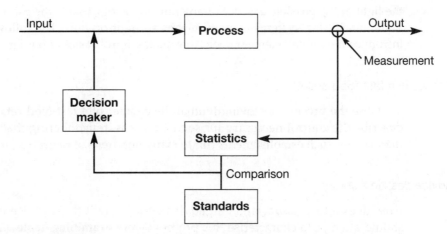

**Fig. 3.1 Control loop**

**Table 3.2 A manufacturing control system**

| | |
|---|---|
| Process | material transformation (but should we also include material handling, testing...?) |
| Output | box lids made to a given specification |
| Measurements | may be the physical dimensions of the lids, smoothness of finish and edges, general appearance, amount of scrap generated... |
| Statistics and standards | will not include all possible physical aspects of the output but should relate to key needs of the customer (for example, tolerances) and the capability of the process |
| Comparison | 'management by exception', that is, only pre-defined differences between statistics and standards will be reported to the decision maker (remember that such a process may be operating continually and be only one of many such in a factory) |
| Decision maker | may be an operator, an engineer or a supervisor. What action does one expect each to make in any given circumstance? In many processes the 'decision' may be programmed, that is the machine may automatically respond to test results with occasional reference to humans. |

## 1. Product manufacture

A machine takes in strips of steel and produces lids for small boxes. This common type of process might be controlled as described in Table 3.2. Notice that this most common of industrial situations is, in fact, highly complex and involves a number of judgements when setting up suitable controls. The reader may find this surprising in the light of the possible absence of any human factors, that is the control of fully automatic machining systems is by no means straightforward. The following situations introduce the human element. Does this make control easier or harder?

## 2. Service in a fast-food outlet

Visualise the process of serving food at the counter of a fast-food retail outlet. Try to describe the control necessary for such a process, remembering that the operations manuals for such establishments run to many hundreds of pages!

## 3. Advice desk in a library

How does a tutor librarian at an advice desk know if their advice is suitable? You should attempt to characterise this process before examining Table 3.3, which shows the possible elements of the control system. As you can appreciate, the control of professional service delivery is far more subtle (though not necessarily more difficult) than that of industrial processes.

**Table 3.3 A service control system**

| Process | talking to students plus distributed materials |
|---|---|
| Output | improved knowledge and satisfaction of student |
| Measurement and statistics | may be easy to define (student can now find location of reference journal) or very hard (student writes better essay); opinion surveys or collection of complaints may be needed to assess value of output |
| Standard | formal service standards may be defined or the opinion of student or librarian that the process was properly performed may be relied on |
| Decision maker and input | presumably the librarians themselves would be relied on to apply their professional judgement to adapting and improving ways of advising students (assuming they have influence over resources available, materials...) |

Having understood the basics of operational control, a number of considerations come to mind. In simple terms, control consists of a:

- basic input–output transformational process
- measurement process based on the output of the basic process
- process of reporting
- process of taking action.

These various processes are all elements of control. It needs to be understood that, for instance, the 'measurement process' must itself be controlled to ensure that its 'output' (data) is valid. Are we sampling properly from the output of the machine, using the measuring devices correctly, recording the data carefully...? Control is a pervasive issue throughout all levels of an organisation.

Furthermore a number of issues can readily be seen in this simple description of control:

- Who does the controlling?
- Who is responsible?
- Who takes action?
- How often do we sample and measure output? Sampling too often may waste resources and cause frequent tinkering with the basic process. Infrequent sampling may miss the onset of a major problem.
- If the output is variable, how can we get a representative picture?
- Can you actually measure the important features of the output (for instance, in service situations)?
- Where do the 'standards' come from? How often should they be reviewed and updated?
- Does the decision maker look only at the direct results of the output? Why not monitor environmental and other changes?

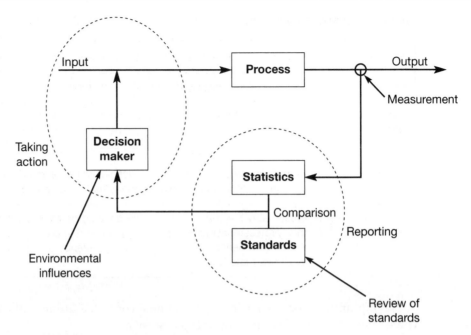

**Fig. 3.2 Control loop – augumented**

In Figure 3.2 we show a more developed view of a control process which incorporates some of the concerns mentioned above. The reader will, however, realise by now that the study of operational control is a major undertaking and our brief description in this book merely scratches the surface.

## STRATEGIES FOR IMPROVEMENT

Since the beginning of the century, there have been a number of attempts to improve what we would now refer to as operational processes. Many of these attempts have been related to manufacturing processes, for instance the rise of 'Work measurement and methods study' was an important facilitating feature of the development of mass production. Such techniques, though, may in principle be applied to any area of operations. Organisation and Methods (O&M) are more likely to be spoken about in the area of office work but the basic principle of studying and measuring work with a view to improvement is universal.

It should be noted at this stage that improvements might be seen to benefit the organisation, customers and the workforce. One of the motivating factors in the original use of work study was to protect the worker from exploitation through unsafe and unhealthy working practices. In the long run, however, all of these methods are driven by organisational objectives.

The necessity of such 'improvement techniques' may be questioned. Surely once a process has been designed either it maintains its validity or it can be gradually adjusted? Everyday experience suggests that this is not the case. Piecemeal adjustments add up in ways which are not consistent with each other or client needs. Costs increase, working practices relax and overall goals are forgotten. In addition competitors learn new ways to organise processes, new technologies become available and the environment changes. Customers become more demanding both in terms of the product or service received and the expected cost. We live in a world of change and learning and have no right to expect that *ad hoc* changes to operational processes are sufficient to maintain overall effectiveness.

More recently the mantle of 'improvement techniques' has been taken over by such practices as Total Quality Management and Lean Manufacturing. The Japanese have demonstrated that dramatic improvements in productivity and quality are possible, often through the application of Kaizen, the philosophy of continuous improvement.

The West has learnt much from this and made changes appropriate for differing working cultures and organisational contexts. Thus the Japanese techniques of Total Quality Control become translated in the West into Total Quality Management with its, necessarily greater, emphasis on the client and on implementation.

Methods such as Just-in-Time manufacturing, though spectacularly successful in some Japanese and Western contexts, have been criticised as being too slow in their application and too tightly tied to manufacturing processes. Thus the basics of Kaizen (a gradual, employee-centred philosophy of continuous improvement) have come under attack and the need for fast, radical, 'breakthrough' performance has been emphasised.

Business Process Re-engineering has been developed in this context. BPR emphasises a planned, top management led approach to process change with the goal of dramatic improvements in customer service and cost reduction, largely through the use of information technology. A slightly different variant is Business Re-engineering with a greater concern for strategic organisational change.

Although only surfacing as an acronym in the early 1990s, BPR uses a range of standard operational planning and systems analysis techniques. It is being criticised already for failing at the implementation stage in a number of cases, and for leading to 'downsizing' and redundancies rather than improved effectiveness for the client. Research is, however, gradually developing on its most appropriate use. It does address the central need of providing a methodology to analyse operational processes and an approach to implementing change.

## IMPROVING MANUFACTURING PROCESSES

In a product manufacturing context, improvements may be possible in a variety of operational processes. To the casual observer, the most obvious improvement will be the use of an altered materials transformational process. In other words we use different machines, materials and techniques to make the product. Thus we may achieve improvements through cost reduction, greater productivity or the facility to make a product with more marketable features. An important, and more subtle, form of improvement is the ability to make a product which meets quality standards more consistently. As we discussed in Chapter 2, variability in manufacture is directly linked with conformance quality and reducing the variability of items produced can be of great value.

In practice, however, improvements in manufacturing come in a wide variety of forms. Typically we may seek to improve testing procedures, materials movement methods, handling and packaging. A concern with improving the quality of supplied parts may bring advantages. More subtle improvements are the changes in materials flow planning and control techniques (see Chapter 11). Improvements must bring increased performance levels for the whole system rather than a small part of it. To make this happen, improvements must be part of a strategic plan to give direction to the whole effort and ensure that resources are available.

A critical strategic issue in practice concerns who is responsible for creating improvements. In a traditionally engineered context, trained professionals study the work process, decide on improvements and implement them. A modern factory is far more likely to give credence to the suggestions and views of all staff, making the reasonable assumption that those who actually carry out a process every day for months and years may have some very good ideas about how to change it for the better!

## IMPROVING SERVICE DELIVERY

A popular idea, derived from the Peters and Waterman *In Search of Excellence* studies, refers to the need to keep close to the customer. Nobody gets physically closer to the actual customer than the service deliverer, though in spirit one can often see that a gulf still exists. As we discussed in Chapter 2, however, the concept of service quality should provide a platform to deliver most services effectively.

Of course, the problem of control remains and the mechanistic forms of control applied easily in a factory might seem intrusive in a service context. Since statistics show that most customers do not complain if they receive poor service but simply move to an alternative supplier, control must be a key issue in service operations.

Rising expectations make the situation even more complex (see Chapter 2). Exceptional service will be appreciated but will soon be expected as the norm. In this case the need for continuous improvement is even more keenly felt.

The model of service quality shown in Figure 2.1 (see page 38) provides a useful guide. Using this approach, quality service depends on a mixture of the following features:

- good interpersonal skills
- sufficient knowledge
- appropriate systems.

Interpersonal skills and knowledge come from training and experience allied with the characteristics of the individual service deliverer, which incidentally shows the need for care in recruitment. Information systems quality depends on appropriate design and resourcing. The success of the total delivery system depends on all three features. Quality control and improvement will therefore be facilitated in different ways depending on the feature under consideration but will require consistency between all three features.

The above shows the value of the 'Front Office and Back Room' view of service operations. Control and improvement in the back room will be achieved through typical office management procedures whilst front office effectiveness is based on more subtle considerations. Essential, however, is the harmonisation of the two, a matter given considerable attention in the specialist service operations literature through such techniques as 'blueprinting', a formal, structured methodology linking activities and information flows in the front office and the back room.

## THE OFFICE CONTEXT

In our classification of operational transformations, the office is the scene of data and information handling. Though manual and paper based procedures are still very much in evidence, most would agree that we are here in the realm of information technology with attention being focused on the design of information systems and on the interface between human and machine parts of the total system.

To some extent office work is similar to the mass production factory. For instance, an insurance company or a financial services organisation must find ways to process a vast amount of data reliably and machine based solutions will usually be appropriate and cost effective. Thus issues of control are similar to those in a factory and improvements are sought through the use of 'big bang' approaches such as Business Process Re-engineering. A particular issue in this context is in the area of software engineering where large application programmes may have grown and been 'improved' over a number of years leading to doubts as to their reliability in all circumstances.

Much office work is less routine and requires tailored solutions. Personal and networked computer systems place a flexible tool in the hands of the service deliverer in order that the service may be adapted to current needs. Typical is the use of query languages to interrogate databases, for instance to build up a market research report from a wide range of sources. In such instances, control and improvement are in the hands of the specific deliverer who will deal directly with the client (internal or external) to meet their needs. This situation is akin to project management and is discussed in Chapter 6. A major problem here is organisational learning and improvement, that is finding ways in which the organisation as a whole can improve its client provision based on the disparate experiences of past service provision.

## TECHNIQUES OF CONTROL AND CONTINUOUS IMPROVEMENT

A great deal of emphasis in recent operational and general management practice has been placed on the use of appropriate structured techniques for controlling activities and encouraging continuous, incremental improvement. These two things are related in that the standards against which one controls a process must be capable of being systematically raised as competition intensifies and learning takes place.

In this section we illustrate some of these techniques through an example involving office operations. It is suggested that, at each stage of the discussion, the reader considers how the techniques described could be used in an alternative situation, preferably drawn from past experience or relating to a current work problem.

## The 'Stone Insurance' Case

The Stone Insurance Company offers household insurance to the general public, mainly through telephone selling. Its customer record system is computer based and just about adequate though problems are increasingly occurring.

One problem relates to previous customers who have not renewed policies and are not being followed up effectively. Non-renewal may be for a variety of reasons, in particular it may simply be case that a renewal notice has been mislaid or that other quotations are being examined. In such instances a telephone call, with appropriate sales advice, may regain the customer. Timing is important, however, and since Stone's sales staff are often late in contacting the customer they discover that alternative arrangements have been made.

(See Chapter 7 for a different view of this case situation in the context of radical change and project management. The specific details given below are for illustration purposes only and are not indicative of current standards of performance in this industry. In the following text, references to the case study are in italics and their analysis should be considered as an ongoing student task.)

*An action team (the Stone Group) is set up to explore this matter. How should it begin its work?*

### Setting objectives and the action plan

Any formal improvement work must begin by determining terms of reference and objectives. This is not from a need to promote bureaucracy but simply to initiate and maintain focus. Any real work problem situation has many facets and links with other problem areas. Progress usually depends on carefully defining which particular issues are to be explored.

An exception to this might be a strategic planning task force which may wish to begin with a clean slate in order not to be bound by past decisions or a group formed to analyse a particularly difficult problem which has not yielded to a direct assault. In other cases, particularly with operational level problem solving, putting a boundary round a problem is a necessary first step, though the boundary might have to be moved if progress proves impossible.

Thus a useful initial phase of group work is to:

- define the problem
- draw a boundary round the system being examined
- determine the aims and objectives of the system being studied.

At the same time the group should reflect on the following:

- membership and ways of working together (when to meet, roles and responsibilities, etc.)

- relationship with other problem solving groups
- group objectives and a timescale for action
- available resources.

At this stage it is also useful to engage in more creative ways of exploring the problem situation. A common difficulty with a team set up to explore, for example, quality problems is that people have differing views about what this means. Is it just about the technicalities of improving production quality and yield or does it relate to suppliers, organisational responsibilities, payment systems and so forth? Such ambiguities should be addressed from the start of group activities. Furthermore a group may feel it has clear objectives but no idea how to proceed. Once again some freeflowing discussions may be important to get things moving.

*The 'Stone Group' meet and answer the above questions. They note that a standard has been set whereby a renewal notice should be sent out 21 days before the renewal date and followed up 14 days later. Doubts have been expressed as to whether this standard is being met consistently, whether it can be met and whether it is a suitable target to meet in the context of the company's objective of having 80 per cent of contracts renewed. What should they do next?*

## Gathering data

Most structured methodologies for systems' control and improvement are based on measuring key parameters of the system's performance over a period of time. There are a variety of ways in which this may be approached. The first is to examine records of inputs and outputs in order to see what has been happening. It may also be necessary to measure in new ways so as to collect fresh data. In a production process for example, measurements of certain key dimensions of the material output may be routinely taken but other features may not have been measured and may now be seen as the possible root of production difficulties.

An interesting extension of this approach is the conducting of detailed studies of some aspects of work. Machine set-up time has for example been filmed on video and discussed with the workers in order to eliminate unnecessary but habitual activities. This may be combined with experiments in which new work patterns are also recorded and analysed to see if improvements result.

Using statistical techniques to analyse data is often essential as the data gathered can vary over time and underlying patterns of behaviour need to be isolated and related to other factors.

Another fundamental form of data gathering relates less to outputs than to production methods. This consists of the use of structured process analysis techniques to record how work is (or should be) carried out. The result is usually expressed in the form of process logic diagrams, workflow maps, activity charts and other devices which are suitable to express the large number of steps involved in commercial and industrial processes. The techniques of systems analysis used by computer systems specialists may well be important in this respect, particularly if automated data processing is part of the overall operational process.

These various means of measuring activities and methods relate to what is often called 'hard systems' analysis. It may profitably be combined with 'soft systems' and other approaches, particularly if it is felt that the hard systems analysis does not address the real problems of effective operations. For instance, if a complex client service process is being investigated it is often necessary to be very careful in reflecting customer expectations and views of quality and not assume that meeting simple performance standards will lead to customer satisfaction.

*What data should the Stone Group collect?*

## Segmentation, priorities, causation and capability

In the context of data gathering, four important issues must be addressed at this stage. The first is that differing processes and times may give dissimilar results and must therefore be considered separately. Data relating to a particular group of customers, factory location, time of the day or any other key feature might be quite idiosyncratic and this may in turn be important in leading us to hypotheses regarding the causes of problems. Such segmentation of the problem area is quite typical of problem solving activity. Unfortunately things might not be quite so clear cut and sophisticated statistical techniques may be required to separate fundamental differences from general chance variability (or 'noise') in the data.

*How might the data gathered by the Stone Group show radical differences between customer groups? Should expected differences be reflected in the ways in which data is collected?*

The second issue is that large amounts of data may suggest to us many possible avenues for future exploration. The novice may fear that data exploration work will yield no ideas and no progress but experienced problem solvers are aware that the opposite difficulty is more likely. Too many lines of enquiry covering many possible variables may also inhibit progress. It becomes increasingly important, therefore, to arrive at priorities, and follow the approach most likely to lead to improved performance and meet objectives. For instance in the Stone Group example it might be noted that the data gathered revealed large differences in the value (and hence potential profitability) of the policies being sold.

One method often used to show differences in data and guide the setting of priorities is Pareto Analysis (see Further Reading for details of this and subsequent numerical techniques).

Our third point is related to the above and leads to techniques often carried out in conjunction with Pareto Analysis. Problems, symptoms and other significant factors are often related; poor performance in one sub-system causes poor performance in another. The web of cause and effect may be highly complex and not obvious from the data collected. This has led to the widespread use of the Ishikawa (or Fishbone) Diagram as a key tool in problem representation. By means of brainstorming, in conjunction with fact finding and data measurement, a cause and effect diagram is drawn similar to that shown in Figure 3.3.

*This relates to the 'Stone Group' example and places 'poor response time' as the main problem symptom on the horizontal axis.*

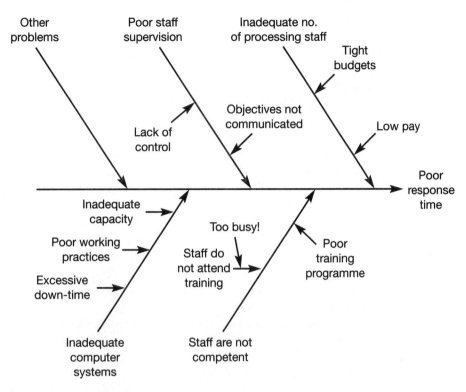

**Fig. 3.3 Ishikawa diagram**

The angled lines joining this axis refer to the main categories of potential cause (either singly or joint) of the problem and these in turn are the bases for other lines denoting 'sub-causes'. The full diagram thus provides a rich illustration of potential causal relationships and the basis for further systematic analysis. Its value can only be appreciated when real diagrams are drawn. These can involve hundreds of lines (often better represented through the use of 'sub-diagrams') and may be the only way in which the action group and other interested parties can comprehend the complexities of the situation.

The fourth issue relates to the capability of the process under consideration. If we observe poor performance from a process then either it is perfectly capable of producing an acceptable performance if executed correctly, or it is incapable of acceptable performance no matter how well it is managed. It is also frequently the case that a capable process (such as a machine) deteriorates over time and requires occasional maintenance to regain its capability.

If a process is basically capable then we must look for the reasons why poor performance has been observed. These might relate to inattention, poor training, poor materials and so forth. If we suspect that this is the case then a capability study should be performed in order to check what performance might actually be achieved under optimal operating conditions.

It may, of course, be the case that the direct process under consideration (for example, a machine) is perfectly capable of good performance but the total system of which the machine is a part is not so capable (for example, previous processes supply inadequate materials to the machine). This situation is quite typical of work systems and capability studies may thus be highly complex as different parts of a system are examined singly and in combination.

If, by contrast, a process is basically incapable then studies may still reveal ways to get the best performance and compensate for inadequacies. It may even be the case that the operating standards are higher than necessary and the customer is quite satisfied with actual, if non-standard, performance. Ultimately an incapable process may have to be redesigned or replaced but this may prove unnecessarily expensive.if some ingenious compromise could be found.

The above discussion may seem somewhat mechanistic and it is certainly the case that such issues are addressed regularly by production engineers and managers in the context of manufacturing systems. In service situations things may not be so clear cut. It may not even be easy to obtain reliable measures of performance and customer satisfaction. In particular where work is not repetitive it is not always straightforward to define what is meant by capability.

*The Stone Group discover that their problems are particularly acute during the summer months, when they are short staffed, and can take action to alleviate this. Detailed computer systems studies, however, reveal that processing times are too long and that the system is close to capacity. It is therefore recommended that a restructuring of customer records takes place in conjunction with a system's upgrading. The question then arises, if these changes take place how can we be sure that new performance levels are maintained? It is in fact possible to collect data regularly and facilitate continuous, rather than occasional, improvement?*

## Control Charts and Statistical Process Control (SPC)

Figure 3.1 suggests controlling a process by comparing measurements of the output with set performance standards. Three problems should, however, be noted with this approach. First, if we take a sample of the output the sample may conform to standards whilst a substantial proportion of the total output may not. Secondly, the standards may not relate directly to the capability of the process. Thirdly, a process may continue to meet standards whilst drifting closer to non-conformance.

Statistical Process Control (SPC) is a key technique designed to provide an adequate process control system whilst addressing the above problems. It bases control on measurements of the continuing performance of a process through the following procedure:

- A capability study is carried out to reveal whether the process, if correctly set up and operated at its best performance level, will actually meet the set standards. If the process is capable we continue with SPC. If not we should redesign the process, possibly incorporating some sorting procedure for the output (note that SPC is still of some use in maintaining an 'incapable' process at its inadequate best!).

- The capability study will reveal performance standards for the 'in-control' process (which may be well within the original product standards). These performance standards are now used to specify control limits for statistics derived from subsequent samples of process output. These control limits take account of the sample size to be used for continuing control.

- Over the period of operation of the process, regular samples of the stated size are taken and plotted on a control chart which incorporates the control limits. If the sample statistics are within permitted limits then the process is allowed to continue operation. If not then further samples are taken and the process operation is reviewed and maintained, with reference being made to the relationship between the control limits and the original standards.

- The measurements taken may be within limits but may show a trend towards those limits indicating that the process may soon drift out of control. This enables action to be taken to rectify the drift or plan future maintenance.

You will have noted that the above, even without the mathematical details, is quite technical but necessary if one wishes to base control through sampling on a sound statistical footing. (See Further Reading – SPC requires careful study to gain an understanding of all its techniques and nuances.)

An alternative approach, regularly found in organisations, is simply to produce and display a graph showing some key feature of a process over time and take common sense action when results appear to be unsatisfactory. The emphasis here is less on statistical validity than on visibility of performance.

As an illustration, let us assume that the Stone Group are concerned with the number of errors made when recording customer details following a first enquiry. Assuming that this can be readily measured (for instance when details are subsequently taken during a sale), we might plot the number of errors per hundred customers at weekly intervals on a graph with time as the horizontal axis. In this case the target value is presumably zero and we would be concerned to see fluctuations in the graph over time and the effects, for example, of staff training on subsequent performance.

A simple approach such as this may be better than nothing in that it attempts to make performance visible. It can, however, be seriously misleading if care is not taken with data specification and measurement. There is also the danger, which is directly addressed by the statistically based methods, of the inherent variability in the data either being given too much attention (for instance when every slight change is interpreted as a major process change) or too little attention (when a gradual drift in the process is masked by day-to-day variability).

One can therefore see why serious quality specialists, such as Deming, place so much emphasis on the correct use of SPC or even the more advanced approaches such as the Taguchi methods. This is not, however, an easy option and requires a very professional approach, not only in gaining a full understanding of the background theory and methods of SPC but also in gaining experience of its practical use.

## FURTHER READING

In addition to the Further Reading listed at the end of Chapter 2 (see in particular Logothetis (1992) for details of the practical techniques and Fitzsimmons (1994) for 'blueprinting' the relationship between front office and back room service systems), the following should be consulted as necessary.

General models of systems and control (in particular the ideas of Stafford Beer):

Flood, R. L. and Jackson, M. C. (1991), *Creative Problem Solving*, Wiley, Chichester.

Background to 'Kaizen':

Imai, M. (1986), *Kaizen*, McGraw Hill, New York.

Statistical Process Control:

Murdoch, J. and Barnes, J. A. (1986), *Statistical Tables* (3ed), Macmillan, Basingstoke.

Oakland, J. S. (1986), *Statistical Process Control*, Heinemann, London.

The original popular text on the 'excellence' movement is:

Peters, T. J. and Waterman, R. H. (1982), *In Search of Excellence*, Harper and Row, New York.

# CHAPTER 4

# The Management of People

All management courses have modules on managing people within organisations. The aim of this chapter is to show some of the ways in which such work is linked to the study of Operations Management. This also gives us the opportunity to focus on some aspects of managing people which are of particular importance to Operations Managers.

**OBJECTIVES**

**This chapter:**

- **shows the range of Human Resource Management issues relevant to operational situations**
- **explores some aspects of job design and motivation, mainly through tasks and exercises**
- **outlines some issues in staff remuneration, training and development**
- **contrasts Japanese approaches to managing people with traditional approaches in the West**
- **discusses briefly the management of change.**

## INTRODUCTION

In this chapter and the next we examine two of the most important aspects of Operations Management in all organisational contexts. In this chapter we consider a range of issues in the management of people. Human Resource Management (HRM), to give it a more resounding title, is one of the major preoccupations of all managers and management courses. Indeed we will assume that the reader has, or is acquiring, background knowledge in theories of organisational behaviour, personnel practices or some similar area of knowledge. If this is backed up by appropriate managerial experience then so much the better but this is not a requirement for understanding the arguments presented here. We will be concerned only with providing a basic map of HRM issues relevant to operations and drawing out some key points. The true richness of this area will be apparent when deeper study is combined with long experience of management.

In Chapter 5 we discuss a range of technological issues in Operations Management. Once again we are outlining an area of great diversity drawing on a range of professional expertise; the manufacturing engineer, computer scientist and specialists in the specific processes underlying manufacturing operations. The Operations Manager has a different role to play in planning and co-ordinating the use of technology in an organisational context but, in order to do this, must have a sound understanding of technological potential and limitations.

Thus, the common theme in these chapters is the way in which the Operations Manager must combine with other professionals to develop suitable operational processes and infrastructures. Part of the argument will relate to the use of people and technology in the direct delivery of services and manufacture of goods. A further part will concern the development of support structures and interfaces, for instance between design and manufacture. Finally we will be concerned with the use of information technology (IT) in all operational processes but specifically the office.

As you may expect, the themes of HRM and technology permeate this book but even so are too extensive to be developed in detail. The intention is to raise issues and show connections with other areas of study. Some illustrative references to more detailed work are given at the end of the chapters. Also note the specific references to the management of people in a project management context in Chapter 6 and the uses of technology in planning and controlling manufacturing operations discussed in Chapter 11.

## HUMAN RESOURCE MANAGEMENT (HRM)

**TASK** We begin this section with a task. Before reading further, try to make a list of the aspects of the management of people which you feel are relevant to operational success.

In carrying out the above exercise with management classes (admittedly including experienced managers, some way into their studies) it would be normal for a group to arrive at around 50 headings! Even allowing for overlapping categories this is a formidable list and leads one to the possibility that the whole of HRM theory and practice is applicable to operations. This is a natural conclusion as 'operations' is often the major employing function in an organisation. In reality, there are some specialist parts of HRM which are not the direct concern of Operations Management and traditionally there are a number of aspects of personnel work, for instance, where the operational manager might rely on others for support. As layers of management and support functions are cut away, however, and line managers are 'empowered' then more and more HRM is devolved to operations. This can lead to problems if line management is inadequately trained and informed, say, regarding new employee legislation. In practice, though, good Operations Managers (whatever their title) have always taken a keen interest in the management of people and used the professional skills of others to inform their actions.

We present a crude classification of HRM issues below, viewed from the perspective of the Operations Manager (hence the primary concern with job design, reward and training).

**Job design:**

- work measurement
- methods study
- productivity
- required skill variety and flexibility
- ergonomics (physical work environment)
- social work environment
- team working
- socio-technical systems design
- motivation
- supervision
- safety.

**Pay systems and structures:**

- staff status
- payment by results
- reward systems (shares, perks, status)
- job evaluation
- performance appraisal
- bonus systems.

**Education and training:**

- on-the-job training
- other training (including company-wide initiatives)
- multi-skilling
- education (internal; external)
- development
- links to the learning organisation.

**General staffing issues:**

- recruitment
- redeployment
- job descriptions
- promotion

- redundancy
- welfare
- employee resourcing (manpower planning).

**Industrial relations:**

- pay and conditions bargaining
- unions
- works councils.

It can readily be seen that our primary three-way classification (design, planning and implementation) is useful in this context. Job design and the design of supporting systems (performance appraisal, pay, training, etc.) is a principal component of Operations Management. We will discuss operational planning in the latter half of the book. Labour is a key resource and expense in plotting a course to a profitable future. Finally, implementation and control (including routine work improvement) are every-day issues for Operational Managers.

In the sections below we explore some of the central issues in operations HRM. In a given context, other issues may be even more critical. Safety is a typical example, as is Industrial Relations. Similarly, the general management of employees (recruitment, welfare, redundancy provisions) is always important but we are assuming that the reader will be informed on such matters through other courses and technical training. The items selected below are deeply embedded in the conceptual framework of opera-tions. For instance, training is seen as a continuing need and prime facilitator of labour flexibility and continuous improvement. Job design is not merely an engineering tech-nique but addresses the fundamentals of who is responsible for deciding how work is to be carried out, a key piece of the operational jigsaw.

## JOB DESIGN AND MOTIVATION

**TASK**

Once again let us begin with a task, on this occasion one particularly suited to group work. Consider a simple service delivery job, for instance a receptionist at a health centre or in a theatre booking office (if time permits, why not observe such work to check whether your ideas reflect reality?).

With reference to your chosen job, choose a particular repetitive task (making an appointment, selling theatre seats):

- What are the customer's objectives?
- Describe what needs to be done from the customer's point of view (points relating to the quality of service).
- What are the objectives of the delivery organisation?

- Describe what needs to be done from the organisation's point of view (for example, maintaining records, receiving payment).
- Describe exactly how the above should be achieved.

(Note: This latter point is quite difficult in that a suitable language of description must be chosen. Do we describe detailed movements of the service deliverer as in classic work study and time measurement? Or perhaps we use data flow diagrams as in information systems design? Unless you are skilled in such techniques, I suggest a common language description will suffice, though examples like this clearly show the need for suitable ways to represent systems activity.)

Having arrived at your task description, answer the following questions:

- Will your method of carrying out the task cope with all eventualities?
- How much initiative and ingenuity is required of the service deliverer?
- Assuming the task is to be repeated continually for several hours, how boring is it?

In the light of answers to the above:

- Are required service levels likely to be maintained?
- Can organisational objectives be met?
- How do you reward the service deliverer?
- What further aspects of service delivery job design are important in your chosen context? (for example, safety, comfort)

(One useful approach in such exercises is to simulate the work, although this provides only a pale reflection of the impact of work carried out for many hours with real customers. Another possibility is to interview individuals with experience of such work.)

The questions listed above are designed to uncover the typical problems faced in job design and addressed in the extensive literature on job design and work motivation. In practice, much of the detailed advice is centred on manufacturing work with service delivery left to the common sense of the deliverer (is this wise?). The above exercise was placed in a service context to make it more approachable and less dependent on a knowledge of manufacturing techniques. The basic principles, however, remain the same: to produce a way of working which meets customer objectives (or specifications in a mass manufacturing context), organisational objectives (cost and productivity for instance) whilst being acceptable to the individual carrying out the task.

This focus on the individual production, office or service worker is typical of writings since the genesis of work study at the beginning of the century. Whether narrowly focused on the technical aspects of work or characterising work as a socio-technical system, a balance between the needs of the customer, organisation and worker must be found. Sometimes a mindlessly boring task has seemed inevitable and the emphasis has been on payment (often linked to productivity) as a motivator. At other times a potentially dangerous or unhealthy task has to be analysed from a safety and an ergonomic perspective to make it acceptable.

One issue of some importance is who designs the job? Traditionally, individuals skilled in particular crafts dealt with the customer and decided on how the work should be done. The industrial revolution led to more directed work with a structure of owners, experts and managers deciding on key parameters of job design (though empirical studies of actual working methods showed that 'the workers' may have had unexpected degrees of discretion). As we discussed in Chapter 3, the philosophy of continuous improvement usually entails tapping into the workers' knowledge and expecting a degree of self-improvement (though in a structured context of team working and the use of approved methods and procedures).

One should also be careful when using concepts such as motivation. All too often, motivation is merely seen as the use of carrots and sticks by managers on workers. This sits uneasily with notions of empowerment and worker autonomy, unless of course the latter are merely the latest design of carrot and stick! The literature on motivation, however, goes some way to help us understand certain facets of organisational work. Typical is the model shown in Figure 4.1 which contrasts repetitive work with job enlargement and job enrichment, the latter being considered more desirable. Similarly the 'Hackman–Oldham Job Enrichment' model attempts to isolate features of industrial work which are more or less motivating. A version of this model is shown in Figure 4.2 with some illustrative jobs.

If we take the example given earlier of the health centre receptionist, we can see in Figure 4.2 how such a job may be more or less motivating. By contrast the other examples shown (some with details left uncompleted to give you a chance to exercise your own knowledge and imagination) indicate both the potential for motivation (or lack of it) in work and the differing ways in which motivation occurs. It should also be remembered that the most motivating tasks (the surgeon, for instance) may also be the most stressful.

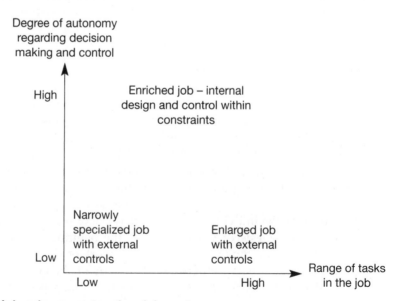

**Fig. 4.1 Job enlargement and enrichment**

| Experienced psychological states: | Meaningfulness of work | | | Responsibility | Knowledge of outcomes |
|---|---|---|---|---|---|
| Job dimensions: | Skill variety | Task indentity | Task significance | Autonomy | Feedback |
| Typical jobs: | | | | | |
| Health care receptionist | Low | Low/ medium | Medium | Low | Medium (some direct from customer) |
| Surgeon | High (possibly specialised) | High | High! | High!! | High |
| Production line worker (traditional) | Low | Low | Low | Low | Low/ medium |
| Retail store manager | ? | ? | ? | ? | ? |
| Manageing director | ? | ? | ? | ? | ? |

**Fig. 4.2  Job motivation**

# REWARDING OPERATIONAL STAFF

Employees at all levels receive a variety of benefits from doing work. These may range from direct payments through to subsidised pensions, health care, welfare and sports facilities. They may include perks of various kinds and the promise of future advancement. Training and education may be intended as a means of moving towards meeting organisational goals but have the additional effect of enhancing the market value of the individual. Finally a variety of status related features of a job may make it desirable.

The design of the total remuneration package is aimed at encouraging high levels of employee performance whilst satisfying expectations of fairness and equity, all in the context of a competitive labour market. In a production operations context the package may vary depending on the type of work, the situation of the employing company and the norms evident in the industry. Some manufacturers in the West have gone for direct links between levels of production and individual bonuses. Others favour a flat wage with group bonuses and it should not be forgotten that overtime working has often provided, in effect, a bonus system linked to the trading conditions of the company. In Japan, the 'salaryman' is accustomed to a modest standard wage (though including payments depending on personal circumstances), extensive facilities provided by the company and large twice-yearly bonuses linked to the global performance of the company. Most important, however, is the use of guaranteed lifetime employment as a means of ensuring employee loyalty (though one should refer to the current literature to assess how things may change in Japan).

The link between performance and reward is not only the concern of operational staff, as current debates on top executive remuneration show only too well. It is central, however, to operations and must be treated with care. Crude linkages between output and pay ignore the rather obvious point that organisational performance is not only about volume of output! Quality, costs (including the costs of administering the payment systems), incentives for improvement and flexibility are also of concern and designing direct, individual payment to reflect performance on all these dimensions is surely to be avoided. As a brief guide, any package must trade-off potential benefits of the following kind:

- individual performance as against group effort
- standardised and simple (low cost) payment schemes as against flexible payment methods targeted on individual or group achievements (requiring complex measurement and administration)
- rewarding spectacular, if uneven, performance (possibly in response to organisational emergencies) against routine merit
- rewarding performance in the context of changing technology as against an unwillingness to change
- current rewards as against promises of future enhancement (depending on individual career or company growth).

## TRAINING, EDUCATION AND DEVELOPMENT

At worst, in the past, training was seen as a marginal activity, the first thing to be cut from budgets if times were hard. Management development was based on experience and common sense with education simply not seen as the concern of an employer. The exception to this was if training or education was indulged in as a perk for an ambitious employee. Certainly there is a danger that a newly trained employee will simply leave an organisation if tempted by a competitor.

If training is poorly planned, unrelated to organisational objectives, poorly controlled and its effects not evaluated then an organisation may feel that it is receiving little value for a considerable investment. Let us examine things from another perspective. If an organisation is investing in plant or technology, a great amount of effort will be taken in the choice of such technology, its adaptation to operating conditions and its maintenance. Similarly, investment in people requires care in recruitment, attention to the working experiences of the recruit and an ongoing concern that the individual is capable of carrying out their allocated tasks. Whether the last point is achieved through on-the-job training, in-company courses or the use of external training agencies is a tactical matter of how to achieve quality and value for money. The strategic concern is for a capable and appropriately skilled workforce. Other issues regarding the control and evaluation of training follow in a simple and logical manner. This separation of the strategic need for competent staff and the tactics of how to achieve this is essential in placing staff development (in all its forms) at the centre of an organisation's agenda of actions.

The Japanese once again give an interesting contrast to Western experiences since World War II. Education is highly valued in Japanese society and people are genuinely considered to be an organisation's prime investment. Training and staff development tend to be in-company (which can cause problems with relationships with individuals from other working cultures) and are central to the role of the manager. This reflects, and pre-dates, the Peters and Waterman *In Search of Excellence* studies which highlight the role of the manager as coach and facilitator. With a different working culture and labour market context, Japanese ideas must be adapted to a Western context but the strategic imperative remains.

Staff training is principally concerned with developing the skills required to carry out current tasks, to allow greater flexibility and to prepare for future planned tasks. Training is also necessary in the techniques of continuous improvement. If we assume that education signifies a broader approach to the acquisition of skills and knowledge then the ability of all staff to adapt to a changing environment may depend on such investment.

The word 'development' often appears with the adjective 'manager' or 'management' and refers to a longer term view of future organisational needs, including the eventual filling of top management positions. With the current attention given to reducing management layers, empowering all staff and working in cells and project teams we might be advised to speak of 'staff development' as a more broad term covering this aspect of ensuring a successful future for an organisation.

In a specifically operational context, one should also remember the need for technical training and development of staff. Indeed one general problem facing organisations which rely on high levels of technology for their products, processes and systems is how to develop and reward top technical specialists. Such individuals may not wish to take on general management roles or be particularly suited for them but have a central place in the organisation and expect suitable career structures and remuneration packages.

## JAPANESE MANAGEMENT

The strength of Japanese manufacturing industry from the 1970s onwards has led a number of observers in the West to speculate whether some Japanese management practices might be directly used to counter perceived weaknesses in Western companies. This idea is partly due to the emphasis Japanese industrialists themselves put on the value of their managerial approach but also comes from the very real differences which exist between Japan and the West. It should be pointed out immediately that it is specifically manufacturing industry which has been noted for its productivity, innovativeness and quality. Though high levels of quality and customer care are typical of Japanese service industries, these are considered to be less cost effective.

It should be noted that several strands may become confusingly interwoven when attempting to import Japanese management. The first is the apparently simple techniques practised on the shopfloor and in the offices of Japanese firms. It should not be surprising that quality circles were one of the first ideas to reach the West and it is tempting to read Schonberger and Deming and see in them merely common sense (see Further Reading at the end of this chapter). Attempts to implement such ideas may be successful but may also lead to disappointment and this has led researchers and practical industrialists to delve further into the Japanese managerial context. This has uncovered other dimensions in the situation, including:

- differences between Japanese and Western industrial structure (that is the relationships between organisations)
- differences in organisational structure and career paths
- differences in attitudes, values and underlying approaches to work
- historical and cultural differences.

It therefore appears that techniques are being imported into a Western context which is quite different from the context in which they were originally developed. We must, however, examine in some detail what is meant by this in order to learn from the Japanese experience lessons which are relevant to the West.

## Industrial structure

For a variety of historical reasons, Japanese industry contains a number of extremely large companies (or groups of tightly inter-related organisations) which exert enormous financial power. Many of the management practices reported in the West relate mainly to such companies which have been able to offer lifetime job security to many employees. These large companies are supported by a network of smaller firms which tend to be dominated by the giant organisations through patterns of ownership and the 'partnership' form of inter-company relationship which is promoted in Japan. This partnership is not between equals but driven by the agendas of the large companies and by the Japanese government which sets strong priorities for long-term future developments.

## Organisations and careers

The large organisations see their long-term employees as forming their backbone. Great care is taken to recruit highly educated and socially suitable staff who are then developed in a range of managerial functions, promotion being by seniority. Such individuals develop extensive networks of contacts both within the firm and with other organisations. Salaries include a large element of group bonus which reinforces the employees' willingness to work towards the success of the organisation as a whole. It is not usual for such 'regular' employees to change organisation in mid-career.

## Attitudes and values

The emphasis is on group working, with co-operation between group members but high levels of competition between organisations. Less reliance is placed on the outward trappings of success as employees are secure in their status. Thus such basic things as office layout (staff work in groups in large common offices) and the accessibility of senior managers reflect a wish to promote communication rather than reinforce individual positions of power. This is reflected in the style of decision making which favours detailed consultation and involvement of all relevant personnel.

## History and culture

The population, homogenous and highly educated, are seen as a principal source of national difference and industrial practices are based on extracting the maximum advantage from this situation. It must, therefore, be an open question whether or not any derived management technique will be applicable elsewhere.

It should be understood that the various aspects of Japanese management reinforce each other. For example, it is far easier to involve staff in decision making if they are all long-term employees and therefore know each other and the organisation in great detail. Similarly people are far more willing to co-operate in group working if they are secure in their jobs, rewards are based on the performance of the organisation as a whole and rivalry for promotion is not as directly expressed as in Western organisations.

A growing literature exists on the practices adopted by Japanese firms when operating in other countries, such as the UK. In this instance it appears that some adaptation of managerial style occurs within the 'foreign' plant, the familiar techniques being used to ensure uniformity and productivity. The real decisions are, not surprisingly, made by the Japanese parent company.

Thus Japanese management practice might be seen as a source of ideas but these should not be implemented unthinkingly within different managerial cultures. Recent work has shown the fundamental differences which exist between many countries in the basic underlying values and beliefs of employees at all levels. Only by increasingly understanding why people work in specific ways can we learn how to take the most appropriate ideas and adapt them to our own organisational situations.

Finally, it should be remembered that the Japanese working culture in the second half of the twentieth century might eventually be seen as a special case suitable only to the environmental conditions pertaining to this period. The real challenge to any organisation is how to manage all its employees effectively in the future!

## THE MANAGEMENT OF CHANGE

Although we have made a number of references to the continuous improvement of operations and the need to develop staff in this context we must not forget that some changes are more radical and need a different approach. In Chapter 6 we mention some such issues in the context of project management, in particular the skills of the project manager and appropriate organisational structures for project management.

Problems in the management of change are particularly evident in the development of technological systems such as Advanced Manufacturing Technology (AMT). In a survey of the barriers to such change, the following were identified as important:

- attitudes of senior management to future planning (a lack of 'future orientation')
- absence of a formal change strategy
- poor managerial integration
- poor in-company educational processes
- poor attitudes to managerial work.

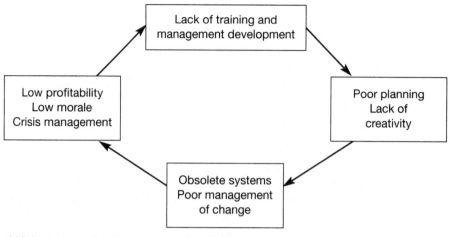

a) Vicious circle of under-investment and failure

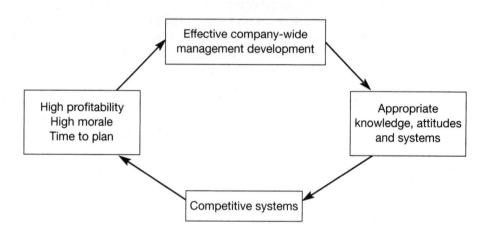

b) Positive circle of management development

**Fig. 4.3 Management development**

It is noticeable that the above barriers relate as much to the organisation's systems and culture as to individuals and that an overall systems view may be necessary. Also such processes work as long-term feedback systems. If this latter comment seems somewhat mysterious, consider Figure 4.3. The top circle shows a vicious circle whereby failure to invest produces a situation where investment is no longer possible. The second circle shows the opposite situation. In both cases training and management development are key strategic factors over a long period of time.

Such ideas are linked to the notion of the learning organisation as a strategic control system which continually reviews its own standards of required performance and organisational practices. In this context we end with a series of questions:

- Can we create 'opportunity structures for people' at the same time as 'hard systems implementation'?

- Can we develop information systems which support individuals in questioning current operational processes and in exploring alternatives?

- Can we create a climate where information and experience are readily diffused within the organisation?

- Can we create a culture which encourages experimentation and systematic learning based on success and failure?

- Can managerial control systems be developed which promote learning as an investment (rather than training as a cost)?

- Can the total process of strategy formulation, investment and implementation be viewed as a learning process?

## FURTHER READING

A useful general text on organisational behaviour, which pays ample attention to operational and technological situations is Huczinski and Buchanan (1991). Hill (1991) is a general Operations Management text which includes much detail on such issues as work study and payment systems.

Schonberger (1982) was an early influence in directing managers in the West to the methods and ideas inherent in Japanese manufacturing. Whitehill (1991) gives a systematic account of Japanese management whilst a reading of Garrahan and Stewart (1993) gives some balance as the latter are critical of Japanese management practices applied in the UK. Hampden-Turner and Trompenaars (1993) is a useful source of ideas on the cultural differences underlying management in different countries.

Twiss (1992) includes some discussion on the organisational issues of the management of change in a technological context, though this subject is extensively referred to in general management texts.

Garrahan, P. and Stewart, P. (1993), *The Nissan Enigma*, Mansell, London.

Hampden-Turner, C. and Trompenaars, F. (1993), *The Seven Cultures of Capitalism*, Piatkus, London.

Hill, T. (1991), *Production/Operations Management*, Prentice Hall, New York.

Huczynski, A. and Buchanan, D. (1991), *Organisational Behaviour* (2ed), Prentice Hall, New York.

Schonberger, R. J. (1982), *Japanese Manufacturing Techniques*, Free Press, New York.

Twiss, B. (1992), *Managing Technological Innovation* (4ed), Pitman, London.

Whitehill, A. M. (1991), *Japanese Management*, Routledge, London.

# CHAPTER 5

# Technology and Information

The objective of this chapter is to show how technology may provide a competitive edge to operations but must be carefully managed, both in terms of justifying its introduction and maintaining its continuing performance.

**OBJECTIVES**

This chapter:

- describes some of the ways in which technology contributes to manufacturing, service and office operations
- introduces some of the issues in technological investment appraisal
- outlines some of the strategies which may be adopted in maintaining the performance of technology-based systems.

## INTRODUCTION

In this chapter we introduce some basic concepts relating to the use of technology in operations. Technology provides one of the key ways in which modern operations may gain a competitive edge. Frequently this relates to information technology which may directly assist operations or may facilitate the effective management of operations through the use of sophisticated planning and control systems. As well as describing some uses of technology in manufacturing, service and office contexts, we address the difficult issue of the financial appraisal of technological investment proposals.

## TECHNOLOGY

The simplest view of the word 'technology' is that it refers to machines. Now, if we wish to use the language of information technology (IT), this identification of technology with 'hardware' is immediately suspect without inclusion of 'software'. If we further follow this route, it leads us to an interesting point. Perhaps technology is not concerned with the specific material components of systems but with the principles on which they are built? Indeed, one very general characterisation of technology is 'the knowledge which supports practical actions'.

This latter point would seem to include all management theory as 'technology'! This is an interesting thought but is somewhat at odds with everyday uses of the word. Therefore we will use 'technology' to refer in general to machines, software, their practical application and the principles which underlie their construction. This systems approach roughly captures current usage and reminds us that one key feature of hardware, software and the procedures for using them is their 'built-in knowledge'. If this seems a slightly strange way of looking at a car engine, it is a very natural way of characterising a computer software applications package. It is also a reasonable way to think about the routine skills of the users of machine systems. All these things embody 'know-how', and one hopes the human parts of the system also have a degree of 'know-why'.

Historically, the most obvious uses of technology have been in the contrasting areas of construction and warfare, although our more general description covers all trades. At the time of the Industrial Revolution, the use of machines as sources of power came to the fore. This led on to the use of machines to manufacture items directly as well as to support the human skills of making things and in this way, machines embody 'know-how'. Machines are also used in the area of transporting materials and eventually of people. In the first section below, we will discuss manufacturing technology as a prime example of the use of scientific and practical knowledge to support wealth creation.

One area of operational activity is the management of transportation systems. This may refer to the movement of materials within a factory (which we include under the heading of manufacturing systems), the movement of materials between factories and warehouses (see the section on supply chain management in Chapter 1) or, at the other extreme, the public transportation of people. This final category tends to receive little analysis in general Operational Management texts, being viewed as a distinct area of expertise. As the management of transport is, however, a key area of public policy and its effectiveness in the use of natural resources becomes ever more critical, it seems natural that Operational Management principles might find further application in this field. Some current ideas regarding road toll and traffic management systems are highly technological and will require great care to ensure safe and cost effective use.

In more recent times, public attention has been caught by the uses of IT in offices and the home. In the second section below we briefly consider 'office technology' whilst remembering that our use of the word 'office' to cover all aspects of data conversion means that we are referring not only to areas of buildings with desks but to activities which permeate all aspects of manufacturing, service and commercial life.

The third area for our attention is obviously the uses of technology in service delivery. One aspect of this has been mentioned already under transportation and others are widespread in areas as diverse as entertainment, health care and education. As the 'front office and back room' model of service delivery reminds us, service and office technology are deeply interlinked as readily seen in such areas as financial services.

As the use of technology often requires considerable expenditure, we continue this chapter with some mention of the techniques of strategic and financial appraisal which are used when considering, possibly risky, investments. It might be remembered that investments in people can also be considerable, and risky, and should also be carefully thought through in a similar manner to those involving technology.

We end by considering issues in the maintenance function. It is of little value investing in equipment if it is not then maintained at optimal performance and even improved as new technologies and working practices become known. It is unfortunate if 'maintenance' is seen merely as a firefighting activity when it can certainly reduce costs and possibly be a source of positive improvement.

# MANUFACTURING TECHNOLOGY

In a UK government report in the mid-1980s, Advanced Manufacturing Technology (AMT) was defined as follows:

> ...any new technique which, when adopted, is likely to require a change not only in manufacturing practice, but also in management systems and the manufacturer's approach to the design and production engineering of the product.

Thus, changes in manufacturing should not be seen in any narrow 'machining' sense but through a total systems concept. It is reasonable to start, however, by noting some of the likely components of this total system. In practice AMT is likely to include technology in some of the following categories:

- direct transformation of materials through cutting, chemical processing, mixing, assembly and so forth
- moving of materials by means of robots, conveyors
- storage and retrieval of materials
- automatic inspection and testing
- product design and engineering
- manufacturing process design
- production management systems (MRP II)
- links to business systems for costing, preparing quotations.

## Material processing

The most obvious use of technology (machines and techniques) in a factory is the material transformations which take place in order to change raw materials and components into the goods required by the customer. This set of activities adds value provided it is planned so that the totality of customer needs are met (that is, specified quality, delivery time and price).

A number of key commercial decisions are involved here, with particular reference to the 'sizing' of a factory (determining its basic productive capacity), process choice (see Chapter 1), timing when to introduce new technologies and the design of the production infrastructure.

Engineering decisions vary greatly between industries. The processing of bulk chemicals is critically dependent on the size and economics of the plant as initially designed. The development of Computer Numerically Controlled (CNC) machining has greatly improved the productivity and flexibility of factories where metals and other materials are worked and similarly electronic assembly can be automated at the individual machine and cell (group of machines) level. In such instances, computer based technologies continue to advance rapidly and the manufacturer faces a difficult decision regarding the timing of new technology equipment purchases.

## Material movement

Though some manufacturing plants are integrated in the sense that material processing and movement are tightly linked (for example, a chemical plant), in many factories decisions have to be made regarding how and when materials are to be moved between individual machines and processes. The timing of movement may be based on engineering considerations (for example, it must arrive at the next process before cooling) or it may depend on scheduling and economic factors (see 'production management systems' on page 77).

The method of movement (which may include some form of packaging or palletisation to prevent damage) is a major problem in manufacturing systems design. Solutions include the use of robots for short range movement, automated guided vehicles and conveyor systems for intra-factory movement and road transportation for inter-factory transfer. It is obviously advantageous to reduce such material movement if possible through redesign of factory layouts and this is a key element of the JIT approach (see Chapter 11).

A trade-off has often to be made of low cost (through processes being close together) against designed product variety (where small batches of product each require differing manufacturing processes). Of course, if the processes used (for example, CNC machines) are themselves flexible enough to do a variety of tasks then this problem is avoided. The general principle here is that the manufacturing system must be designed as a totality to cope with varied outputs in an economical manner.

A final point to note is the importance of reliable information regarding the position of materials in a factory, warehouse and during transit. The use of bar coding systems is invaluable to avoid what can easily become a bane in the life of the production manager – losing things! Even a temporary loss can create havoc with tight schedules, quite apart from the security problems caused by poor control of quantity and location.

## Material storage

In spite of the popularity of the JIT philosophy, which views stock holding as a waste to be eradicated, materials and finished goods often do have to be stored. This is true both in manufacturing and retailing, though in both cases one would wish to facilitate as fast a turnover of materials as possible. This leads to the need for good storage input and retrieval systems and good information systems to track the location and quantity of stored items. Automated warehousing is a well developed technology used in many industries.

## Automated testing

It should be obvious from our previous discussion on quality management and control that the frequent testing of materials is important both for product and process control. Quality testing is itself a process and incurs a cost; it may disrupt processes and may even destroy some of the product. It is therefore an advantage if testing can be made as unobtrusively and automatically as possible. Hence the use of sophisticated testing devices (for instance in electronic assembly) with real-time feedback of results and indications of problems can be an essential part of a production process.

## Flexible manufacturing systems (FMS)

While the previous sections have dealt with separate issues, the resulting technological solutions are not separate but involve the design of inter-related engineering processes. Thus our use of the word 'machine' could well be replaced with 'system' (despite the over-use of this word). The idea that a group of processing machines along with robots, test equipment and so forth be considered and operated as an integrated cell is obvious. On a larger scale, the operation of many cells can be looked on as an FMS. The practical problems to be solved here often relate to the interfaces between cells and to the overall planning of flow though the FMS.

There is nothing new about large, integrated production systems. The classic 'production line' of mass manufacture is engineered in this way and the making of large numbers of identical products is a well understood manufacturing task (see Chapter 1 on process choice). The key point to note is the word 'flexible' which entails considerable sophistication in the design and operation of the FMS. It is perhaps not surprising that reports of the performance of FMS suggest that they are sometimes used as straightforward production lines. Flexibility is not easily achieved but may be the key to success in highly competitive markets with frequent product changes.

## Computer aided design (CAD)

CAD is now one of the most widely used techniques in engineering, whether based on the global networks of the major manufacturers or the personal computer of the student or small company. Ranging from simple 2D draughting packages to 3D modelling, computer based solutions to the needs of most designers can now be found. Particularly impressive are the emerging possibilities for visualising the final results of the design, for instance through the use of virtual reality techniques allowing a tour to be made of a proposed building.

The issue here is not simply facilitating the work of the designer but also of allowing new forms of interaction with the customer. We are technologically at the point where a customer is able to go into, say, a car showroom and 'design' their own car (in fact, choose from a set of options). It is surely not unreasonable to expect this facility for a wide range of goods, a service which adds value for the customer and can therefore create a differentiated product/service package thus commanding a higher price.

For the Operations Manager, one key advantage of CAD is that it leads on to CADCAM (Computer Aided Design and Manufacture). If all relevant product details are available as electronic data, then surely such data can be directly used for manufacture and also for planning the best way in which the product can be manufactured. Thus we have here a technology which directly supports an important type of competitive edge, the rapid design and implementation of a new product. The practical problems inherent in such a move should not be underestimated but barriers to rapid product innovation may now be managerial and organisational as much as those due to problems of engineering and technology.

## Production management systems, CIM and CIB

Whatever the manufacturing technology, there remains a need for planning and controlling the flow of materials through a production plant. This is particularly crucial for a batch manufacturer and is the subject of Chapter 11 where the contrast between human hands-on control and computer based planning is very evident. Computer based systems have the advantage of interfacing with the data produced by the actual processes (for example, CNC machining, automated warehouses, bar coding for shop floor control) and also with an organisation's commercial systems relating to order taking, cost control and so forth.

As the problems of communication between computer based information systems are being successfully addressed, the way is increasingly clear for the use of Computer Integrated Manufacturing (CIM) and Computer Integrated Business (CIB) within the organisation as a whole. This in turn can lead to enhanced inter-company communication and the co-ordination of planning and control through the use of Electronic Data Interchange (EDI).

Whilst the argument in favour of such total information system approaches is strong, the need for continual adaptation and improvement is also evident. What is the place of Kaizen and the very human activities of creative problem solving in such a context? Business Process Re-engineering addresses such issues but it would be unfortunate if the technologies intended to increase flexibility and responsiveness to the customer themselves produced a bureaucratic rigidity.

**Points for discussion**

1. What is meant by 'flexibility' in the context of a CNC machine? Is this different from 'commercial flexibility'?

2. As a manufacturer, would you always re-equip your factory with the very latest machine technology? On what principles would you base decisions involving the purchase of high technology production processes?

3. Material logistics is concerned with the movement and storage of materials throughout a supply chain. Choose some everyday manufactured item or food and trace through the totality of the supply chain from obtaining the basic raw materials to its arrival at the place of consumption.

4. The ultimate automated manufacturing system, in some people's minds, is the unmanned (or 'lights out') factory. Apart from problems of unemployment, is this really a good idea?

5. Choose a consumer product (preferably a major purchase) and discuss the extent to which you would like to be able to customise the product, that is, to change the design to suit your own particular needs. What are the implications of such customisation for the product's designers and the managers of production operations?

6. Is CIB inevitable?

7. In what ways might newer developments in computer systems (knowledge based systems, virtual reality...) facilitate radically new approaches to manufacturing management? (Note: you may have to do some background reading to even begin to answer this question!)

## THE USES OF TECHNOLOGY IN SERVICE DELIVERY

Whilst we have not assumed any prior knowledge on the part of the reader regarding the uses of manufacturing technology, and have therefore described such applications in some detail, examples of the use of technology in service delivery are all around us so, as a preliminary task, you might like to list some of them.

You should not, of course, have assumed that all technologies are new. For instance railways, airlines, diagnostic X-rays, cinemas and food preparation technologies are not fundamentally new. Some uses of technology are of comparatively recent origin:

- hole-in-the-wall cash dispensers
- laser based surgery
- computer aided learning
- theme parks
- national lottery.

Many traditional services (mail order shopping for instance) are also made more cost effective through using computer based office technology.

One point we must consider clearly is whether a particular technology is directly visible to the service client (used in the front office) or supports the delivery of the service from the back room. Thus, a financial adviser may use a computer system directly to show off his products to a potential client and the same system will eventually record and monitor all aspects of transactions in the future with only occasional direct reference to the client.

Front office systems may be used by a service deliverer working with a client or may be used directly by the client. In both cases the system must be carefully designed to cover all eventualities of client need (including safety and confidentiality) and be robust in case of misuse. The latter point, of course, relates both to hardware and software. Back room systems are general office systems but care must be taken when inter-facing with front office systems.

When considering technology which is used in direct contact with the client, the flexibility of response of the system will be very much in evidence. This is particularly true if the technology is replacing a human service deliverer who, in theory at least, could be very flexible in approach. Thus a client will expect a narrower range of behaviours from a car park barrier than a cash dispenser or a vending machine. Still greater sophistication will be expected from an expert system used for medical diagnosis or an electronic share trading system. Another issue to bear in mind is the client's perception of service and the SERVQUAL model (mentioned in Chapter 2) is a useful starting point in this respect.

## OFFICE TECHNOLOGY

Considerations of Computer Integrated Manufacturing and the front office–back room service model lead us on to a brief discussion of the uses of technology in the office. This area is dominated by two major considerations:

- the use of computer based information systems
- the use of electronic communication systems.

The former continues to be one of the areas of greatest technological advance in the late twentieth century whilst the latter has transformed management communication through simple devices such as mobile phones, fax machines and other enhancements to telephone and data transfer systems. It may seem ironic that this vast area of work receives little detailed coverage here but we will assume coverage in other modules and subject areas of a management course.

Two points are of particular relevance to the Operations Managers:

- How can such technology facilitate manufacturing and service operational processes?
- How can such technology directly help in their own managerial work?

We leave the consideration of these to you as a final task in this section.

## INVESTMENT APPRAISAL

Though not exclusively a technological issue, the problems of investment appraisal in an operational context often have a technological dimension. In particular, major changes in technology may take a number of years to show substantial benefits and hence it is useful to consider such long-term financial issues in the context of the management of operational process technology.

The problem we are concerned with can be stated quite simply. Through a process of strategic decision making, or perhaps merely due to current circumstances, we feel the need to spend considerable amounts of money in the near future in order to improve existing operations, to develop new capabilities or simply to increase capacity. This may apply to production equipment, service delivery technology and computer systems. The financial benefits of such expenditure may, however:

- occur at some time in the future
- be hard to measure (amount and timing)
- carry some risk.

More bluntly, you are asking your senior management for £500 000 for a new state-of-the-art computer controlled production line. The hoped for result is increased sales of a better product at lower cost. Unfortunately, you don't know exactly how much it will cost, whether or not it will work effectively, whether the market is really there or what the competition will do! Even more alarmingly this is a relatively straightforward investment example compared with long-term product development and IT systems changes.

The real argument for change may well be strategic in the sense that a competitor who successfully makes such an investment may drive you out of business. An interesting current speculation is the rise of telebanking. As a strategic planner in a large financial institution delivering services to customers through high street branches can you ignore the possibility that in the future customers may prefer virtual to physical banking? In such a case you may decide to invest, albeit cautiously, in appropriate technologies in order to keep your options open.

Some investment decisions are less hair-raising. In many cases you will be concerned with more modest changes, with shorter time horizons and better understood environments. The decision may not be whether or not to invest but when to invest and which equipment to choose. Furthermore the investment may be inevitable in that ageing equipment must be changed in order to maintain operations. It should also be emphasised that much expenditure will not relate directly to equipment but to training, systems and the general cost of upheaval associated with change.

Most medium and large organisations have well documented systems for investment appraisal and these usually involve significant financial estimation. Whether such systems are genuine attempts at rational decision making or merely a test of the persistence of the middle manager is hard to say but the Operations Manager must be capable of understanding and using them. The strategic aspects of investment assessment are beyond the concerns of this book but some knowledge of the basic details of the financial methods is important to grasp at this stage.

The key points we will be concerned with (only a fraction of the issues addressed in a text on financial appraisal) are as follows:

- What is the basis for measuring cost and benefit?
- How do we allow for differences in the timing of cash flows?
- How do we allow for risk?

## Measuring cost and benefit

The main point to grasp here is that costs and benefits are characterised by expected changes in cash flow in some suitably defined system. For instance suppose we are considering putting in a computer system with terminals for staff taking bookings at several recreational centres in a town. In this case we should imagine two future scenarios; the centres without computers and the centres with computers. We will then construct forecasts of cash flows for each scenario and look at the differences between the two.

Obviously, if we invest in the terminals we will have an immediate cost in the second scenario over and above the first. Presumably we expect this to be balanced by increases in revenue in the second relative to the first over a period of years. The result of this kind of exercise is usually a time-based profile of cash flow differences which we can use in the next stage of the appraisal exercise.

A word of warning is, however, appropriate here. Let us suppose that the decision had been whether or not to invest in terminals at a health centre. In this instance, the costs would have been obvious but the benefits, relating to quality of service and effective flow of patients, more subtle. Would this form of analysis still have been meaningful?

## Differences in cash flow timing

This is a standard issue in financial mathematics and is handled through the use of discounted cash flow (DCF). Assuming that the organisation incurs a cost for its capital which can be measured and forecasted into the future we discount future cash flows through a process which is in effect the reverse of compound interest calculations. (See the illustration given on page 82.)

The decision rule for whether or not to invest is that the sum of the discounted benefits should exceed the sum of the discounted costs (or that the Net Present Value (NPV) of benefits and costs should exceed zero). Of course in practice a failure in the NPV to attain a non-negative value is the signal for a re-appraisal of the figures used rather than abandonment of the proposal.

## Allowing for risk

All the events and cash flows described above relate to the future and hence are estimates which are liable to error. Unfortunately, with investments the costs may well occur but the benefits may fail to materialise.

The problem of risk is usually handled in one of two ways. The first is to raise the cost of capital of the investment artificially by applying a risk premium. This makes it more difficult for the NPV to attain positive values without substantial benefits. The second method is to apply probability estimates to various assessments of cash flows (that is the use of what is usually termed 'Statistical Decision Theory').

### Example of the use of discounted cash flow

Your company is considering investing in a replacement production system at a cost as shown in Table 5.1 (costs and timing being given in the 'cash out' column). The benefits of the new system lie in reduced costs relative to the existing system and the possibility of using the new equipment to produce an innovatory new product. The benefits are also shown in Table 5.1 (in the 'cash in' column). The net improvements in cash flow are then calculated as shown in the 'net cash' column (note that all these figures are estimates of differences relative to the existing system).

**Table 5.1 Example of DCF calculation**

| Time (years) | Cash out | Cash in | Net cash | Discount factors (25% discount rate) | Discounted net cash |
|---|---|---|---|---|---|
| 0 | 250 | 30 | −220 | 1.0000 | −220.00 |
| 1 | 70 | 80 | 10 | 0.8000 | 8.00 |
| 2 | 20 | 120 | 100 | 0.6400 | 64.00 |
| 3 | | 130 | 130 | 0.5120 | 66.56 |
| 4 | | 130 | 130 | 0.4096 | 53.25 |
| 5 | | 70 | 70 | 0.3277 | 22.94 |
| 6 | | 40 | 40 | 0.2621 | 10.49 |
| 7 | | 20 | 20 | 0.2097 | 4.19 |
| 8 | | 5 | 5 | 0.1678 | 0.84 |
| Net Present Value | | | | | 10.26 |

All data in £000 (except discount factors)

It can readily be seen that the total cash out is less than the cash in (or alternatively the total 'net cash' is greater than zero) and therefore the investment might appear to be a good idea. The benefits tend to occur, however, somewhat later than the costs and hence we must allow for the cost of the capital investment which is tied up in this project until paid off. We do this by applying discounting factors to each item of cash flow. These factors depend on the cost of capital (here taken as 25 per cent per annum) and the timing of the cash flow (in years from the start of the project)

(Note: For simplicity we have considered the 'year' as the unit of time and have assumed that all cash flows occur at the ends of years. In practice a more detailed calculation, following the same principles, must be carried out with more specific timings.)

The discounting factors (found from published tables or by using standard spreadsheet functions) are given in Table 5.1 along with the discounted values of the cash flows and the sum of the latter, the Net Present Value (NPV). The NPV for the project is greater than zero and hence the investment seems to be a good idea, although alternative systems and timings should also be explored as well as changes in the cost of capital. (See Further Reading at the end of the chapter for details of other information sources regarding this complex issue.)

# MAINTAINING THE PERFORMANCE OF TECHNOLOGICAL SYSTEMS

In this section we describe some of the major issues in maintenance. Most Operations Management texts describe this area of work in terms which relate mainly to manufacturing, where it is a key concern. Naturally these principles can also be applied to service uses of technology (for instance heavily used photocopying machines appear to require high levels of maintenance) and to IT hardware. In the latter case one might argue for the need for maintenance of software though the methods described below may require some reinterpretation in such an instance.

We begin with a discussion of the strategic issues in maintenance, if for no other reason than the past tendency to assume that, whilst technology investment was a strategic concern, maintenance is the sole preserve of men in overalls and service engineers!

## Maintenance strategies

There is little point in investing heavily in buildings and equipment if we do not make the best use of them. A key function in this regard is maintenance, by which we mean something more comprehensive than simply repairing machinery.

In the 1980s the term 'terotechnology' was invented to stand for a broader view than the traditional maintenance approach. Though we will not explicitly use this term, its definition (from BS 3811 (1984)) is useful in showing the full range of ideas covered by a modern approach to maintenance:

> Terotechnology ... a combination of management, financial, engineering, building and other practices applied to physical assets in pursuit of economic life cycle costs. Its practice is concerned with the specification and design for reliability and maintainability of plant, machinery, equipment, buildings and structures, with their installation, commissioning, operation, maintenance, modification and replacement and with feedback of information on design, performance and costs.

We should note within this definition the following factors:

- design of physical and information systems
- purchasing of equipment
- a long-term economic approach
- job design (the man/machine interface)
- training and education (part of the 'social systems' aspect of maintenance)

- organisational structure and the allocation of responsibilities
- communication
- actual continuing maintenance of engineering systems.

Thus, if we accept this approach we have a genuine integrative managerial methodology with considerable implications for operations management as well as other functional areas. This is an important concept as maintenance, even in this wider setting, can easily become seen as an exclusively engineering issue.

An alternative way forward, originating in Japan, is Total Productive Maintenance (TPM). This begins at the point where the above approach ends by focusing on the implementation of a comprehensive approach through employee participation. It might crudely be characterised as the continuous improvement philosophy of Kaizen and Total Quality Management applied to maintenance over the full life-cycle of equipment.

The main features of TPM are as follows:

- optimising the effectiveness of equipment
- establishing a thorough maintenance system based on the lifespan of the equipment
- involvement of all departments, functions and individuals in this approach
- motivation through the use of small group activities (similar to quality circles with an inter-disciplinary base).

In many ways this approach is similar to the Just-in-Time philosophy with its emphasis on the elimination of waste (see Chapter 11). In this instance, waste (principally of time and money) is due to:

- breakdowns
- set-up and adjustment
- idling and minor stoppage
- reduced operating speed
- process defects
- reduced yield.

One important aspect of all good maintenance approaches is a regular reporting of relevant control information relating to the operational systems under consideration. Within TPM it is recommended that the format displayed in Figure 5.1 is used, the figure also including a worked example. Thus overall equipment effectiveness is divided into three factors:

- operation time ratio (which reflects losses due to unplanned downtime)
- quality
- operational performance ratio (which reflects the speed at which the machine was running and the period of actual running time relative to standard speeds and available running times).

| | | | Example: | | |
|---|---|---|---|---|---|
| | | | | Data | Calculated values |
| A | Running time | mins | | 480 | |
| B | Planned downtime | mins | | 20 | |
| C | Loading time | mins | **A–B** | | 460 |
| D | Downtime loss | mins | | 60 | |
| E | Operating time | mins | **C–D** | | 400 |
| T | Operation time ratio | | **E/C*100%** | | 86.96% |
| | | | | | |
| G1 | Quantity processed (good) | items | | 392 | |
| G | Quantity processed (total) | items | | 400 | |
| H | Quality ration | | **G1/G*100%** | | 98.00% |
| | | | | | |
| I | Standard cycle time | mins/item | | 0.5 | |
| J | Actual cycle time | mins/item | | 0.8 | |
| M | Operation speed ratio | | **I/J** | | 0.625 |
| F | Actual processing time | mins | **J*G** | | 320 |
| N | Net operation ratio | | **F/E** | | 0.8 |
| L | Operation performance ratio | | **M*N* 100%** | 480 | 50.00% |
| | Overall equipment effectiveness | | **T* L* H** | | 42.61% |

**Fig. 5.1 TPM – overall equipment effectiveness**

This disaggregation of a crude effectiveness measure into readily identifiable factors shows how a problem can be broken down in order to target areas for improvement. In the example quoted, low machine speed seems the main source of ineffective working, followed by poor use of operating time. These factors must not, however, be seen in isolation from the schedules used by production planning staff (see Chapter 11). Equipment may only be working for half the time available because there is little demand for the products made on such machines! Once again this shows why a broad systems perspective must be taken when interpreting control data and taking remedial action. Communication and integration are not merely managerial buzzwords – they really are important in managing operational systems effectively, particularly in areas which have traditionally been considered the narrow concern of one type of specialist.

## Maintenance tactics

Although we have emphasised the strategic nature of maintenance activities, we should also note some of the details and terminology which are central to this area of work. There are three main ways in which equipment can let us down:

- it may fail, resulting in unplanned losses of output and high repair or replacement costs. Engineers classify failure modes in a number of ways, including by frequency, degree of warning, completeness and implications.

- it may deteriorate, thus lowering quality and output levels and giving a higher probability of failure

- it may become obsolescent, that is its economic performance is no longer competitive compared with other manufacturing methods.

In each of these situations we must consider aspects of productivity, cost and safety as well as environmental concerns if equipment failure can lead to pollution and public danger. In particular, the risk of unexpected failure in key equipment must be borne in mind as this may incur extremely high costs due to contract penalties and damages.

We may seek to reduce the impact of the above in three main ways:

- increased investment in more reliable and robust equipment

- the use of equipment performance monitoring systems and Statistical Process Control

- planned maintenance.

We concentrate our attention on the last of these by considering the fundamental ways in which we can approach the maintenance problem. One possibility is simply to react to problems as they occur (reactive maintenance). In many cases this can be economical and effective and is a form of planned maintenance if we spend time and attention ensuring the means to respond and in improving response times. A comparison may be made with the emergency services: we cannot predict where a road accident or a fire may occur but we can plan to respond effectively.

The second possibility is preventive maintenance whereby regular maintenance is carried out in order to reduce the probability of problems occurring, such work being timed to occur when operations will not be disrupted. This approach may be enhanced through the use of condition based maintenance which seeks to monitor equipment in order to plan maintenance schedules and bring forward maintenance on items which are showing signs of deterioration.

A final possibility is to use stand-by equipment or to develop flexible uses of production facilities so that work can be routed away from trouble spots until repairs have been carried out.

Planned maintenance programmes have a large number of benefits and yet may not be preferred over the classic comment 'if it's not broken, then don't mend it'! Unfortunately, this piece of advice can also be used to counteract attempts at systems improvement in many contexts. The best response is to benchmark performance against other organisations and to make determined attempts to measure costs of breakdowns in the same way as quality costs should be measured in order to inform and motivate programmes of quality improvement.

There will undoubtedly be some instances when failure has not been anticipated but the 'leave well enough alone' approach ignores the myriad of cases when constructive action could have been taken in advance, if only to plan an effective emergency response. The fundamental problem here may well relate to attitudes, working culture and organisational structure rather than the technicalities of engineering maintenance.

## FURTHER READING

The literature on the uses of technology in operational systems is vast and ever-changing. Engineering texts should be sought on the subject of manufacturing operations and IT texts on office systems. Texts describing the general principles of production management systems are listed at the end of Chapter 11 but Kerr (1991) gives some details of the use of Knowledge-Based systems in this area.

Texts on financial management give full details on investment appraisal methods but also see Harrison (1993). An interesting historical introduction to the uses of technology in industry is Buchanan (1992).

Buchanan, R. A. (1992), *The Power of the Machine*, Penguin, London.

Harrison, M. R. (1993), *Operations Management Strategy*, Pitman, London.

Kerr, R. (1991), *Knowledge-Based Manufacturing Management*, Addison Wesley, Sydney.

# CHAPTER 6

# Managing Projects

This chapter and the next are devoted to one of the major areas of Operations Management which is, to a large extent, self-contained. The methodology of project management has been developed to address a specific form of work organisation yet has much to tell us about practical management. As an increasing amount of work is carried out as 'projects', this area of operations is growing in importance.

In the past, texts on operations tended to concentrate on the quantitative aspects of project scheduling whilst a number of industry specific texts related to, for instance, construction projects with an emphasis on practical issues such as forms of contract. More recently, some useful work has been done on the human resource issues of project management. Our intention here is to provide a brief summary of this work. As a result, these chapters contain a balance of discussion and numerical technique.

It should be understood that the increased availability of project management software has made a detailed knowledge of the intricacies of network analysis less essential. The principles of such relevant quantitative techniques must, however, be fully understood in order to use computer packages effectively. Though this text cannot contain a full exposition and comparison of available software (the manuals for any one package will be longer than this entire book) the modern project manager is likely to be a skilled user of such packages and the examples given should be seen in this light.

## INTRODUCTION

Many operational processes are, to a greater or lesser extent, 'one-off' in character. Such processes are called projects. Typical examples of large projects, such as building the Channel Tunnel, are regularly mentioned in the media. Smaller scale activities, including student projects, share some of the characteristics of large projects as we show below. One should not carry this comparison too far, however. Large scale industrial and commercial projects provide a challenge to all staff involved in them which may be far beyond that met in other aspects of organisational life. Fortunately they also provide a focus for effort and managerial attention which has produced stunning results over the ages.

The building and civil engineering industry was one of the main areas where the techniques of project management were developed. Historically one can view construction projects from the building of the pyramids, through castles and cathedrals to modern buildings and major road, bridge and dam projects as examples of large numbers of people working together to produce single items with stunning properties. Though inspiring, this is a narrow view. Many current, major projects are concerned with developing software and information technology systems, creating films and TV programmes, developing new products and installing new industrial manufacturing processes. Projects may have less tangible outcomes such as a better trained workforce or customers who are more aware of your product range.

There is one further reason, however, why we are concerned with large projects. They may be a disaster! Bridges have been known to fall down, even before completion. Companies may spend vast amounts of money on, say, developing new drugs in the pharmaceutical industry with little to show at the end of the day. Even when a project is completed it may have involved excessive time and cost and be considered a financial disaster. Developing a new car which arrives in the marketplace a year after its rivals and must be sold at a loss to be competitive (that is, it cannot recoup its development costs) is not a happy situation to be in.

Such examples of misfortune should be studied in detail in order to learn how to improve project management. This brings us to another key point. If each project is unique, how do we learn how to manage them? Many organisational processes are repetitive and thus naturally provide a vehicle for continual experimentation, learning and adaptation. If we have to do a job a number of times we have the opportunity to improve the way we work, our choice of materials and the way we control the process. This gradual improvement may even be quantified as the 'learning curve' effect.

Though each project will have unique elements, much of the work will be similar to that carried out in other projects. It is possible to arrive at some principles of project management which appear to hold, or at least provide convenient 'rules of thumb' when applied to a range of projects. Experience and learning gained in one project situation is valuable in others. Techniques and procedures encapsulate the learning which has taken place by many staff working on many projects, and some of these are presented below. It should always be remembered, however, that project management is as much an art as a science, particularly in relation to the management of people and negotiating with clients.

## WHAT IS A PROJECT?

General definitions of the word 'project' can be unhelpful in that they are often either circular, too abstract or too restrictive. It is possible, however, to arrive at certain characteristics of organisational projects which appear to be common and widespread. Even if we do not agree with all of them, at least they provide a vehicle for debate and learning. In summary, we can characterise a project like this:

- Projects have an identifiable beginning and end.
- Projects have identifiable clients.
- Projects have objectives.
- Projects have constraints.
- Projects require individual, continual management.

## Projects have an identifiable beginning and end

It would, of course, be quite wrong to say that projects always start or end on time! Their beginning and their end should, nevertheless, be important and readily definable events, whenever they occur. Some problems may occur with, say, defining the ends of research and development projects which, if successful, lead naturally into the marketing of a new product or service. In such cases it is often of particular importance from the point of view of managerial control to decide at what point the R&D ends and routine operations begin.

Many projects, particularly in construction, have ceremonies or social rituals to mark beginnings and ends. In particular if the end of a project means breaking up a project team, then there are a number of human resource issues to be faced at such a time.

Thus the key point is that projects have an identifiable life span and it makes sense to talk about a project in terms of the stages in its life cycle. In particular we are drawing attention to the importance of time management in a project context.

## Projects have identifiable clients

This may seem a more controversial assertion, but we are going to assume that for any project it is possible to identify a client. This client may be an organisation, may change over the life of the project or may be a member of our own organisation (though external to the project team). The client may not be the intended end user of the output of the project and may use a professional agent to represent their needs and wishes.

The point of this assertion is that project management requires an external reference point with which to negotiate issues of required outcomes, time and cost. A practical example might be a computer software engineer constructing a special system for a client. The engineer may deal directly, for example, with a consultant employed by the client firm. They may never meet the staff who will eventually use the system (though this could be unwise) but will always have some way of referring back problems and issues regarding the intended working of the system as well as development costs and timescales. This is in contrast to repetitive operational processes which work to specifications based on the general perceived needs of a population of customers.

## Projects have objectives

Projects exist to meet the needs of the identifiable client. They should aim towards specific outcomes as encapsulated in their objectives.

Objectives may change as a project continues, though not so dramatically that the project becomes unidentifiable. Clients needs change, the working environment changes and the project team may learn new ways to do things. Objectives may be modified to be less demanding as opinions change regarding what is feasible. Objectives may even become more ambitious if progress is outstanding.

There should always, in any project, be mechanisms for the regular review of progress against objectives and for the modification of objectives (with accompanying changes to costs and timings) through negotiation with the client.

## Projects have constraints

In any project situation there are limits to the time available, resources which can be obtained, cash which can be spent and the feasibility of intended operations. Project management inevitably involves the balancing of scarce resources against costs and intended outcomes, as does all management!

## Projects require individual, continuing management

This is usually stated as the need for:

- a team of people
- a project manager
- dedicated resources (at least for a given period of time)
- accounting and control systems based on the project as an identifiable unit of work.

Although it is possible to envisage more fluid working arrangements, almost all project specialists emphasise the importance of the above, in particular the project manager as a key player.

The project manager is the individual responsible for the overall achievement of the project's objectives, within cost and time constraints. This role definition can, of course, become problematic if client needs or the environment (and hence the stated objectives) continually change but the principle of the individual as project champion, manager and controller remains and has the added virtue of great motivational potential.

### Clients and projects

Issues of client interaction in project management leads to a particularly interesting general point regarding the relationship between an organisation and its customers. If you are making, say, washing machines then you are likely to work to standard designs based on market research. Suppose the customer can walk into a shop and specify a particular colour of washing machine along with particular mechanical properties (presumably from a predetermined list). This information is fed to the factory which now schedules a specific machine to be made for this customer. The machine may have a unique set of characteristics, be made for a particular client and its manufacture takes place at a given time but we would not refer to this as a project as the overall context is one of repetitive manufacture. If we were manufacturing high quality pottery figures, however, and a client was willing to pay for a genuinely unusual item then perhaps the management of this process would have all the characteristics of project management. The key point is not to be dogmatic about what characterises a project but to use the concepts and techniques of project management as appropriate.

Incidentally, the information technology and manufacturing systems required to tailor individual products to customer needs have been in existence for some time and major car manufacturers are now considering their use. The problem of implementation of such systems may be as much an issue of customer attitudes, cost and organisational flexibility as of technical feasibility.

## THE KEY MODELS OF PROJECT MANAGEMENT

Though we will introduce a number of specific project management techniques, some general ideas are of central importance. One very simple idea is illustrated in Figure 6.1 and shows in readily identifiable form the relationship between three features of any project:

- *Outcomes*: what the client will actually get
- *Time*: when the client gets it
- *Cost*: what the client pays.

Alternatively 'Cost' may mean 'cost of the project from the project team's point of view' if we are looking at the internal control of the project rather than adopting a client perspective.

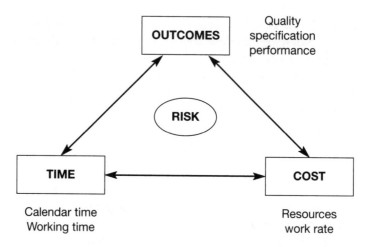

**Fig. 6.1 Project management – the basics**

Before the physical start of any project, negotiations will take place in order to arrive at a balance between intended outcomes, time and cost. The actual form of negotiation depends on context. An external client may wish to draw up a project contract or may put work based on a previous design out to tender. The latter case, common in the construction industry, may fix both the outcomes and times and leave cost as the only topic for negotiation. Alternatively, a client and service provider may adopt a more fluid relationship but must initially agree on some basic parameters of outcome, time and cost. Outcomes will at this stage be expressed as some form of specification.

As the project progresses, this balance between intended outcomes, time and cost may need to be reviewed. For instance in a college based student project, what seemed to be a good idea at the start may prove impossible as time goes by and the student's tutor (in the 'client' role) may be consulted to agree a change of plan or an extension to deadlines. The important point here is the need for formal systems to agree and record such changes in the student or the industrial situation.

At the end of the project, performance against time schedules will be known (and penalties for lateness a possible issue) and outcomes will be actual rather than intended. The client and the project manager will be concerned with conformance to specification (that is quality, in its classic definition), with actual cost incurred and with the amount of payment due from the client.

The triangle shown in Figure 6.1 can be extended to show relationships with resources. In particular time is seen as calendar time, the dates at which events take place. Time may also be seen as a resource (for example, the number of hours it takes to write advertising copy as part of a product promotion project) and as such is linked with other resources (the availability of staff to do the writing) and cost (the expense involved in employing extra staff if the work is late).

If we wished to extend the basic triangle of 'outcomes, time and cost' further, a favoured candidate would be 'risk'. As with all complex processes extending some

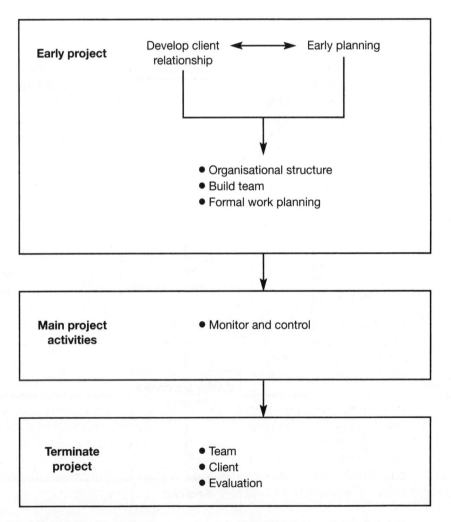

**Fig. 6.2 Life cycle of a project**

time into the future, there is always a chance that the project team will not deliver the outcomes, meet the schedules or keep to budget. Though the formal techniques of risk management are beyond the scope of this introduction, the sources and magnitude of risks should always be borne in mind by the project manager.

Underlying this notion of a dynamic balance between outcomes, time and cost is the idea of the life cycle of a project. This is illustrated in simple form in Figure 6.2 using terms which have been covered above.

In Figure 6.3 we provide a more extended map of project management using a number of new terms which will be explained later. In particular we draw attention to the following:

- the relationship between the team for a specific project and its organisational context

- the techniques employed to manage projects, with particular reference to the management of time and money.

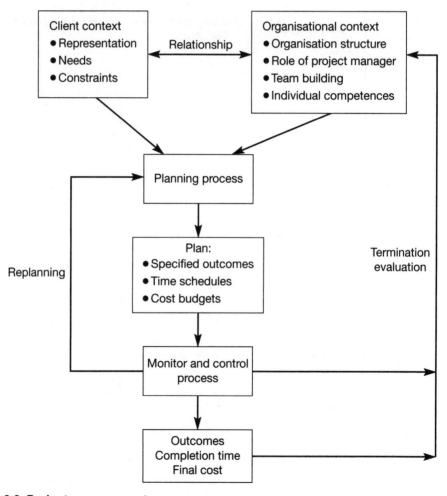

**Fig. 6.3 Project management**

In this context we should now draw attention to another key issue in project management. Underlying our earlier discussions is a contrast between the management of large industrial projects and small, personal projects (for example, student projects). Naturally one should not expect the same formality in the use of project management techniques at both ends of this spectrum. Whilst the ideas of large project management are of some interest when managing small projects, it is appropriate that simpler management controls are used for the latter. In practice, however, there is a third context of importance, that is the management of a portfolio of projects.

Typically an engineering department in a company might be involved with many projects. Some of these will be large, say the design of a major new component, whilst others will be small. A major management challenge is the overall management of this situation involving overlapping project teams, resource sharing, controlling the progress of many projects at the same time and so forth. Much recent project management software addresses this problem of multi-project management.

Alternatively, large projects can often conveniently be broken down into a number of smaller projects and managed on a multi-project basis provided the overall relationships between them are carefully monitored.

# LIFE-CYCLE MANAGEMENT

The life-cycle management concept illustrated in Figure 6.2 is of particular value whether applied to small or large projects. It provides a framework of key issues for the project manager as described in the following. This material is then developed in later sections.

## Early project planning

It is tempting to describe the first stages of a project as 'pre-project planning'. In this case we would be characterising the 'project' as, for example, building things or designing things and implicitly assuming that a 'pre-project' phase exists in which planning occurs, contracts negotiated and so forth. We will adopt the alternative view, however, in which early planning through to termination are all part of a total project which must in itself be planned and controlled. This is consistent with large project management where early project work may take many years to complete and involve substantial resources. It is also a valuable discipline for small project management in focusing attention within an organisation and freeing resources.

One problem with this approach is that it begs the question, 'when do you plan the total project?' Obviously, one of the first stages in a total project is some rough planning of the project itself, often by senior management and based on the assumption that further refinements will take place as experience is gained. First contact with a client may involve some outline agreement on the general parameters of the project, using the 'outcomes, time and cost' framework shown in Figure 6.1. It should therefore be remembered that the 'project' for which detailed plans are made, resources scheduled and so forth in a formal manner (see below) is only a part of the 'total project'.

This hierarchical model of projects containing other projects is central to the approach we are adopting here. The important point is to be clear about the boundaries of any given project and to be clear as to who is managing a given project (or sub-project or portfolio of projects). Problems of definition and responsibility are likely to be most acute at the early stages of a project and at termination.

The early project planning stage involves the following activities:

- developing a relationship with the client, negotiating agreement on outcomes, time and cost and drawing up appropriate documentation (for example, contracts) based on this agreement
- relating the project to its organisational framework (see below) and appointing a project manager
- formally planning project activities, determining resources required and preparing appropriate control mechanisms for quality, time and cost.

In the context of formal planning, some important terminology needs to be introduced at this stage. The key to such planning is determining a 'Work Breakdown Structure' (WBS) for a project. In simple form this is a list of tasks to be carried out, their relationship (for instance, Must task A be completed before task B can be started?, Can tasks C and D be carried out at the same time?), time estimates for their completion and resources required for each task.

Now such a list of tasks may be easy to produce for a small project but is quite impractical for a project of any size. Thus two further concepts are of importance. The first is the hierarchy of tasks whereby a major project is first of all broken down into smaller projects, which are in turn broken down until eventually some discrete, recognisable tasks are obtained.

For instance our project may be to move a library from one building to another. Our first level of sub-projects may involve such things as:

- refurbish new building
- erect shelving in new building
- sort stock of books, discard unwanted material etc.

The second of these sub-projects, 'erect shelving', cannot commence until the first, 'refurbish new building', has been completed though it can be continuing while the books are being sorted. We can presumably allocate a time (say two weeks), some resources and some cash to this sub-project. We could also divide this sub-project into a detailed set of physical tasks, though this may be unnecessary at the planning stage. Indeed we may intend to employ a sub-contractor to carry out this work and therefore not plan the work in any more detail than necessary to convey our needs to the sub-contractor.

One point that must be emphasised is the need for the responsibility for carrying out of this, and every other, sub-activity to be clearly designated. One of the most obvious ways in which project management fails is when doubts exist about who is responsible for any piece of work. This responsibility relates to outcomes, time and cost.

A further idea of importance here is the 'Rolling Wave' concept. In a large project it might be impossible to plan in detail sub-projects which will not be attempted for months or years in the future. Thus we will produce an outline plan showing details of sub-projects and will plan in detail the sub-projects which must be carried out in the near future but will only produce detailed plans of later sub-projects when necessary.

An example to illustrate the Rolling Wave concept is a research and development project for a radically new product. Though we will eventually have to determine production arrangements for when the product in launched, such details cannot be settled until the basic properties of the product have been designed. Therefore our initial plan may include re-tooling a production line and may even include estimates of cost and time but further refinements of the plan will only be possible in the future.

This idea of continually refining a project plan as experience and information is gained and problems overcome is a valuable way of looking at project management. All too often in the past, excessively detailed initial plans have simply been discarded as they proved impossible to work with, thus wasting planning time and losing control of the project. It is far better to start with a sound outline plan and then to fill in the details when necessary and using current information. This may sound like common sense but some of the classic project planning techniques are highly mechanistic and complicated and the inexperienced project manager may lose sight of the fact that planning is only a means to an end – producing quality outcomes for a client at the right cost and time.

A word is appropriate at this point on the subject of project planning software. Along with spreadsheets, database management systems and word-processing packages, computer software suppliers have not been slow to realise that project planning can to some extent be automated. When such packages allow outline planning and provide facilities to improve productivity and control, they are highly recommended, although with the warning that it takes some time to learn how to use them effectively. They can, however, also be seen as fascinating distractions from practical project management. Also, within a bureaucratic organisation, the production of glossy project reports may be viewed as more rewarding than keeping in touch with client needs.

## Main project activities

As we move from planning and negotiating to starting work on the main project (that is actually producing outcomes for the client) the attention of the project manager moves towards team building, establishing patterns of work, detailed planning of daily work, problem solving and control.

At this point, or earlier, project managers must think carefully about their role, their competence to carry out this role and their place in the structure of the organisation. This set of issues is explored later in this chapter where the management of projects and change are contrasted with functional organisational styles.

Since the 1950s, much has been written on project management techniques such as PERT, CPA and such like. Detailed coverage of the basic theory of such techniques requires a textbook in itself but the underlying ideas can be illustrated by means of a simple example as shown in the next chapter (see 'Moving the Office' on page 108).

This example shows a complete approach suitable for a very small project and it should be understood that although the general ideas are relevant to larger projects, their application may be very demanding, even with the help of the more sophisticated software packages.

A further major aspect of this phase of project management is continual control relating, as usual, to outcomes, time and cost. Such control may be subjective and intuitive or highly formal and rigorous. It may be carried out by members of the project team or by external staff (from the parent organisation or acting for the client). It may occur at any time or relate to specific points in time and project milestones.

A variety of forms of control are likely to be relevant with short projects requiring more hands-on control and major long-term projects needing formal documentation. Though the latter sounds bureaucratic it is essential to keep track of the many decisions and changes made in a large project and to provide one of many communication devices for internal and external staff.

Some simple ideas of cost and time control are explored later in the next chapter in the form of the 'Curec Design Project' example.

## Termination

Whilst it is natural to spend much time and attention on setting up and running projects, this final phase may unfortunately be neglected, except to the extent that it may be crisis oriented and involve large final payments! Yet this is a time of maximum impact for the client when final outcomes are realised. It can often be a time of stress for project staff as the uncertainty of their future careers becomes evident (specifically in the context of large projects and staff specifically committed to the project).

A further difficulty should be noted: many projects do not reach their intended outcomes. Some simply fail to produce the outcomes; on some occasions the environment changes and the outcomes are no longer required (as can often happen with protracted new product development); internal politics may move against a project (usually where the client is internal, for instance developing new in-house systems); money can run out or the project can become amalgamated with other work. A key task of the project manager is to be watchful for the symptoms of such forms of project malaise.

An alternative problem presents itself when the project is successful and leads on to further activity. A typical example is a new product (or service) development project where design leads naturally into process development, customer trials, launch and continuing delivery (presumably with continuing improvement). On the one hand it seems good management practice for designers and development project staff to have a continuing involvement. Indeed it can lead to major problems if they simply abandon the work done (or 'throw it over the wall' that traditionally separates designers from production staff!). Yet a never ending project can pull valuable creative staff into inappropriate roles, can inhibit the market realisation of their ideas through unnecessary changes and adjustments and make it difficult to evaluate the success or otherwise of the project.

Whilst this whole area of project management is a subject in itself (see Further Reading), the following should be noted as guidelines for the final phase of any project:

- a final reckoning must be made in terms of outcomes, time and cost, often in terms of a project final report
- there must be a handover to the client or an end user of a system
- arrangements must be made for final payments to be made by external clients (unfortunately this can often involve litigation in major development and construction projects)
- plans must be made for the redeployment of project staff, including the project manager
- a formal evaluation of the project should be carried out in order that lessons may be learnt for project management in the future, relating to similar and dissimilar projects.

## PROJECT MANAGEMENT IN AN ORGANISATIONAL CONTEXT

An issue we have not addressed so far in this book is the place of the Operations Manager in the management structure of an organisation. When considering project management we cannot assume that this issue is capable of straightforward resolution. Many projects do not easily fit within traditional organisations and it is important that we consider why this is the case and what might be done about it.

(Note: 'organisational structure', that is the roles, responsibilities and authority of various managers in an organisation, is a topic normally considered in depth in general management and HRM texts. Our comments here should be seen only as a brief indication of the complexities of this subject.)

The traditional company is organised on hierarchical and functional lines, that is each individual has only one direct line manager (the principle of unity of command) who is likely to have similar professional interests (for example, also be an engineer) or similar area of business responsibility (for example, also be concerned with selling pottery figurines in the USA). Delegation of responsibilities comes down through the hierarchy whilst the promotional path is upwards through the same hierarchy. This structure is seen as being permanent and dealing with recurring tasks which are allocated to parts of the hierarchy depending on skills and areas of business concern (often factories, products or markets). Whilst there are a number of advantages of this arrangement, problems may occur in communication and the co-ordination of activities across the hierarchy.

Projects, as we have seen, are not permanent. They require the bringing together of a mixture of skills relevant to meeting the clients needs. One way in which this may be achieved, common in, say, major project civil engineering, is to employ the appropriate individuals for the duration of the contract. A project manager is directly responsible for such personnel. This leaves some residual problems of project team organisation but the overall situation is clear and team members are probably quite experienced in working in such an environment. Once again this arrangement has a number of obvious advantages but can lead to the duplication of resources across several projects. It is also not necessarily a suitable structure for smaller projects with differing skill requirements over their life cycle.

A simple solution often adopted is to locate a small project within one functional arm of an organisation, with the possibility of buying in extra staff for short periods if required. This may be adequate if most of the required skills are within this arm (for example, product development engineering) but can easily divert the focus of a project from the needs of the client to the capabilities of available staff, quite apart from a very human tendency towards empire building.

Thus we can readily visualise project situations where neither functional nor project forms of organisation seem quite appropriate. Can some compromise be reached between them or do we need another form of organisation? One possibility which has been known about for some time is the idea of 'matrix management'. In practice there are a number of quite distinct ways to implement matrix management and we introduce three of these below (see references at end of chapter for further details).

## Functional matrix

In this situation, a project manager is appointed who co-ordinates efforts amongst the existing functional specialisms. Such an individual has budget responsibility and negotiates proposed outcomes with senior functional managers who are then responsible for directing staff to achieve those outcomes within agreed budget allocations. Though a useful compromise model, this arrangement may not solve problems of co-ordination between the functions involved. The success of the project (in terms of cost and time management) may very much depend on the negotiating and troubleshooting skills of the project manager.

## Project matrix

An alternative is to appoint a project manager who then has staff assigned to the project for definite periods of time. The project manager thus becomes, in the short term, the line manager of all project staff and is responsible for their work, possibly with limited reference to a functional manager for technical advice. This method of working directly addresses issues of control and communication and maintains client focus for project staff. Problems can be caused for the functional managers who may lose key individuals and skills for periods of time. This arrangement can lead to an ineffective use of resources within functions who may now be hard pressed to cover other tasks and projects.

## Balanced matrix

This is a sophisticated solution where functional and project managers have joint responsibility for the work to be done. Whereas the structures given above maintain unity of command at any one point in time (though with different line managers at different points of time with a project management structure), the balanced matrix assumes a more fluid form of work where an individual is responsible to differing managers for differing aspects of their work. This is an ambitious way of working seeking the best of both worlds – good communication and co-ordination as well as effective resource allocation and low cost.

The simplest conclusion is that a balanced matrix is a good solution if it can be made to work but it requires great skill on the part of all managers concerned as frequent compromises will be inevitable. Empirical evidence seems to suggest that the project matrix is considered more effective by team members and may well be the pragmatic solution if resources can be made available.

For some modern organisations who have embraced team working and the outsourcing of many operational activities, continual negotiations over outcomes, cost and time are an accepted way of life and the above discussion may seem redundant. Many organisations, however, appear to be engaged in a continual struggle to reconcile project and recurring activities and hence need to think clearly about how they wish to organise projects.

## THE ROLE OF THE PROJECT MANAGER

We have now dealt with the basic structure of projects and their place within the organisation. Where does this leave the project manager in terms of:

- appropriate role and responsibilities
- required skills and competences
- desirable personal attributes.

The responsibilities are quite clear and identical with the formal aims of the project, the client and the parent organisation (assuming any differences between the above have been, or can be, reconciled through negotiation). The project manager's role will partly depend on the organisational structure adopted but will certainly include providing an interface between the environment and the project team.

It is in this latter area that many of the project manager's skills must lie, that is in a combination of communicating and building up an agenda and a consensus for future action. In addition, technical skills and formal project management and control skills are likely to be required.

**TASK**

> An interesting final task for this chapter is for you to attempt to list, on the basis of what you have read so far as well as your own experience, the most useful personal qualities to be possessed by a project manager.

Perhaps your list included enthusiasm, optimism, energy, a thick skin, courage, tenacity, maturity, drive, ambition, credibility, political nous, inter-personal sensitivity, leadership, honesty...

and the ability to handle stress!

## FURTHER READING

There are a number of specialist texts on project management but the following are particularly recommended, the former specifically relating to the role and skills of the project manager:

Boddy, D. and Buchanan, D. (1992), *Take the Lead*, Prentice Hall, New York.

Meredith, J. R. and Mantel, S. J. (1995), *Project Management* (3ed), Wiley, New York.

# CHAPTER 7

# Project Management Techniques

In Chapter 6 we introduced the main concepts of project management, concentrating on the basic process and organisational issues. In this chapter we are concerned with the technical side of project management, that is the practical techniques which have been developed in the past 50 years as aids to project planning and control.

## OBJECTIVES

This chapter:

- shows how practical project management is based on a **Work Breakdown Structure**
- illustrates project scheduling in a case exercise context
- illustrates cost and schedule control in a case exercise context.

## INTRODUCTION

Techniques such as Critical Path Analysis (CPA) pre-date the discussions of organisational issues presented in Chapter 6. A glance at texts on project management of 30 years ago would reveal a great deal of arithmetic and some practical, common-sense management advice. Many students in the past might be forgiven for identifying project management with CPA as the latter was all they were taught!

This concentration on learning the details of numerical techniques was more understandable before project planning software was readily available on personal computers at low cost. Almost all individuals now involved in planning medium and large scale projects will use appropriate packages. There are, however, two good reasons for gaining a basic understanding of the techniques. The first is to appreciate the language of technical project planning and gain some feeling for what the computer packages can and cannot do in terms of planning and control. The second is to be able to plan and control a small, everyday project where computer based planning would give little advantage.

It should be noted at this stage that one of the major advantages of computer based networked systems is their potential for controlling a group of projects which share resources. In such situations it is important to use the system as a basis for planning and managing all projects of whatever size.

We begin the chapter by providing further details of Work Breakdown Structures and some insights into the problems of time and cost estimation. We then move onto the key technique areas of project scheduling, resource allocation and cost and schedule control. In each case we demonstrate the techniques presented through the use of small examples. It should be remembered that a full mastering of project planning and control techniques will require detailed study beyond the material presented here, which is intended as an introduction to the basic principles. We end the chapter with a small case example to be attempted by the reader as an individual or group assignment.

In working through the following material, you should attempt every exercise before looking at the solutions. This will help you to gain an appreciation not only of how to carry out the arithmetic techniques but also of why things have to be done in certain ways. As presented here, the techniques are not highly mathematical though the more advanced texts will show alternative and more complex ways of attempting to improve on this simple approach. It is by no means clear that such advances are necessary for controlling small and medium sized projects and, as in much operations management, a simple and robust approach is often the best.

## WORK BREAKDOWN STRUCTURE (WBS)

In order to provide the specified outcomes for the client, a number of activities (sometimes called 'work packages') will have to be carried out as part of the project. The organisation of these activities is a prime concern of the project manager. In particular, to ensure effective work planning, we need to be able to satisfy a number of criteria, including the seven criteria following:

1. Label each activity for it to exist in the project management information system.
2. Relate the activities to one another.
3. Assign responsibility for the completion of each activity.
4. Estimate how long it will take to complete each activity.
5. Decide what resources are required to complete each activity.
6. Budget for the costs involved in each activity.
7. Set appropriate control mechanisms to monitor the progress of each activity.

*But what do we mean by an activity?*

At the base of our plans will be pieces of work which can be recognised by involved parties as coherent and reasonable tasks and which require no further subdivision. For instance if redecorating our office is the project, then we may decide that wallpapering one particular wall is one of our basic tasks. In a different context, 'redecorate the office' may be seen as a basic activity in a larger project (renovate the building) and may be sub-contracted, say, with no further detailed planning.

Thus the decision as to what tasks are basic is a matter of convenience and subjective judgement. This is not to say it is an arbitrary decision. The above seven criteria must be capable of being met. In particular we must be able to relate the task to others and assign responsibility for its completion.

Two ways to relate activities are obviously important:

- *Inclusion* – some activities are parts of other activities
- *Precedence* – some activities may need to be completed before others can begin

The first of these, inclusion, suggests that it may be appropriate to view projects as hierarchies of activities. The project itself may be subdivided into a small collection of sub-projects which, in turn, may be subdivided further. This process continues until basic tasks are reached. This structure is illustrated in Figure 7.1. The primary project, renovating the building, is built up from three sub-projects: 'offices', 'roofing', and 'basement'. We have no information at this stage of the precedence relationships between these three but each may now be separately planned. In particular we see that 'offices' is itself built up from four sub-sub-projects, which we may, for convenience, term activities. These may in turn be further subdivided if this is appropriate.

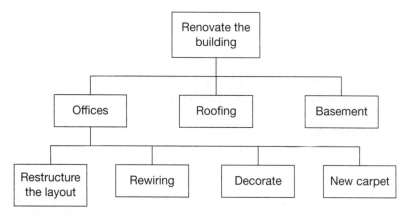

**Fig. 7.1 Work breakdown structure**

One complication which may arise is that an activity in one leg of the hierarchy may be related in some way to an activity in another leg. Though such a relationship may be handled in the detailed planning stages which follow, the existence of a large number of such relationships is a sign that the hierarchical structure we are using is not appropriate.

Such a structure is one example of a Work Breakdown Structure (WBS). Many representations of a WBS are possible but all must facilitate planning by addressing the seven criteria given above.

Precedence relationships may be of a number of types with the most common being of the form 'activity A must be completed before B can begin'. In the absence of a stated relationship we may assume that activities may proceed in parallel, that is work may *logically* be carried out on each at the same time. In practice, however, we may not have sufficient *resources* for this to take place. One should note that logic and resource issues are seen as separate at this stage. When scarce resources are allocated at a later stage in the planning process, a number of activities may then be forced into sequential rather than parallel relationships.

## TIME AND COST ESTIMATION

Having arrived at a Work Breakdown Structure for a project, we now need to estimate the likely cost and duration of each activity. There are several ways in which this might be performed as shown below.

### Time-driven estimation

Some activities will take a given length of time to complete regardless of the resources allocated to them. For instance an external organisation may be involved or a fixed duration process included in the activity. In such cases the activity time estimate will be resource independent, though there may still be some uncontrollable uncertainty present. Resources will then presumably be allocated in such a way as to minimise costs.

### Resource-driven estimation

Frequently activity durations will be dependent on resources utilised. If the resource is fixed and available then activity duration can be directly estimated from work rate. If not then some initial estimate of resource availability must be made with the proviso that this may be changed later in the planning process. It should not be assumed that doubling an available resource will inevitably lead to halving the activity duration. Indeed studies have shown that beyond certain limits an increase in resource may be counterproductive.

An example to illustrate resource-driven estimation is as follows. Assume an activity will require 20 'person-months' of work. Thus if we allocate four people to the activity then its duration may be estimated at five months. Alternatively, we might be tempted to allocate ten people hoping for a duration of two months but may be frustrated in this expectation due to the difficulties of the ten people organising their work on the activity and communicating progress effectively with one another. In practice the relationship between resources allocated and resulting activity duration may be very complex.

Similarly, the link between resources allocated and costs incurred may be difficult to state accurately as differing payments for resources (for example overtime payments, sub-contractor charges and so forth) may be necessary.

### Top-down estimation

Based on past experience of similar work, it may be possible to estimate directly the likely time for completion of a whole project or at least its principal sub-projects. In this case the total duration provides a framework for setting target durations for component activities. There is a danger, however, that a needlessly generous amount of time is allocated to the project. To counter this, audit and evaluation of past projects is necessary to review time and resource usage standards.

## Bottom-up estimation

An alternative approach, similar to the use of method study and work measurement in repetitive operations, is to use estimates of time based on the 'ground-level' tasks of the Work Breakdown Structure in order to build up the time needed for completion of the project as a whole. This obviously logical approach contains a major potential problem in that individual time estimates may be excessive in order to cater for unforeseen contingencies. Though it is natural for an individual manager to add a little to a time estimate in case of emergencies, such padding may add up over the project as a whole to produce project times which are costly and unacceptable to the client.

A similar problem can obviously arise when estimating costs and needed resources and therefore strict discipline is required when estimating activity parameters in this way.

## Development projects

Some projects require us to do things which are quite new or potentially open-ended. This is obviously a potentially difficult situation but some form of duration, resource and cost estimates must be made in order for effective management control to be exercised. In such cases an added emphasis must be placed on top-level reviews of project progress and a determined effort made to measure outcomes and predict likely future performance.

## The rolling wave concept

In a project which extends some way into the future or is subject to a considerable degree of uncertainty, detailed planning of all but immediate activities may be impractical. In this case top-down planning for the whole project is necessary but with the disaggregation of plans to lower levels in the hierarchy delayed until such planning becomes necessary. Thus the detailed planning of activities 'rolls like a wave' through the project as time goes by.

This is by no means as radical a concept as it may appear. In many projects a considerable amount of replanning is necessary as events unfold, the environment changes and learning takes place. The rolling wave concept builds such continual replanning into the basic administration of the project.

## SCHEDULING IN A PROJECT CONTEXT

We now move on to the technical aspects of project scheduling. The methods we show below are widely known and will normally be carried out by specialist computer software, though simple projects can easily be analysed by hand or by using spreadsheets. It is important to understand the principles on which these calculations are based even if there is no need to carry out such calculations manually.

The method described in this section is usually known as critical path analysis and is an important preliminary to project resource allocation and budgeting.

Note: In this basic introduction we will make a number of assumptions in order to simplify the presentation, in particular:

- The pre-requisites of activity X are those other activities which must be completed before X can begin. If Z is a pre-requisite of Y and Y of X then we need not explicitly state that Z is a pre-requisite of X.

- Activity durations are given as definite lengths of time (that is deterministic rather than probabilistic estimates). Naturally they should be considered provisional until plans and schedules have been agreed as changes in resource levels are likely to affect actual activity durations.

- Activity on Arrow networks have been used throughout as they contain, in conjunction with activity tables, all the information we need. Some texts and computer programmes use the alternative Activity on Node presentation which is simpler but does not explicitly include event times.

Once we have arrived at a set of activities, their pre-requisites and estimated durations we can then set about the task of analysing the logical implications of this structure. This is best demonstrated through the use of a simple example. It should be remembered that real projects may involve many hundreds of activities at each level of their WBS and that most will not be on the 'critical path'.

## Moving the Office – a project scheduling example

In Table 7.1 we show the activities associated with this project. The pre-requisites show the logical relationships between activities as described above. The simplest way to proceed is to draw up a project activity analysis table as shown in Table 7.2. You may like to fill in the empty boxes as we proceed and then compare your results with those given in Table 7.3.

**Table 7.1 'Moving Office' project – activities**

| Activity code | Activity description | Pre-requisite activities | Estimated activity duration (days) |
|---|---|---|---|
| MO1 | Discuss new layout with staff | | 3 |
| MO2 | Re-structure walls and fit new carpet | MO1 | 12 |
| MO3 | Order furniture and equipment | MO1 | 10 |
| MO4 | Install new telephone lines | MO2 | 6 |
| MO5 | Decorate office | MO2 | 4 |
| MO6 | Equipment delivered and installed | MO2, MO3 | 5 |
| MO7 | Move in – office party! | MO4, MO5, MO6 | 2 |

**Table 7.2 'Moving Office' project – activity analysis sheet**

| Code | Pre-requisites | Successor activities | Time (days) | Earliest start | Earliest finish | Latest start | Latest finish | Float |
|------|----------------|----------------------|-------------|----------------|-----------------|--------------|---------------|-------|
| MO1 | | | 3 | | | | | |
| MO2 | MO1 | | 12 | | | | | |
| MO3 | MO1 | | 10 | | | | | |
| MO4 | MO2 | | 6 | | | | | |
| MO5 | MO2 | | 4 | | | | | |
| MO6 | MO2, MO3 | | 5 | | | | | |
| MO7 | MO4, MO5, MO6 | | 2 | | | | | |

The first step is to fill in the 'Successor Activities' column. These are the opposites of pre-requisites and, whilst they contain no new information, are very useful when calculating some of the statistics below. To fill in this column we simply transcribe the 'Pre-requisites' column, for instance as MO1 is a pre-requisite for MO2 then MO2 is a successor to MO1.

We then carry out a forward pass through the table by calculating 'Earliest Start (ES)' and 'Earliest Finish (EF)' times for all activities using the following rules:

- for all activities, $EF = ES + Time$
- for all activities with no pre-requisites, $ES = 0$
- for all other activities, ES is the largest EF of all the pre-requisites
- the project duration is the largest EF.

Using these rules we might proceed as follows:

MO1 has no pre-requisites so its ES = 0 and its EF = 0 + 3 = 3. (Time is measured in days in this example. As a working convention, assume that points of time refer to the end of a working day. Thus ES = 9 means that an activity can start at the end of day nine, in fact, the start of day ten)

MO2 has pre-requisite MO1 so its ES = 3 and EF = 3 + 12 = 15. *(You should now complete MO3 to MO5)*

MO6 has pre-requisites MO2 and MO3 and hence its ES = 15 (why?) and EF = 15 + 5 = 20. *(You should now complete MO7).* The project duration is 23 days (why?)

**Table 7.3 'Moving Office' project – activity analysis results**

| Code | Pre-requisites | Successor activities | Time (days) | Earliest start | Earliest finish | Latest start | Latest finish | Float |
|------|------|------|------|------|------|------|------|------|
| MO1 | | MO2, MO3 | 3 | 0 | 3 | 0 | 3 | 0 |
| MO2 | MO1 | MO4, MO5, MO6 | 12 | 3 | 15 | 3 | 15 | 0 |
| MO3 | MO1 | MO6 | 10 | 3 | 13 | 6 | 16 | 3 |
| MO4 | MO2 | MO7 | 6 | 15 | 21 | 15 | 21 | 0 |
| MO5 | MO2 | MO7 | 4 | 15 | 19 | 17 | 21 | 2 |
| MO6 | MO2, MO3 | MO7 | 5 | 15 | 20 | 16 | 21 | 1 |
| MO7 | MO4, MO5, MO6 | | 2 | 21 | 23 | 21 | 23 | 0 |

If a project duration of 23 days is not acceptable then the WBS and time estimates should now be examined and revised if possible.

We now carry out a backward pass through the table by calculating Latest Start (LS) and Latest Finish (LF) times for all activities using the following rules:

- for all activities, LS = LF – Time
- for all activities with no successor, LF = project duration
- for all other activities, LF is the least LS of all the successors.

Thus we proceed as follows:

MO7 has LF = 23 and LS = 23 – 2 = 21

MO6 has LF = 21 and LS = 21 – 5 = 16 *(You should now complete MO5 to MO3)*

MO2 has LF = 15 (why?) and LS = 15 – 12 = 3 *(You should now complete MO1)*

Note that at least one activity has an ES = 0 and none have negative ES. This is a useful, though not comprehensive, check on our calculations.

We can now complete the Float calculations as follows:

for each activity, Float = LF – EF (or alternatively LS – ES gives the same answer)

Activities with zero float are on the critical path of a project, that is any delay with their completion will delay the project as a whole. Other activities have some discretion in their planning but it should be remembered that if one activity uses up some float then it will not be available for later activities.

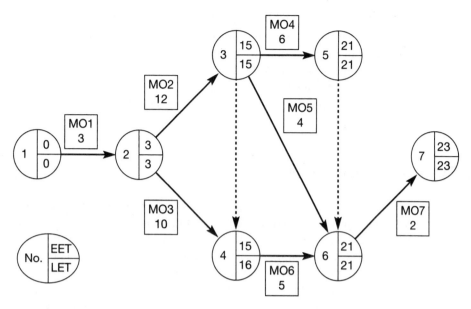

**Fig. 7.2 CPA diagram**

An alternative way to proceed which gives us a slightly different perspective on the project is to draw an Activity on Arrow (AoA) diagram. The diagram for this project is shown in Figure 7.2. AoA diagrams require some practice in construction but the basic principles are as follows.

Each activity is represented by an arrow drawn between two circles (the 'tail' and 'head' events). The pattern of the arrows reflects the pre-requisites, which requires the use of a strange device called a 'dummy activity' (shown by a dotted line and arrow-head). Dummy activities have no duration and are necessary to preserve the logic of the network. For example, MO6 must follow MO2 and MO3 but MO4 need only follow MO2. Dummies are also necessary when two activities would otherwise have the same head and tail events, as with MO4 and MO5. The AoA diagram must start with only one event node and end with another single tail node.

Analysis of this diagram consists of working out Earliest Event Times (EET) and Latest Event Times (LET) using rules which are similar to those for calculating activity statistics. First we make a forward pass by calculating the EETs as follows:

- for the first event, EET = 0
- for each succeeding event, the EET is the largest of the (EET + Time) for incoming activities
- project duration is the EET of the final event and is also the LET of that event (assuming the project duration is acceptable).

The backward pass is now entirely predictable:

- for each event, the LET is the smallest of the (LET – Time) for outgoing activities
- the LET of the first event should be zero.

For each event, the difference between the LET and EET for a given event is termed the 'slack' for that event. Though not the same as activity float, slack is useful for project planning. In addition, the actual event times can be related to a calendar and to events in other projects and the environment. This is particularly useful when relating sub-projects within a hierarchy of projects. With experience you should be able to relate activity and event statistics, in particular it is quite easy to calculate activity float from the AoA diagram (can you work out how?).

## RESOURCE ALLOCATION

Having identified the WBS, estimated activity times and analysed the result using CPA, we have now discovered the time for completion of the project and the amount of float relating to activities and paths. This work is summarised in Figure 7.3 where it is noted that the next stage may well be to revise the above as the total project time is unacceptable to the client. Assuming that such problems can be resolved (noting that the work we have done so far provides an excellent basis for discussion and for resolving conflict) we move on to the next stage of planning and resource allocation.

It may come as a surprise to discover that a next stage is necessary after the rigours of CPA. Indeed for activities on the critical path we have no room for manoeuvre; they must be carried out as soon as possible or the total project will be delayed. Other activities, which will be the majority for any project of reasonable size, have a 'window of opportunity' (i.e. the period of time between their earliest starts and latest finishes) as shown in Figure 7.4. We can imagine the activity being planned on a time-

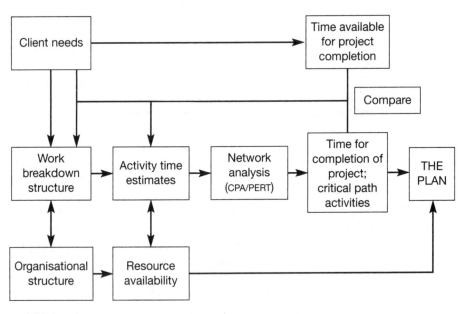

**Fig. 7.3 Project planning – time and resource issues**

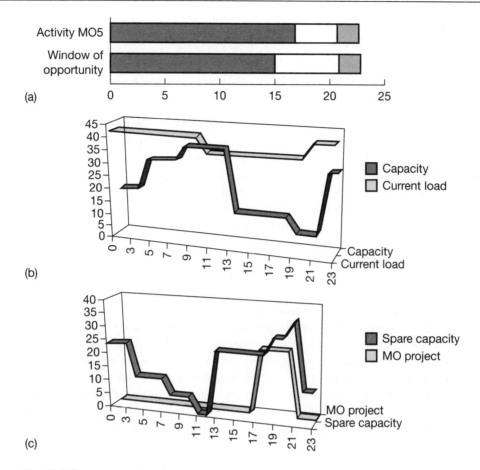

**Fig. 7.4 Resource planning**

scale ranging from its earliest start to its latest finish. It should be noted, however, that a planned early start will constrain previous activities on the same path to early starts and may also affect other activities on related early paths. Similarly, a planned late start has an effect on subsequent activities. The exact effect depends on the logical relationships in the network. Some texts use the concepts of free, independent and total float in order to clarify this situation.

Thus the planning of activity start times is a complex matter. It should be approached in an integrated manner and computer software is most useful in showing the implications for other activities of a particular planned start time. Some principles to bear in mind when setting activities early or late within their windows of opportunity are as follows:

- what are the implications for resources which are shared with other projects (is resource smoothing possible to avoid peak workloads)?
- what are the implications for cash flow (for example, setting all activities early in their windows may result in bringing forward some expenditures but also may produce some early revenue)?

- what are the implications for the management of risk (for example, starting early might provide extra time if things go wrong)?
- what are the implications for the management of learning (for example, an early start on a development activity might provide new knowledge for the benefit of the total project)?

In Figure 7.4 we take one of the activities in our simple Moving Office project and show its window of opportunity. We also show a chart indicating how available capacity overtime, based on the assumption that this activity shares resources with other projects. Here we see that a later start is more appropriate from the point of view of resource smoothing. It should be noted that this form of chart (showing variations in capacity and planned resource usage over time) is a particularly useful form of presentation in many areas of operational planning beyond project management.

There are a number of further strategies which might be useful to facilitate resource allocation. It might be possible to split the activity, to lengthen it (requiring less intense resource usage) or to shorten it (through the use of extra resources or different working methods). Most of these strategies have cost implications. Indeed it should be noted that we have here been discussing times and schedules with little mention of cost. Some more advanced project planning techniques explicitly handle both cost and time and a 'cost and time' project control method is shown in the next section. This is the point at which project planning may become very complex and where computer packages can be of most use. It should be remembered, however, that an over-complex plan which aims at fine-tuning a project to maximise profit may be destroyed by one unforeseen delay near the start of a project. The best plans are robust in the sense that they allow opportunities to cope with emergencies whilst maintaining an acceptable profit level.

## COST AND SCHEDULE CONTROL

Having planned the project and commenced work, we now move on to the next phase of project management. It would be highly over-optimistic to assume that all will now go according to plan. Common sense, and the accumulated evidence of project failures, tells us that things are likely to go wrong to a greater or lesser extent. We therefore have to exercise control in the manner described in Chapter 3, that is we must monitor outcomes, compare with standards and take corrective action as necessary.

Since control is an ongoing activity, possibly over a range of projects, it is desirable to set up a routine system for reporting and drawing to management's attention the need to take action. Such a system should include measurements of cost, time and performance against plans and schedules. One possibility is a series of milestones to be reached at agreed review points of time. The system described below collects cost and time information on a regular basis as an input to such a review process.

Much of our work above has concentrated on the time dimension of project management and it is useful at this point to consider a technique which is based on cost information. The basis of this methodology is the regular calculation of three types of statistic as shown below:

### 1 BCWS = Budgeted Cost of Work Scheduled

This is built up at the project planning stage, based on the Work Breakdown Structure, time estimates and agreed costings.

### 2 ACWP = Actual Cost of Work Performed

This is measured as the project proceeds.

### 3 BCWP = Budgeted Cost of Work Performed

This hybrid statistic is calculated as the project proceeds. It reflects the amount of money which would have been spent on work actually performed if there had been no changes in the cost rates used when charging for the work.

The above may be stated for a given time period or may be cumulative from the start of the project. They may refer to the project as a whole or to a given sub-project or activity. They thus give the basis for a very flexible control system. A graphical presentation of these statistics (showing cumulative costs for the whole project) is given in Figure 7.5. Note how the BCWS can be shown until the end of the project but the ACWP and BCWP can only show progress until the current time.

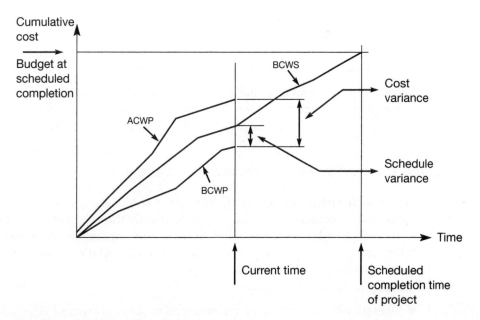

**Fig. 7.5  Cost and schedule control**

The three statistics are likely to differ and the differences may be presented in two forms. The first is variance analysis:

**Cost Variance = BCWP – ACWP**

By showing differences between budgeted and actual costs for the same work (that is, the work actually performed), this statistic gives a measure of change in costs incurred for work.

**Schedule Variance = BCWP – BCWS**

By showing differences between work performed and work scheduled (through the medium of budgeted costs which should have been incurred for the work performed and the work scheduled), this gives a measure of progress against schedule. It is, somewhat surprisingly, expressed in terms of cost rather than time.

Note that the apparent total variance = BCWS – ACWP = Cost Variance – Schedule Variance. Thus a project may have high cost and schedule variance but together these may give little apparent total variance. Hence a situation where corrective action is needed may go unheeded if we only track the difference between budget and actual spend. This form of variance presentation is illustrated in Figure 7.5.

The second form of presentation is through the use of cost and schedule indices:

Cost Performance Index, CPI = BCWP/ACWP

Schedule Performance Index, SPI = BCWP/BCWS

For each index, I:

I < 1 means poor performance

I = 1 means par performance

I > 1 means good performance

The above indices do a similar job to the cost and schedule variances but use a ratio rather than a difference form of presentation. This is complementary to the more usual variance analysis used in cost accounting and is illustrated in the example below.

## The Curec Design Project – a project control example

The Stone Insurance Company is a medium sized, though growing, company offering household insurance to the general public, mainly through telephone selling. In order to conduct their business effectively they need to improve their customer records (the 'Curec' project) and this requires the design and installation of appropriate computer based software.

A project is currently underway to meet this need. The major groups involved are:

● Operational managers and systems staff of Stone Insurance (the 'internal' group) who are charged with project management, providing general guidance and advice and any hardware changes that might be necessary

- Marketing management and staff of Stone Insurance (the 'research' group) who are conducting some limited customer research but whose main task is to validate existing customer records and ensure they are in a suitable form for the new system
- An external software design consultancy (the 'design' group) who are designing the new application software in consultation with the other groups.

The project manager has arrived at the following table as representing an agreement on the costs involved and the timescale for this project as shown in Table 7.4.

**Table 7.4 'Curec' project – BCWS**

| Budgeted Cost of Work Scheduled, BCWS (by month) | | | | |
|---|---|---|---|---|
| 1996 | £ | | | |
| Month | Internal | Research | Design | Total |
| Feb | 50 000 | 20 000 | 20 000 | 90 000 |
| Mar | 50 000 | 40 000 | 50 000 | 140 000 |
| Apr | 10 000 | 70 000 | 100 000 | 180 000 |
| May | 10 000 | 30 000 | 100 000 | 140 000 |
| Jun | 10 000 | 30 000 | 110 000 | 150 000 |
| Jul | 50 000 | 30 000 | 10 000 | 90 000 |
| Total | 180 000 | 220 000 | 390 000 | 790 000 |

**TASKS**

1. Set up an appropriate cost and schedule control system for this project. What further and ongoing information would you need to run such a control system?

2. A review of the project is carried out at the end of April 1996 with the following results as shown in Table 7.5 (overleaf). This represents a considerable cost overrun and furthermore it appears that customer record validation may not be progressing at the necessary rate. Review progress based on the above data. What further information is essential for a fair picture of project progress to be available?

3. The data as shown in Table 7.6 (overleaf) has been gathered in order to enable judgements to be made on project progress and appropriate control actions. Present the above data in an appropriate form using tables, graphs and indices as necessary.

Describe the state of the project as shown by this analysis and suggest an approach that might be taken by the project manager in a further attempt to explore past events and eventually to bring the project back on track for completion by the end of July.

**Table 7.5 'Curec' project – ACWP**

| Actual Cost of Work Performed, ACWP (by month) | | | | |
|---|---|---|---|---|
| 1996 | £ | | | |
| Month | Internal | Research | Design | Total |
| Feb | 50 000 | 22 000 | 30 000 | 102 000 |
| Mar | 60 000 | 39 000 | 80 000 | 179 000 |
| Apr | 15 000 | 68 000 | 140 000 | 223 000 |
| Total | 125 000 | 129 000 | 250 000 | 504 000 |

**Table 7.6 'Curec' project – BCWP**

| Budgeted Cost of Work Performed, BCWP (by month) | | | | |
|---|---|---|---|---|
| 1996 | £ | | | |
| Month | Internal | Research | Design | Total |
| Feb | 49 000 | 16 000 | 32 000 | 97 000 |
| Mar | 47 000 | 31 000 | 83 000 | 161 000 |
| Apr | 11 000 | 59 000 | 135 000 | 205 000 |
| Total | 107 000 | 106 000 | 250 000 | 463 000 |

## Analysis of Curec Results

The key to this analysis is the use of the cost and schedule indices. In Figure 7.6 we show the cumulative cost and schedule indices as calculated for the project as a whole as well as a graph showing progress to date. We can readily see that the ACWP differs from the BCWS but why is this the case?

The cumulative CPI for April is 0.92, that is, costs are approximately 8 per cent above what one would expect for the work done (remember that an index less than one denotes poor performance). Thus, quite apart from the progress made, Curec have a cost control problem.

**Budgeted cost of work performed, BCWP (by month)**

| Month | Internal | Research | Design | Total |
|---|---|---|---|---|
| Feb | 49 000 | 16 000 | 32 000 | 97 000 |
| Mar | 47 000 | 31 000 | 83 000 | 161 000 |
| Apr | 11 000 | 59 000 | 135 000 | 205 000 |
| Total | 107 000 | 106 000 | 250 000 | 463 000 |

**Cumulative for project**

| Month | End month cumulatives | | | Indices – Project | |
|---|---|---|---|---|---|
| | BCWS | ACWP | BCWP | CPI | SPI |
| Jan | 0 | 0 | 0 | | |
| Feb | 90 000 | 102 000 | 97 000 | 0.95 | 1.08 |
| Mar | 230 000 | 281 000 | 258 000 | 0.92 | 1.12 |
| Apr | 410 000 | 504 000 | 463 000 | 0.92 | 1.13 |
| May | 550 000 | | | | |
| Jun | 700 000 | | | | |
| Jul | 790 000 | | | | |

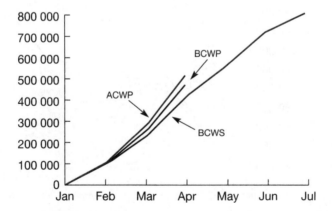

**Fig. 7.6 Curec Results – project**

The cumulative SPI for April is 1.13, that is work has progressed to around 13 per cent ahead of schedule. This may be desirable but will also give us cash flow problems if it relates to work done by outside contractors.

To analyse the situation in more depth we now calculate the cumulative indices for April for each of the contributing major groups. These results are shown in Figures 7.7 to 7.9 and show a varying picture of cost control and progress made.

| Budget cost of work performed, BCWP (by month) | | | | |
|---|---|---|---|---|
| Month | Internal | Research | Design | Total |
| Feb | 49 000 | 16 000 | 32 000 | 97 000 |
| Mar | 47 000 | 31 000 | 83 000 | 161 000 |
| Apr | 11 000 | 59 000 | 135 000 | 205 000 |
| Total | 107 000 | 106 000 | 250 000 | 463 000 |

| Cumulative for internal | | | | | |
|---|---|---|---|---|---|
| Month | End month cumulatives | | | Indices – Internal | |
| | BCWS | ACWP | BCWP | | |
| | | | | CPI | SPI |
| Jan | 0 | 0 | 0 | | |
| Feb | 50 000 | 50 000 | 49 000 | 0.98 | 0.98 |
| Mar | 100 000 | 110 000 | 96 000 | 0.87 | 0.96 |
| Apr | 110 000 | 125 000 | 107 000 | 0.86 | 0.97 |
| May | 120 000 | | | | |
| Jun | 130 000 | | | | |
| Jul | 180 000 | | | | |

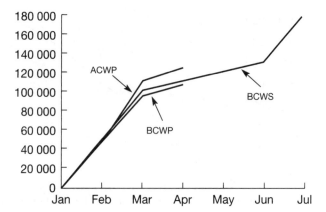

**Fig. 7.7 Curec Results – internal cost centre**

The 'internal' group is incurring costs around 14 per cent above budget (CPI = 0.86) and is slightly behind on schedule. This shows a major cost control problem which must be directly addressed.

The 'research' group is incurring excessive costs (CPI = 0.82) and is also making poor progress (SPI = 0.82). This is a potentially disastrous situation which would have not shown up if we had simply compared their expenditure to date (ACWP) against budget

**Budget cost of work performed, BCWP (by month)**

| Month | Internal | Research | Design | Total |
|-------|----------|----------|--------|-------|
| Feb   | 49 000   | 16 000   | 32 000  | 97 000  |
| Mar   | 47 000   | 31 000   | 83 000  | 161 000 |
| Apr   | 11 000   | 59 000   | 135 000 | 205 000 |
| Total | 107 000  | 106 000  | 250 000 | 463 000 |

**Cumulative for research**

| Month | End month cumulatives | | | Indices – Research | |
|-------|------|------|------|-----|-----|
|       | BCWS | ACWP | BCWP | CPI | SPI |
| Jan   | 0       | 0       | 0       |      |      |
| Feb   | 20 000  | 22 000  | 16 000  | 0.73 | 0.80 |
| Mar   | 60 000  | 61 000  | 47 000  | 0.77 | 0.78 |
| Apr   | 130 000 | 129 000 | 106 000 | 0.82 | 0.82 |
| May   | 160 000 |         |         |      |      |
| Jun   | 190 000 |         |         |      |      |
| Jul   | 220 000 |         |         |      |      |

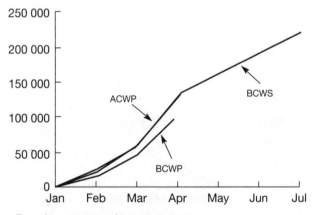

**Fig. 7.8 Curec Results – research cost centre**

(BCWS). Of course we would have found the problem by the end of the project but by then it would have been too late to take effective control action.

The 'design' group (which is an external consultancy) are incurring the correct costs (presumably as these are detailed in a contract) and is way ahead of schedule (SPI = 1.47). We may consider this to be good progress but are likely to be charged for it and the difference between this good progress and the poor progress being made by 'research' could cause additional problems.

| Budget cost of work performed, BCWP (by month) | | | | |
|---|---|---|---|---|
| Month | Internal | Research | Design | Total |
| Feb | 49 000 | 16 000 | 32 000 | 97 000 |
| Mar | 47 000 | 31 000 | 83 000 | 161 000 |
| Apr | 11 000 | 59 000 | 135 000 | 205 000 |
| Total | 107 000 | 106 000 | 250 000 | 463 000 |

**Cumulative for design**

| Month | End month cumulatives | | | Indices – Design | |
|---|---|---|---|---|---|
| | BCWS | ACWP | BCWP | CPI | SPI |
| Jan | 0 | 0 | 0 | | |
| Feb | 20 000 | 30 000 | 32 000 | 1.07 | 1.60 |
| Mar | 70 000 | 110 000 | 115 000 | 1.05 | 1.64 |
| Apr | 170 000 | 250 000 | 250 000 | 1.00 | 1.47 |
| May | 270 000 | | | | |
| Jun | 380 000 | | | | |
| Jul | 390 000 | | | | |

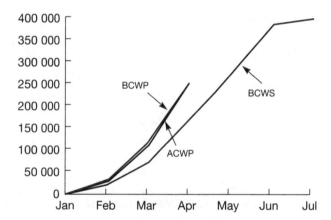

**Fig. 7.9 Curec Results – design cost centre**

Thus we can see how the application of a simple, though carefully structured, cost reporting system provides the basis for timely and targeted control actions. Such a system is essential for any project but is not in itself a complete control device. Control has also to relate to the actual quality of the outcomes, to adapting the project as the environment changes and to the taking of decisive action if things are going wrong.

## The Training Programme Project – an integrated exercise

As a final exercise in this chapter, we present an integrated case which gives you the opportunity to practise a number of the skills shown above in a new context. Some solution guidelines are given as the case proceeds and it is suggested that this exercise be handled as a group task.

You are the Operations Manager of a medium sized manufacturing organisation, H L Rogers and Co. HLR (as they will be referred to below) design and assemble specialist office equipment for individual clients. Each office layout is considered as a separate project and your main responsibility is to manage the totality of projects whilst drawing on the expertise of a variety of functional specialists who are either employed directly by HLR or act as sub-contractors. Unfortunately, a variety of problems have recently occurred in the co-ordination of individual projects.

Following a critical report by a team of consultants into the management effectiveness of your organisation, you have been asked by the Managing Director to design a training programme to improve the personal effectiveness of all individual project managers as well as functional specialists at HLR. The emphasis on this programme will be their ability to communicate with one another and to work as members of a team. HLR does not have a specialist training and development function though the personnel department can be relied upon to provide some assistance as required.

The core of the programme is an operational simulation (that is, a business game based on current HLR projects). Participants in the programme will work in teams to solve typical problems associated with the scheduling of tasks, cost control and ensuring client satisfaction. This activity is to be supported by a variety of learning materials relating to project management techniques and to the management of human resources. The latter will include a simple questionnaire which helps respondents analyse their own strengths and weaknesses when working as part of a group.

In addition to personnel staff you may call on the services of your own central planning staff and outside bodies as required.

**TASKS**

1. How do you begin?

2. Having formed your small action team and set out your objectives (agreed with the Managing Director), you set about deciding on a Work Breakdown Structure for the design of the training programme. The following activities shown in Table 7.7 (on p. 124) are seen as essential and some time estimates are included. What should you do next and what problems do you anticipate in continuing with this planning exercise?

3. The completed activity analysis grid is shown in Table 7.8 (on p. 125). From this it can be seen that the Critical Path is D, F, J, M, N and the estimated project duration is 80 days.

   In order to be able to plan this project effectively we also require information on the work content and organisational responsibility for each task. This information is provided in Table 7.9 (on p. 126). The data gives the number of persons and number

▶

of days required in each resource centre to complete each activity. 'Maximum People' is the number of people in each resource centre qualified to work on a particular activity.

The launch date for the training programme (that is, the end of your programme design project) is in 15 weeks time. Normally a five day week is worked with costs increasing by 25 per cent for activities outside the normal working week. The standard costs for staff are as given below:

| Personnel | £150 per day |
|---|---|
| Systems staff | £200 per day |
| Consultant | £300 per day |
| Print Dept. | £120 per day |

Analyse the above information and produce a plan for the project using standard project planning techniques as appropriate.

**Table 7.7 'Training Programme' project – activities**

| | Activity description | Pre-requisite activities | Estimated activity duration (days) |
|---|---|---|---|
| A | Consultation with senior management and project managers | | 5 |
| B | Consultation with target participants for the programme | A | 10 |
| C | Consultation with functional specialists and other middle managers | A | 20 |
| D | Background investigations of structure of simulation | | 20 |
| E | Write up detailed objectives for programme participants | B | 15 |
| F | Outline design of simulation | D | 10 |
| G | Preparation of technical learning materials | D | 15 |
| H | Development and trial run of personal skills questionnaire | C | 5 |
| I | Specification of 'Human aspects' inputs | C, E | 5 |
| J | Detailed design of simulation | C, F | 30 |
| K | Analysis of sample questionnaire returns | H | 10 |
| L | Detail design of 'Human aspects' learning materials | I, K | 20 |
| M | Trial run of simulation | G, H, J | 5 |
| N | Printing of materials and preparation of presentational aids | L, M | 15 |

**Table 7.8 'Training Programme' project – activity analysis**

| Activity code | Prerequisite activities | Successor activities | Estimated activity duration (days) | Earliest start | Earliest finish | Latest start | Latest finish | Float |
|---|---|---|---|---|---|---|---|---|
| A | | B, C | 5 | 0 | 5 | 5 | 10 | 5 |
| B | A | E | 10 | 5 | 15 | 15 | 25 | 10 |
| C | A | H, I, J | 20 | 5 | 25 | 10 | 30 | 5 |
| D | | F, G | 20 | 0 | 20 | 0 | 20 | 0 |
| E | B | I | 15 | 15 | 30 | 25 | 40 | 10 |
| F | D | J | 10 | 20 | 30 | 20 | 30 | 0 |
| G | D | M | 15 | 20 | 35 | 45 | 60 | 25 |
| H | C | K, M | 5 | 25 | 30 | 30 | 35 | 5 |
| I | C, E | L | 5 | 30 | 35 | 40 | 45 | 10 |
| J | C, F | M | 30 | 30 | 60 | 30 | 60 | 0 |
| K | H | L | 10 | 30 | 40 | 35 | 45 | 5 |
| L | I, K | N | 20 | 40 | 60 | 45 | 65 | 5 |
| M | G, H, J | N | 5 | 60 | 65 | 60 | 65 | 0 |
| N | L, M | | 15 | 65 | 80 | 65 | 80 | 0 |

**Table 7.9 'Training Programme' project – resource requirements**

| Activity code | Personnel | | | Systems staff | | | Consultant | | | Print Dept. | | |
|---|---|---|---|---|---|---|---|---|---|---|---|---|
| | People | Days | Max. People | People | Days | Max. People | People | Days | Max. People | People | Days | Max. People |
| A | 3 | 5 | 6 | | | | | | | | | |
| B | 1 | 10 | 2 | | | | | | | | | |
| C | 1 | 20 | 2 | | | | | | | | | |
| D | | | | 2 | 20 | 2 | | | | | | |
| E | 1 | 15 | 2 | | | | | | | | | |
| F | | | | 1 | 10 | 1 | | | | | | |
| G | | | | 1 | 15 | 2 | | | | | | |
| H | | | | | | | 1 | 5 | 1 | | | |
| I | | | | | | | 1 | 5 | 2 | | | |
| J | 1 | 30 | 6 | 1 | 30 | 2 | | | | | | |
| K | | | | | | | 1 | 10 | 2 | | | |
| L | 1 | 20 | 6 | | | | 1 | 20 | 2 | | | |
| M | 2 | 5 | 6 | 1 | 5 | 2 | | | | | | |
| N | | | | | | | | | | 2 | 15 | 2 |

## FURTHER READING

In addition to Meredith and Mantel (1995) (see further reading for Chapter 6), a useful reference for the techniques of Critical Path Analysis is:

Lockyer, K. (1984), *Critical Path Analysis*, Pitman, London.

# CHAPTER 8

# Managing Supply and Demand

The objective of this chapter is to introduce some of the fundamental issues in the long-term and medium-term matching of supply and demand in an operational context. This is partly achieved through the demonstration of a number of techniques in a simplified form appropriate to an introductory text.

## OBJECTIVES

This chapter:

- introduces the key issues in forecasting, capacity management and the aggregate planning of operations
- demonstrates a basic forecasting technique
- shows in some detail how aggregate plans are developed in a manufacturing context
- shows how a simple product mix planning problem may be handled through a graphical form of linear programming.

## INTRODUCTION

In this chapter we continue with our method of learning through handling data and working through examples but in a different context. We move away from the world of project management to more regular and recurring situations and concentrate on the issues involved in matching supply and demand.

Much of practical Operations Management consists of developing plans and controls to ensure that, as far as possible, products and services are available at the time required by the customer. We here have to make a sharp contrast between manufacturing and service operations. In the former we at least have the option of building up stocks of goods in anticipation of demand. We may forgo this option and attempt to match supply and demand by producing goods 'Just-in-Time' for the customer but this requires a specific set of circumstances as described in Chapter 11. In many cases we anticipate demand and hold stocks, and occasionally we may even backlog demand, that is only manufacture some time after an order is placed. In service operations, the presence of the customer requires real time matching of supply and demand and this presents us with a different range of problems.

A further classification of the problems of matching supply and demand is the timescale under consideration. For instance in manufacturing we have to ensure that the capacity of our plant is sufficient to handle the required demand over a long period. This will not ensure day to day matching of supply and demand as both will fluctuate over time but a failure to reach either a long-term balance or an excess of capacity will mean that demand cannot be met. This may not worry us in the sense that we may be satisfied by a limited market share and can make a good profit on this basis whereas an expansion of capacity might be risky. We may simply allow our competitors to take the extra demand or even raise prices to adjust the demand downwards to our capacity level. In the long term, therefore, operational planning is closely linked with the underlying strategy and economics of our firm.

We refer to this long-term view as the strategic planning of production, when issues of capacity, plant location and process are settled. In the medium term we must work within these constraints to arrive at an 'aggregate plan of production'. Such plans are usually expressed in monetary terms or standard output units (the exact product mix is only roughly represented). In some situations this may be misleading and a more detailed plan involving actual products must be derived, although this may be hard to achieve as new products are continually being brought into production. The subtle relationship between aggregate planning, product scheduling and ongoing control in batch manufacturing is a very difficult area to understand and manage (see Chapter 11 and Further Reading on MRPII).

Similar problems arise with service situations, although in this instance the capacity decision may be related to peak demand rather than average demand. We explore this in Chapter 10 through a consideration of capacity management, aggregate planning and queue management in service operations.

In both service and manufacturing we require some form of demand forecast in order to arrive at even the most provisional aggregate plans. Therefore, we begin this chapter with a discussion of the principles of forecasting, followed by some illustrative techniques based on one of the simpler methods of statistical forecasting. This is followed by a further discussion on capacity management.

The remainder of the chapter is based on a series of examples showing the problems of medium term aggregate planning in a manufacturing context. This consists of two case examples demonstrating a spreadsheet presentation of manufacturing aggregate planning, followed by an introduction to the problems of planning when product mix is taken into account.

## FORECASTING

As business decisions relate to the future, then it should be obvious that forecasts of some kind will be relevant. Despite the large number of forecasting techniques in the business literature, however, it should not be thought that forecasting is in any way a simple activity. It is fraught with problems and difficulties, not least because of the turbulent nature of the economic environment and the effects of competitive action.

Before looking at the practical issues of statistical forecasting, we must clarify the very nature of forecasting in the context of managerial decision making and control. All forecasting is based on regularities which we have observed in the past and which we assume will continue, perhaps with some practical adjustments, into the future. This is true of our everyday lives but some additional factors relate to the organisational context. In particular:

1. Organisations interact with economic, social, political and technological environments. They are certainly affected by such external influences and may indeed affect them through their market actions and innovations (for instance, the development of a new manufacturing process).

2. Organisations interact in a competitive and a co-operative way with individuals and other organisations in a variety of markets.

3. Having 'looked into the future' (that is, having examined the logical consequences of continuing with existing plans), organisations will often actively seek to change it to avoid poor performance.

4. Forecasts are linked to plans and budgets and as such enter the arena of organisational politics. Many managers will seek to exceed a forecast performance to look good, increase bonus payments and so forth and hence a low initial target is desirable. This may be unhelpful for financial planning and control.

5. Forecasts are linked to expectations, morale, motivation and an organisation's whole vision of where it is going. Optimism can lead to a positive cycle of success whereas pessimism may be self-fulfilling in fostering a spiral of decline.

The above influences have led some recent writers to downgrade the whole activity of planning and forecasting as a delusion. References are made to the Butterfly Effect in the Chaos Theory whereby wing movements of a tiny insect in one country affect the weather elsewhere in the world. While it is perfectly reasonable to draw attention to the problems of establishing cause and effect relationships in large, inter-connected systems, it is also perfectly valid to emphasise the merits of flexibility and adaptiveness in facing the future. Surprisingly, one can often be more flexible within a framework of objectives and broad plans than in an unstructured environment lacking basic performance information.

Some form of forecasting and planning will need to be faced by the operational manager because in many operational situations resources have to be committed in advance of a detailed knowledge of demands. For instance factories and retail outlets must be built and equipped, research and development carried out on processes, personnel must be employed and trained and working methods and infrastructure put in place far in advance of orders being received or customers turning up at the door. One can see why many commercially sophisticated individuals prefer to 'downsize' their organisations and to rely on sub-contracting and franchising. In this way they pass on much of the risk to others, but genuine creation of wealth requires taking a view of the future and investing in processes and products for future markets.

Looking towards a more medium term horizon, the Operational Manager must form some view on how supply and demand may be balanced in the coming months. This will have a considerable effect on resource allocation, the size of the required workforce, sub-contracting arrangements, dealing with suppliers, building up of stocks and on cash flow planning. This whole exercise is called Aggregate Planning and is dealt with later in this chapter with reference to manufacturing operations.

In the short term, the Operational Manager must literally balance supply and demand as far as possible in order to minimise customer dissatisfaction and under-utilised resources. Whilst long and medium term forecasting and planning may be carried out in terms of broad families of products or in financial terms, short term Operational Management is a highly complicated exercise involving actual orders, products, services, staff and other resources. The need now is often for effective, automated and computer based procedures and this is where statistical forecasting techniques are of particular value.

In the next section we consider some of these techniques before moving on to a consideration of aggregate planning. The following exercise is, however, included to help bring the problems of forecasting into perspective.

---

**TASK**

You have been appointed Operations Manager of a small but rapidly growing manufacturing firm whose products are based on a new, innovative process.

1. What decisions will have to be made about the long-term structure of operations? What types of forecast will be useful to inform such decisions? (Hint: Look ahead to Chapter 12 for ideas on typical policy decisions.)

2. You have to produce plans and budgets for the next 12 month period. To do this task, what features of the environment do you need to forecast?

3. How much faith would you place on forecasts relating to such time periods? What can you do to reduce your reliance on the accuracy of such forecasts (that is, how can you manage things so that the inevitable forecasting errors will have less effect on operations)?

---

## STATISTICAL FORECASTING TECHNIQUES

Statistical forecasting techniques are concerned with the analysis (or 'decomposition') of past data in order to facilitate the projection of basic regularities (such as average levels, trends and seasonal variations) into the future. An essential part of such techniques is an assessment of the likely errors in such forecasts.

Although a number of specialist forecasting packages exist, it has been found that quite simple methods often yield results comparable with the most mathematically sophisticated techniques. Such methods are often included in readily available general packages such as spreadsheets and hence are perfectly accessible to any business which requires their use.

We can illustrate this general approach by building a simple forecasting system to handle demand where no strong trends or seasonal variations exist. Texts which concentrate on quantitative techniques in business and management usually contain a considerable amount of material relating to statistical forecasting and there are a wealth of specialist forecasting texts and computer packages available. Our simple example is intended mainly to show what statistical forecasting is and to look at some of the assumptions on which it is based (see Further Reading for details of more comprehensive techniques).

Statistical forecasting aims to look back over a time series of data (for instance showing product demand for each of the past few weeks), extract certain key details from this past data (such as average demand, trends, etc.) and produce a forecast through extrapolation of such details into the future. This is obviously a risky exercise and therefore most techniques not only update such forecasts at regular intervals but also include an error checking system to reflect the performance of the forecasting system.

This can all be illustrated through 'Simple Exponential Smoothing' which, despite its name, really is an intuitively straightforward exercise. We consider Figure 8.1 and imagine we have just received data (which could reflect anything of interest, say product demand) for Period 3 and are looking to produce a forecast for Period 4. Our forecast for Period 3 was 54 units but the actual data was 36 units. Thus our forecast was out by 36 – 54 = –18 units (note that we preserve the minus sign to show the direction in which the forecast was wrong). This deviation of data and forecast is commonly called the forecasting error, but the word 'error' does not mean avoidable mistake in this context. Forecasting 'errors' are inevitable!

We might simply ignore this error and continue with a forecast of 54 units for Period 4. Alternatively, we might panic completely and give a forecast of 36 for Period 4. Experience shows that both of these alternatives, complacency and panic, are not usually desirable. An interesting third possibility is to adjust our forecast by some proportion of the error. The proportion used is the 'alpha' factor for the system and is usually taken as some value between 0.05 and 0.3 (thus we only panic by somewhere between 5 per cent and 30 per cent!). In the example given we take alpha as 0.1 and this gives us a forecast adjustment equal to 10 per cent of –18, that is –1.8 and the new forecast for Period 4 is 54 – 1.8 = 52.2. This is rounded to 52 and carried forward as the forecast for Period 4. This whole process may be expressed as a mathematical formula as follows:

$$F_{t+1} = F_t + \alpha \, (D_t - F_t)$$

Expressed in words, we have the following:

- we are working at period '$t$', the current period (assuming periods are equal lengths of time). Therefore the next period will be '$t+1$' and so forth
- $F_t$ is the forecast for the current period and $F_{t+1}$ is the forecast for the next period
- (alpha) is the percentage adjustment or smoothing factor
- $D_t$ is the data in the current period.

Therefore we may read the formula as 'the forecast for the next period is the current forecast plus an adjustment due to the current forecast error. This adjustment is calculated as a constant (for example, 0.10, which relates to a 10 per cent adjustment) multiplied by the difference between current data and forecast. If this difference is negative then the adjustment is subtracted from the current forecast.'

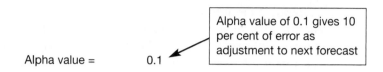

Alpha value of 0.1 gives 10 per cent of error as adjustment to next forecast

Alpha value = 0.1

| Week | Data | Forecast | Error | Adjustment | New forecast | Rounded new forecast | Absolute error |
|------|------|----------|-------|------------|--------------|----------------------|----------------|
| 1 | 56 | 55 | 1 | 0.1 | 55.1 | 55 | 1 |
| 2 | 40 | 55 | −15 | −1.5 | 53.5 | 54 | 15 |
| 3 | 36 | 54 | −18 | −1.8 | 52.2 | 52 | 18 |
| 4 | 72 | 52 | 20 | 2 | 54 | 54 | 20 |
| 5 | 51 | 54 | −3 | −0.3 | 53.7 | 54 | 3 |

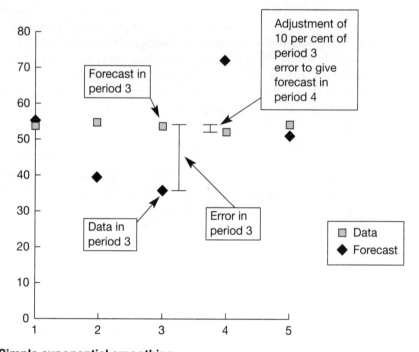

**Fig. 8.1 Simple exponential smoothing**

We may refer to the difference between data and forecast in a given period as the forecast error, that is:

$$E_t = D_t - F_t$$

Hence we can write:

$$F_{t+1} = F_t + \alpha E_t$$

If we continue this process for 15 periods we obtain the results as shown in Figure 8.2. The data used here illustrates a situation in which demand is basically stable (its average is either constant or shows only very gradual trend) but where there are fluctuations about the average. Simple exponential smoothing is a useful technique to adopt in such circumstances. We address some frequently occurring questions at this point.

| Week | Data | Forecast | Error | | New forecast | Rounded | Absolute error |
|------|------|----------|-------|------|--------------|---------|----------------|
| | | | | Alpha value 0.1 | | | |
| 1 | 56 | 55 | 1 | 0.1 | 55.1 | 55 | 1 |
| 2 | 40 | 55 | −15 | −1.5 | 53.5 | 54 | 15 |
| 3 | 36 | 54 | −18 | −1.8 | 52.2 | 52 | 18 |
| 4 | 72 | 52 | 20 | 2 | 54 | 54 | 20 |
| 5 | 51 | 54 | −3 | −0.3 | 53.7 | 54 | 3 |
| 6 | 78 | 54 | 24 | 2.4 | 56.4 | 56 | 24 |
| 7 | 74 | 56 | 18 | 1.8 | 57.8 | 58 | 18 |
| 8 | 25 | 58 | −33 | −3.3 | 54.7 | 55 | 33 |
| 9 | 65 | 55 | 10 | 1 | 56 | 56 | 10 |
| 10 | 49 | 56 | −7 | −0.7 | 55.3 | 55 | 7 |
| 11 | 55 | 55 | 0 | 0 | 55 | 55 | 0 |
| 12 | 57 | 55 | 02 | 0.2 | 55.2 | 55 | 2 |
| 13 | 83 | 55 | 28 | 2.8 | 57.8 | 58 | 28 |
| 14 | 70 | 58 | 12 | 1.2 | 59.2 | 59 | 12 |
| 15 | 38 | 59 | −21 | −2.1 | 59.6 | 57 | 21 |

Mean error = 1.2
Mean absolute error = 14.13333

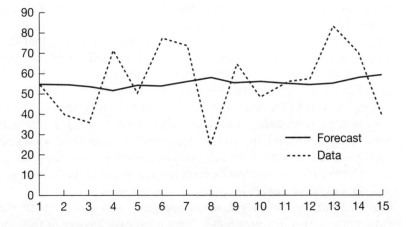

**Fig. 8.2 Simple exponential smoothing – example 1**

*Does the time interval have to be a week?*

Any period of time may be used provided all time periods are the same. This method is likely to work best, however, with short time periods (that is, it is a Short Term Forecasting Technique) as the data is less likely to be stable and trend free in the longer term.

*Does the data have to relate to product demand?*

Any operationally significant time series may be forecasted, for example cost, usage, quality yields and so forth. It is important, however, that the past history is relevant, for instance can past sales be used to forecast future demand?

*How do you find the first forecast?*

The forecasts are derived iteratively and hence the above question obviously arises. A simple average of a few initial periods of data will suffice and the forecasts should then quickly adjust if the time series is stable.

*How do you find the alpha value?*

Alpha gives you a balance between smoothing (low alpha value) and response (high alpha value) so its numeric value is one of choice. A low value will lead to less re-planning of stocks and production levels but be slower in adapting to change. A higher value will be more adaptive but if you feel you need a value greater than 0.3 then this technique is probably inappropriate to the circumstances.

In Figure 8.2 we show a longer run of data and forecasts and a graph showing the way in which the forecast acts as a continually updating average for the time series. Of considerable importance are the two statistics shown at the bottom of the table. The mean error is the mean value of the error column and should, ideally, be zero as the positive and negative errors cancel out. The table includes a final column labelled absolute error, and merely consists of the error figures with the negative signs removed, showing the magnitude of the errors rather than their direction. Thus, the mean absolute error gives some measure of the amount of fluctuation in the time series. Though, in practice, the mean error will not be zero, it should be substantially less than the mean absolute error. A useful rule of thumb is that the magnitude of the mean error should be less than 30 per cent of the mean absolute error.

The point of these statistics is made clearer in Figure 8.3 where we use the technique in an inappropriate context. From Period 6 onwards we have introduced a strong trend into the data and, as the graph readily shows, the forecasting system begins to perform badly from that point onwards. This is also reflected in the large mean error figure (relative to the mean absolute error) and shows how an error monitoring system, based on the ratio of mean error to mean absolute error for example, could be used to give information on the suitability of the technique used.

This, of course, leaves one rather large question unanswered. How does one forecast in situations of trend, or of seasonal variations where simple exponential smoothing is also inappropriate? There is no easy answer to this, though a number of

|  |  |  |  | Alpha value 0.1 |  | Rounded |  |
|---|---|---|---|---|---|---|---|
| Week | Data | Forecast | Error |  | New forecast | new forecast | Absolute error |
| 1 | 56 | 55 | 1 | 0.1 | 55.1 | 55 | 1 |
| 2 | 40 | 55 | −15 | −1.5 | 53.5 | 54 | 15 |
| 3 | 36 | 54 | −18 | −1.8 | 52.2 | 52 | 18 |
| 4 | 72 | 52 | 20 | 2 | 54 | 54 | 20 |
| 5 | 51 | 54 | −3 | −0.3 | 53.7 | 54 | 3 |
| 6 | 128 | 54 | 74 | 7.4 | 61.4 | 61 | 74 |
| 7 | 124 | 61 | 63 | 6.3 | 67.3 | 67 | 63 |
| 8 | 75 | 67 | 8 | 0.8 | 67.8 | 68 | 8 |
| 9 | 115 | 68 | 47 | 4.7 | 72.7 | 73 | 47 |
| 10 | 99 | 73 | 26 | 2.6 | 75.6 | 76 | 26 |
| 11 | 105 | 76 | 29 | 2.9 | 78.9 | 79 | 29 |
| 12 | 107 | 79 | 28 | 2.8 | 81.8 | 82 | 28 |
| 13 | 133 | 82 | 51 | 5.1 | 87.1 | 87 | 51 |
| 14 | 120 | 87 | 33 | 3.3 | 90.3 | 90 | 33 |
| 15 | 88 | 90 | −2 | −0.2 | 89.8 | 90 | 2 |

Mean error = 22.8
Mean absolute error = 27.8667

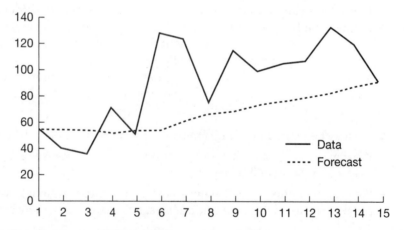

**Fig. 8.3 Simple exponential smoothing – example 2**

techniques exist to cater for a wide range of contingencies. For details, consult the Further Reading at the end of the chapter, bearing in mind the following:

● Dramatic changes in time series may not be capable of being forecasted in practice.

● Some changes are due to your own actions, for instance an advertising campaign or poor quality goods being sold.

● The more complex techniques do not necessarily perform better than the simple ones.

- Simple techniques are often better to use in practical management situations and their results may be more meaningful to a wide range of staff.
- You should always update forecasts frequently and include an error monitoring system.

## CAPACITY MANAGEMENT

Inherent in our discussion on matching supply and demand is the idea that there will be a limit on available supply. Whether we are talking about a shop or a factory, a warehouse or a hospital there is always some upper limit on the service which can be provided or product made.

A warehouse provides one of the simplest examples. Here the obvious limit is storage space, though the facility to handle goods at receiving and despatch may also be a constraint. In a shop, floor space may limit the number of customers but it is more likely that the ability of service assistants to cope with customer demands in a given time is the major constraint. In a factory the engineering characteristics of machinery may limit production flow, or again the constraint may be availability of skilled labour.

We refer to the limit of supply as the capacity of a system and often speak of bottlenecks when discussing specific constraining parts of a system. Thus the capacity of a factory may be 100 standard production units per week due to a bottleneck in the assembly department.

From these simple examples we see that constraints and bottlenecks may relate to size (for example, space in a warehouse, dimensions of a machine) but most frequently relate to flow. We may be talking about the flow of materials in a factory or of people in a service situation but time is usually a key dimension.

We must also be careful about whether we are referring to tactical or to strategic decisions when discussing capacity. For instance, when planning how many of product X we can make in a factory:

- We may be limited to 50 units tomorrow because machine A has broken down.
- We may be limited to 600 units in a typical week because of a shortage of skilled workers in the assembly department.
- We may be limited to 40 000 units next year because, although we have a retraining programme for labour, the equipment cannot handle any more than this number.

Of course, the year after this we may buy new equipment! Most capacity limits can be changed given sufficient time and resources. As operational managers planning within a given time and resource framework we must, however, obviously recognise capacity constraints.

Organisational issues may also present themselves at this point. Perhaps next week we could make 600 units of product X to meet our order backlog but our sales team in Germany want us to make 700 units of product Y as a more profitable alternative. Thus a production plan has to be agreed which meets the objectives of the whole organisation within the identified constraints, some of which may arise due to decisions made in other parts of the organisation.

At this point we should also note a key difference between traditional ideas of production planning and those of service planning. In the former we could often avoid short-term capacity constraints by the use of stock. We cannot stock a service and, similarly, if we wish to use Just-in-Time production we will expect to match supply and demand continuously. In these situations short term supply constraints and demand fluctuations become more of a problem.

Thus we are led to consider the use of excess capacity as an organisational buffer (see Chapter 9 on the similar use of stock). Such capacity has to be paid for, however, and capacity decisions, which often involve fixed assets and the size of the workforce, have a major impact on profitability. In particular, unused capacity may readily be visible as under-utilised or idle resources and be seen (perhaps unfairly) as a visible sign of poor Operational Management.

A solution appears to present itself in the form of flexibility. If resources can be put to a variety of uses within a reasonable operational timescale (that is, they have range and response flexibility) then excess capacity can find alternative uses. Alternatively capacity itself may be flexible to some extent. For instance, tills in a supermarket need not all be manned continually and thus provide an important degree of tactical capacity flexibility. Excess production facilities may be mothballed for a period of months, or even years, until required again. Such strategies have a cost but this may be far less than under-utilising assets or failing to meet peak demands.

Thus we can readily see that capacity management (ensuring that supply constraints are tolerable and economic) is a key ingredient in profitable Operational Management in both manufacturing and service contexts. It also raises a number of problems of intra-organisational communication and co-ordination and also a number of strategic issues regarding the aggregate amount of service or product an organisation wishes to make available to its customers.

**TASKS**

In order to explore the implications of capacity management for an organisation, consider each of the following in either a service or manufacturing context and show how it relates to capacity management:

1. yield and internal quality management (Hint: See Chapter 1, Milon part 2, for an illustrative calculation showing how capacity and quality might be inter-related and dramatically affect profitability)

2. new product and service introduction (Hint: New product introduction may have an impact on existing facilities and also require new ones)

3. productivity improvement and the learning curve (Hint: Higher levels of productivity make better use of capacity; can we learn how to maintain capacity?)

4. human resource management (Hint: Though capacity is often seen in terms of fixed assets, many bottlenecks are human)

(Note: The above are emphasised as the key operational routes to strategic business improvement in Garvin (1992).)

## AGGREGATE PLANNING IN MANUFACTURING

We now examine some basic procedures for aggregate planning in a manufacturing context. Whether working in batch or repetitive (mass) manufacturing, a company must look forwards, usually over a budget period of a year, to gain a view of how its manufacturing capacity might be profitably used in the context of forecast demand (see Chapters 6 and 7 for a view of planning in a project management context). Now if demand were to be known in detail, which is not impossible but rarely happens, then a detailed production plan based on actual products might be attempted. It is more normal for a mixture of orders and forecasts to be available for the months ahead. Some forecasts of individual product sales will be too optimistic and some pessimistic but hopefully, though the final mix of items sold may differ from that shown in long-term plans, the total business done will be within predictable limits. Therefore it is often convenient to plan in monetary terms, or in terms of a 'standard product', and then to resolve details of product mix to a later stage, always assuming that sufficient flexibility exists to change production from one product to another. Where a product requires a specific manufacturing process which has no other use, then it may be directly planned.

The purpose of *aggregate planning*, therefore, is to define a framework for the year ahead within the capacity constraints governed by major investments. Tactical capacity changes (for example, involving labour or sub-contracting) may well be made during the year. In addition a policy of stockholding must be agreed. This whole process is best illustrated through an example and therefore in the next section we revisit the Milon Manufacturing Company.

## The Milon Case, continued

(Note: See Chapter 1 for Parts 1 and 2 of the Milon case. Parts 3 and 4 are contained in this chapter and illustrate a range of issues in medium term manufacturing planning.)

Part 3
Aggregate planning in 1996

The management of Milon are now looking in more detail at how supply and demand may be balanced in 1996. Demand forecasts for 1996 have been produced and these are shown in Table 8.1 along with amounts of basic production capacity available in various months of the year.

(Note: In this exercise, supply and demand are expressed in terms of standard units of production, so in January 1996 we forecast a demand for 20 000 units of a standard product. Actual demand will be for various products in our range but we express the total potential impact on production facilities to be equivalent to 20 000 of this standard product.)

We see that over the year, supply and demand are balanced, but this is not the case for individual months. In order to explore the monthly effects we expand this table as shown in Table 8.2. 'Cumulative demand' is an important column in our calculations and gives the demand forecast up to and including the current month. Thus the cumulative demand for December is also the total demand forecast for the year. In this case

**Table 8.1 'Milon Part 3' – demand and capacity**

| Month | Forecast demand | Base capacity |
|-------|-----------------|---------------|
| Jan | 20 000 | 30 000 |
| Feb | 30 000 | 35 000 |
| Mar | 45 000 | 35 000 |
| Apr | 55 000 | 35 000 |
| May | 60 000 | 35 000 |
| Jun | 30 000 | 35 000 |
| Jul | 30 000 | 35 000 |
| Aug | 30 000 | 25 000 |
| Sep | 30 000 | 35 000 |
| Oct | 25 000 | 35 000 |
| Nov | 25 000 | 35 000 |
| Dec | 20 000 | 30 000 |
| Total | 400 000 | 400 000 |

Note: all data is in Standard Units of Production

the 'Total production' column is the same as base capacity (which will not be the case in later tables where total production will also include overtime working, sub-contracting and the effects of hiring and firing workers). Cumulative production may be directly compared with cumulative demand to see what imbalances occur between demand and supply up to a particular month. The 'Opening stock' for January is carried forward from the previous year whilst other opening stock figures are merely the closing stocks of the previous month. The 'Closing stock' figures are calculated as opening stock for the month plus production in that month minus sales.

We have assumed that we began the year with a modest stock of 10 000 units and of course end the year with the same amount as supply and demand eventually balance out. Unfortunately, during the year there are times when stock builds up to as much as 25 000 units and other times when we have a demand backlog of up to 30 000 units (seen in this table as 'negative stock'). Indeed in the middle part of the year we appear to be a month behind in meeting demand. (Note: This is based on a monthly planning interval – the stock situation might be worse within some months and therefore judgement must be applied in choosing the most practical planning interval.)

**Table 8.2 'Milon Part 3' – initial plan**

| Month | Forecast demand | Cumulative demand | Base capacity | Total production | Cumulative production | Opening stock | Closing stock |
|-------|------|------|------|------|------|------|------|
| Jan | 20 000 | 20 000 | 30 000 | 30 000 | 30 000 | 10 000 | 20 000 |
| Feb | 30 000 | 50 000 | 35 000 | 35 000 | 65 000 | 20 000 | 25 000 |
| Mar | 45 000 | 95 000 | 35 000 | 35 000 | 100 000 | 25 000 | 15 000 |
| Apr | 55 000 | 150 000 | 35 000 | 35 000 | 135 000 | 15 000 | –5 000 |
| May | 60 000 | 210 000 | 35 000 | 35 000 | 170 000 | –5 000 | –30 000 |
| Jun | 30 000 | 240 000 | 35 000 | 35 000 | 205 000 | –30 000 | –25 000 |
| Jul | 30 000 | 270 000 | 35 000 | 35 000 | 240 000 | –25 000 | –20 000 |
| Aug | 30 000 | 300 000 | 25 000 | 25 000 | 265 000 | –20 000 | –25 000 |
| Sep | 30 000 | 330 000 | 35 000 | 35 000 | 300 000 | –25 000 | –20 000 |
| Oct | 25 000 | 355 000 | 35 000 | 35 000 | 335 000 | –20 000 | –10 000 |
| Nov | 25 000 | 380 000 | 35 000 | 35 000 | 370 000 | –10 000 | 0 |
| Dec | 20 000 | 400 000 | 30 000 | 30 000 | 400 000 | 0 | 10 000 |

An alternative way of depicting this situation is in Figure 8.4 where a graph showing cumulative demand and cumulative capacity is shown. Where cumulative capacity is above cumulative demand we have a build up of stock and where the reverse applies we have a backlog of demand.

What will happen when we delay meeting demand? One possibility is that customers will reluctantly wait but another possibility is that they will go elsewhere. Neither are desirable so we must look at how we might handle this situation. Some possibilities are as follows:

1. Expand capacity earlier in the year through working overtime or sub-contracting, though this will lead to overproduction in the year as a whole and a build up of stock.
2. Attempt to make capacity more 'flexible' to meet current demands, but how could this be done?
3. Introduce an 'order promising' system so that although customers will have to wait, they have a clear idea when their orders will be met.
4. Expand capacity over the year as a whole and seek to expand sales at times of excess capacity.

Let us analyse each of these in turn using a common format. In Table 8.3 we show the effect of expanding capacity early through the use of overtime and sub-contracting.

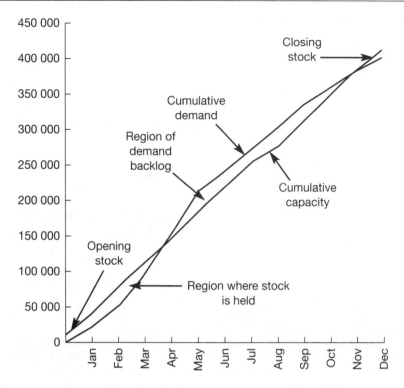

**Fig. 8.4 Milon Manufacturing Company – aggregate planning 1996**

## Table 8.3 'Milon Part 3' – plan with overtime

| Month | Forecast demand | Cumulative demand | Base capacity | Planned overtime | Sub-contract | Hire & fire | Total production | Cumulative production | Opening stock | Closing stock |
|-------|-----------------|-------------------|---------------|------------------|--------------|-------------|------------------|-----------------------|---------------|---------------|
| Jan | 20 000 | 20 000 | 30 000 | | | | 30 000 | 30 000 | 10 000 | 20 000 |
| Feb | 30 000 | 50 000 | 35 000 | 5 000 | | | 40 000 | 70 000 | 20 000 | 30 000 |
| Mar | 45 000 | 95 000 | 35 000 | 5 000 | | | 40 000 | 110 000 | 30 000 | 25 000 |
| Apr | 55 000 | 150 000 | 35 000 | 5 000 | 10 000 | | 50 000 | 160 000 | 25 000 | 20 000 |
| May | 60 000 | 210 000 | 35 000 | 5 000 | | | 40 000 | 200 000 | 20 000 | 0 |
| Jun | 30 000 | 240 000 | 35 000 | | | | 35 000 | 235 000 | 0 | 5 000 |
| Jul | 30 000 | 270 000 | 35 000 | | | | 35 000 | 270 000 | 5 000 | 10 000 |
| Aug | 30 000 | 300 000 | 25 000 | | | | 25 000 | 295 000 | 10 000 | 5 000 |
| Sep | 30 000 | 330 000 | 35 000 | | | | 35 000 | 330 000 | 5 000 | 10 000 |
| Oct | 25 000 | 355 000 | 35 000 | | | | 35 000 | 365 000 | 10 000 | 20 000 |
| Nov | 25 000 | 380 000 | 35 000 | | | | 35 000 | 400 000 | 20 000 | 30 000 |
| Dec | 20 000 | 400 000 | 30 000 | | | | 30 000 | 430 000 | 30 000 | 40 000 |

**Table 8.4 'Milon Part 3' – plan with redundancies**

| Month | Forecast demand | Cumulative demand | Base capacity | Planned overtime | Sub-contract | Hire & fire | Total production | Cumulative production | Opening stock | Closing stock |
|---|---|---|---|---|---|---|---|---|---|---|
| Jan | 20 000 | 20 000 | 30 000 | | | −10 000 | 20 000 | 20 000 | 10 000 | 10 000 |
| Feb | 30 000 | 50 000 | 35 000 | | | −10 000 | 25 000 | 45 000 | 10 000 | 5 000 |
| Mar | 45 000 | 95 000 | 35 000 | 5 000 | 10 000 | −10 000 | 40 000 | 85 000 | 5 000 | 0 |
| Apr | 55 000 | 150 000 | 35 000 | 10 000 | 20 000 | −10 000 | 55 000 | 140 000 | 0 | 0 |
| May | 60 000 | 210 000 | 35 000 | 10 000 | 25 000 | −10 000 | 60 000 | 200 000 | 0 | 0 |
| Jun | 30 000 | 240 000 | 35 000 | 5 000 | | −10 000 | 30 000 | 230 000 | 0 | 0 |
| Jul | 30 000 | 270 000 | 35 000 | 5 000 | | −10 000 | 30 000 | 260 000 | 0 | 0 |
| Aug | 30 000 | 300 000 | 25 000 | 5 000 | 10 000 | −10 000 | 30 000 | 290 000 | 0 | 0 |
| Sep | 30 000 | 330 000 | 35 000 | 5 000 | | −10 000 | 30 000 | 320 000 | 0 | 0 |
| Oct | 25 000 | 355 000 | 35 000 | | | −10 000 | 25 000 | 345 000 | 0 | 0 |
| Nov | 25 000 | 380 000 | 35 000 | | | −10 000 | 25 000 | 370 000 | 0 | 0 |
| Dec | 20 000 | 400 000 | 30 000 | | | −10 000 | 20 000 | 390 000 | 0 | 0 |

Not surprisingly we end the year with considerably more stock than when we started.

By contrast in Table 8.4 we start by reducing the workforce by an amount equivalent to the manufacture of 10 000 units (we do this once in January, although the effect lasts all year). We then use overtime working and sub-contracting as our 'flexibility' in matching supply and demand continuously over the year.

At each stage of this exercise you should remember that what we are producing here is only a plan based on current information. Neither demand nor supply will have exactly these values as the year progresses so we must always bear in mind the need to re-plan and adapt to current circumstances. Bearing this in mind, the second plan given above has advantages of flexibility but the social disadvantage of initial redundancies.

The effect of an order promising system can be directly seen from Table 8.2. It will involve customers waiting for around a month at the most, which may or may not be acceptable.

The final alternative is to plan for growth. Suppose we could increase demand to 600 000 per year, with pro-rata increases each month. How could this be handled? You might like to attempt some aggregate planning before looking at Table 8.5 which shows one possibility, which involves backlogging demand towards late summer. Can you find a better plan?

Following the example above, we can see how important decisions are made in this medium-term form of planning. It can, however, be a frustrating exercise as much will change over the year. With manufacturers attempting to satisfy customers in terms of

**Table 8.5 'Milon Part 3' – final plan**

| Month | Forecast demand | Cumulative demand | Base capacity | Planned overtime | Sub-contract | Hire & fire | Total production | Cumulative production | Opening stock | Closing stock |
|---|---|---|---|---|---|---|---|---|---|---|
| Jan | 30 000 | 30 000 | 30 000 | | | | 30 000 | 30 000 | 10 000 | 10 000 |
| Feb | 45 000 | 75 000 | 35 000 | 10 000 | | | 45 000 | 75 000 | 10 000 | 10 000 |
| Mar | 60 000 | 135 000 | 35 000 | 10 000 | | 10 000 | 55 000 | 130 000 | 10 000 | 5 000 |
| Apr | 80 000 | 215 000 | 35 000 | 10 000 | 20 000 | 10 000 | 75 000 | 205 000 | 5 000 | 0 |
| May | 90 000 | 305 000 | 35 000 | 10 000 | 20 000 | 10 000 | 75 000 | 280 000 | 0 | –15 000 |
| Jun | 65 000 | 370 000 | 35 000 | 10 000 | | 10 000 | 55 000 | 335 000 | –15 000 | –25 000 |
| Jul | 45 000 | 415 000 | 35 000 | 10 000 | | 10 000 | 55 000 | 390 000 | –25 000 | –15 000 |
| Aug | 45 000 | 460 000 | 25 000 | | | 10 000 | 35 000 | 425 000 | –15 000 | –25 000 |
| Sep | 45 000 | 505 000 | 35 000 | | | 10 000 | 45 000 | 470 000 | –25 000 | –25 000 |
| Oct | 35 000 | 540 000 | 35 000 | | | 10 000 | 45 000 | 515 000 | –25 000 | –15 000 |
| Nov | 35 000 | 575 000 | 35 000 | | | 10 000 | 45 000 | 560 000 | –15 000 | –5 000 |
| Dec | 25 000 | 600 000 | 30 000 | | | 10 000 | 40 000 | 600 000 | –5 000 | 10 000 |

product availability whilst making a profit based on a narrow margin between revenue and cost, it shows how easily things can go wrong even if annual supply and demand are roughly balanced. Unfortunately, further problems await us when we disaggregate our medium-term plans in terms of product mix, but we will delay this for a short while and consider a case exercise in aggregate planning, included as an exercise for the reader.

The following case, James Woods and Sons, is a major exercise and should preferably be attempted using a computer spreadsheet package to handle the arithmetic and continual experimental planning involved. The exercise is particularly suitable as a group activity.

## James Woods and Sons – a case exercise

The management of James Woods and Sons would be insulted if the company were to be called a 'traditional' manufacturing company, as the word has connotations of 'old-fashioned' and 'inefficient'. The company is small, having been founded in the early 1960s, but has until recently made a good profit from the manufacture of locks and similar household and office security equipment. It has, however, experienced little growth and invested little in the development of new products and new equipment, preferring to remain at around 35 employees and £2.3m turnover in 1995.

The Managing Director of James Woods and Sons, Neville White, has been with the company for three years, is highly capable and looking forward to improving growth and profits. Bob Smith has recently been appointed as Operations Director to strengthen the middle management of the company and to undertake a series of small projects aimed at improving the company's competitive potential in a currently buoyant market.

The company sells a very wide range of security equipment manufactured mainly in small batches for a variety of local retailers. Some success is being experienced in interesting major retailers in the most successful of the Woods products. Though the company is quite capable of achieving required quality levels and competing on price terms, difficulty is being experienced in meeting delivery dates and scheduling work through the factory.

In order to simplify medium term planning, work done and factory capacity are described in terms of Standard Production Units (SPUS). Each product manufactured by the company is given a number of SPUS. Fortunately different products require roughly the same mix of labour and machine resources and therefore SPUS provide a useful device for aggregate planning.

### Table 8.6 'James Woods' and Sons – demand and capacity

| Month | Demand (SPUS) | Basic production (SPUS) |
|---|---|---|
| Jan | 260 | 270 |
| Feb | 360 | 300 |
| Mar | 460 | 300 |
| Apr | 500 | 300 |
| May | 500 | 300 |
| Jun | 480 | 300 |
| Jul | 280 | 270 |
| Aug | 240 | 250 |
| Sep | 280 | 300 |
| Oct | 480 | 300 |
| Nov | 480 | 300 |
| Dec | 280 | 240 |

Demand for the company's products in 1995, along with some useful production statistics, are given in Table 8.6. The Basic Production SPUs refer in this case to the factory capacity with no overtime or sub-contracting. In January to March an additional 10 per cent of production was achieved through overtime working. From April to December overtime production was 20 per cent of basic production. In each of May, June and July a further 200 SPUs were achieved through sub-contracting.

The opening stock in January 1994 amounted to only 20 SPUs with no demand backlog. In the early summer, a backlog of several weeks' work existed for many items, a situation which caused considerable problems with major customers and which must be avoided as far as possible in the future.

Recent trends in crime and householders' interest in security products has led to a potentially favourable situation for James Woods and Sons. Forecasts suggest that demand for their products in 1996 could be 50 per cent higher than in 1995 (with a similar monthly pattern). Firm orders and contracts suggest at least a 20 per cent increase. In addition the company is negotiating with a new customer, DIYNow, for an order equivalent to 75 SPUs per month commencing in April 1996. DIYNow, however, are a notoriously tough customer in requiring high quality levels and Just-in-Time deliveries. Neville Jones's view is that this order should only be accepted if Woods are completely sure that deliveries can be maintained as per contract.

To respond positively to this buoyant market situation, Woods will have to increase production capacity in 1996. Basic production can be increased by 25 per cent by the employment of new labour, though new equipment will be required beyond this point. Overtime working could possibly increase to 25 per cent throughout the year. A similar sub-contracting arrangement to that in place in 1995 could be used up to a maximum of 200 SPUs for each of up to four months in a continuous stretch, though the sub-contracting arrangement in 1995 was not entirely satisfactory due to quality and delivery problems. It was also rather expensive!

A more radical solution would be to buy out the firm which carried out the sub-contracting. Woods already have an interest in this company, which has premises on the same industrial estate and is in financial difficulties. It is estimated that Woods could double its basic capacity in this way with effect from May 1996.

For analysis and planning it may be assumed that one SPU sold generates revenue of around £50 with a variable cost of £20 per SPU (basic production) and with a 30 per cent increase in variable cost if overtime working is used. If items are produced by the sub-contractor then an equivalent cost is £30 per SPU. Fixed costs (which include marketing and the production infrastructure of buildings, equipment and so forth) are £900 000. Stockholding cost is assessed at £1 per SPU per month. It is difficult to estimate the true cost of order backlogs in terms of lost future orders and administrative costs. For the purposes of analysis, a rough estimate of £10 per SPU per month may be taken as indicative of the impact of backlogs.

The same basic costs and prices may be used for 1995 and 1996. If the sub-contractor is taken over then its variable cost of production will be the same as Woods but an extra fixed cost of £400 000 must be allowed for.

**TASKS**

1. Analyse Woods 1995 production and delivery performance and comment on their apparent effectiveness.

2. Adopting a variety of scenarios for demand and capacity, show how Woods might achieve profitability in 1996.

3. What course of action would you recommend for Woods, taking into account the potential risks in each of your suggested scenarios?

4. What performance indicators would you suggest to measure the impact of order backlogs?

## PRODUCT MIX PLANNING

Earlier in the chapter we mentioned the need to extend aggregate planning into a consideration of the product mix. This may happen at a later stage of tactical planning or may be a necessary part of aggregate planning if critical decisions are involved.

In this section we introduce some basic concepts in the analysis of multi-product situations through a simple extension of the Milon case. We will only consider a two product situation which can easily be handled through a simple diagram. If a greater number of products are involved we must extend this approach through the use of Linear Programming (LP). This topic is considered in depth in the more advanced quantitative and Operational Research (OR) texts and small scale examples can easily be solved through the use of spreadsheet routines. Industrial problems may involve the use of large-scale models and more sophisticated software.

The underlying mathematics of LP was developed in the 1950s and the subject became an important part of OR and economics. LP in itself is part of the general area of mathematical optimisation theory and has applications way beyond product mix planning. As part of OR, it is readily identified with the hard systems approach to Operations Management and is therefore, at the very least, an important part of the Operations Manager's toolkit.

We will restrict our discussion here to the '2 variable' situation and therefore do not need to invoke the formal mathematical apparatus of LP problem solving. The language in which we express the problem, however, is typically that of LP, the optimisation of a linear profit function with linear resource constraints.

### The Milon Case continued

Part 4

The Milon Manufacturing Company is considering the manufacture of two products on an automated production line. As this specialised line is necessary for these products and has no other current uses, it is essential that the company plans its product mix carefully to make the best use of its dedicated facilities.

The products are as follows:

- Standard (Code X1)
- Special (Code X2).

Some key facts and forecasts for these two products are given in Table 8.7 for the coming year. Fixed costs are estimated as £700 000 per year.

**Table 8.7 'Milon Part 4' – key facts**

|  | X1 | X2 |
|---|---|---|
| Maximum sales | 130 000 units | 40 000 units |
| Material cost | £2.00 per unit | £3.00 per unit |
| Variable machine cost | £0.30 per unit | £0.60 per unit |
| Labour cost | £1.00 per unit | £5.00 per unit |
| Selling price | £10.50 per unit | £24.50 per unit |

Three capacity constraints have been identified:

1. Machine capacity is available to manufacture at most 120 000 units of X1 or 60 000 units of X2 or some pro-rata combination in the year.
2. Labour can handle 150 000 units of X1, 30 000 units of X2 or some combination as above.
3. Materials are available for either 120 000 units of X1, 80 000 units of X2 or some pro rata combination.

If we wish to maximise contribution to fixed costs for this profit centre, what product mix should we choose (that is, how many of X1 and X2 should we plan to manufacture in the year)?

First of all we analyse the cost and price information in order to set up the 'Objective function' (which, in this instance, is based on the assumption that we wish to maximise contribution to fixed costs, i.e. the difference between revenue and variable costs). This analysis is shown in Table 8.8.

We then construct a graph of the 'Product space' for X1 and X2 as shown in Figure 8.5. Possible manufactured quantities of product X1 are shown on the horizontal axis and those for product X2 are shown on the vertical axis (note that either product could have been shown on either axis).

Lines are then drawn denoting the limits of manufacture of X1 and X2 relative to the known constraints. As the sales constraints relate to each product individually, they appear as horizontal and vertical lines on the graph. Other constraints allow some pro-rata substitution of the products and hence appear as angled lines. One

**Table 8.8 'Milon Part 4' – cost analysis**

| Unit variable costs and prices £ | X1 | | X2 | |
|---|---|---|---|---|
| Selling price | | 10.50 | | 24.50 |
| Material cost | 2.00 | | 3.00 | |
| Machine cost | 0.30 | | 0.60 | |
| Labour cost | 1.00 | | 5.00 | |
| Total cost | | 3.30 | | 8.60 |
| Unit contribution | | 7.20 | | 15.90 |

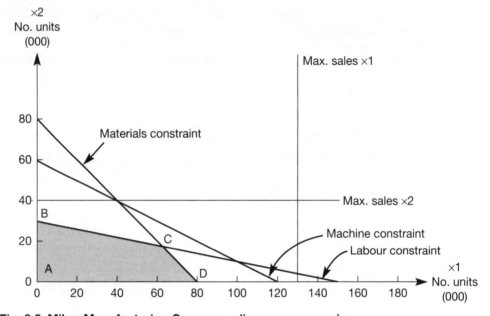

**Fig. 8.5 Milon Manufacturing Company – linear programming**

notes that as the substitution is directly proportional, the lines are straight – hence linear programming.

The only feasible product mixes (to use LP jargon) are those which satisfy all the constraints, that is the area bordered by the polygon ABCD in the diagram. Note that only labour and materials actually constrain production in this instance. The optimal mix (using both the jargon and a theorem of LP) must lie at one of the vertices of the polygon and therefore we calculate which of these gives us the greatest contribution (remembering that each unit of X1 gives £7.20 per unit contribution to fixed costs and each unit of X2 gives £15.90). The results are shown in Table 8.9.

**Table 8.9 'Milon Part 4' – results**

| Point | X1 units | X2 units | X1 contribution £ | X2 contribution £ | Total contribution £ |
|---|---|---|---|---|---|
| A | 0 | 0 | 0 | 0 | 0 |
| B | 0 | 30 000 | 0 | 477 000 | 477 000 |
| C | 62 500 | 17 500 | 450 000 | 278 250 | 728 250 |
| D | 80 000 | 0 | 576 000 | 0 | 576 000 |

Thus the optimal product mix (at point C) is to produce and sell 62 500 of X1 and 17 500 of X2. This gives a contribution to fixed casts of £728 250 and hence a profit (after deducting £700 000 fixed costs) of £28 250.

A full description of LP is found in a number of specialist Operational Research texts (see Further Reading). Industrial situations usually lead to LP models with hundreds of variables and constraints but the basic principle is a straightforward extension of the 2 variable method shown above.

## FURTHER READING

The basics of forecasting and aggregate planning are in Vollman et al. (1992) and most full texts on operations. Garvin's four ways of competing are in Garvin (1992). Slack et al. (1995) contains much on the advantages of operational flexibility.

Linear Programming is a complex technique to study beyond the simple 2 variable model. Full details are in Taha (1992). If you are interested in the possible applications of Chaos Theory to management see Stacey (1993).

Garvin, D. A. (1992), *Operations Strategy*, Prentice-Hall, New York.

Slack, N., Chambers, S., Harland, C., Harrison, A. and Johnston, R. (1995), *Operations Management*, Pitman, London.

Stacey, R. D. (1993), *Strategic Management and Organisational Dynamics*, Pitman, London.

Taha, H. A. (1992), *Operations Research* (5ed), Macmillan, New York.

Vollman, T. E., Berry, W. L. and Whybark, D. C. (1992), *Manufacturing Planning and Control Systems*, Irwin, Homewood.

# CHAPTER 9

# Inventory Decisions

This chapter introduces fundamental issues in the management of stock control systems and includes numerical examples showing stock related decision techniques.

## OBJECTIVES

This chapter:

- introduces the basic language of stock control
- outlines the various costs involved in a stock-holding system
- shows, through an extended numerical example, how an 'economic ordering quantity' may be achieved
- shows one simple method for calculating stock re-order levels
- provides a structured guide to the implementation of stock control systems change.

## INTRODUCTION

The basic ideas and techniques in the area of 'independent demand' stock control systems were extensively developed up until the 1970s when the techniques were computerised. It suffered something of a reversal of fortunes when Just-In-Time became fashionable – why concentrate on holding the right amount of stock when you needn't hold stock at all!

As this is a naive argument and quite inappropriate for many operational systems, it is important that the fundamental building blocks of stock control systems are understood so that an appropriate system may be chosen. If it is argued, as in JIT, that stock represents idle material and hence is a waste which should be eliminated then, if we do hold stock, we must be able to show clearly how the holding of stock does add value for some external or internal customer. If this cannot be done then we should indeed find a way of eliminating it though this may in turn require considerable changes in working practice (see Chapter 11).

This chapter, therefore, follows a tight and quite technical argument without losing sight of the organisational context. It does, however, only represent the briefest introduction to a large and demanding area of theory and practice which must eventually be explored further by anyone wishing to specialise in manufacturing planning and control or, alternatively in retailing logistics.

# STOCK CONTROL

One important practical question which faces Operations Managers in a wide variety of organisational contexts is:

*'How much stock should we hold?'*

This question obviously arises in a retail context where shelves full of a wide variety of goods may well attract the customer but represent a major expense to the business. The complexity is increased in a manufacturing context where a multiplicity of decisions must be made.

*'How much raw material stocks should we hold?'*

If we hold too little then our machines and labour may be standing idle whilst waiting for materials to arrive.

*'How much work-in-progress should we hold?'*

Work-in-progress (wip) may be in the form of materials actually being worked on or materials in queues waiting for spare productive capacity to become available. It also includes stocks of partly finished goods held between major processes.

*'How much finished goods stock should we hold?'*

In some situations we may be manufacturing to a given customer's order, though even then we may hold some finished goods stock until the order is complete or a sufficient quantity has been built up for transport to the customer to be economical. In many situations, however, we are manufacturing in the expectation of customer purchase and some finished goods stocks may be seen as inevitable.

*'Should we hold spare parts for customers or for our own equipment in case of breakdown? What about office supplies?...'*

The list of possible types of stock we may hold is very long. To the shop floor worker or the individual in direct contact with the customer there may seem to be excellent reasons for holding a wide variety of items in anticipation of need. If we engage in extensive stock holding then many operational tasks seem superficially easier. For instance if quality problems or equipment breakdowns occur then we may fall back on stocks of materials or products to keep things going until the problems are rectified. Planning and scheduling are less critical if stocks can be used to handle demand fluctuations. There may be economies of scale in producing large quantities of the same product before resetting machinery. If prices go up we may even make money through speculation in materials!

To summarise, the following are common reasons why stocks of materials are held:

- Finished goods stocks may be held as a buffer against variations in demand or to allow for seasonal demand.

- Raw material stocks may be held as a buffer against variations in supply (such as delays or poor quality of supply) or as a precaution against shortages or price rises.
- Work-in-progress may be held in order to 'decouple' our processes, that is to allow them to operate independently to some extent in case of breakdowns or quality problems.
- Any type of stock may be held in order to build up a batch of sufficient size to make transportation economically feasible.
- Economies of purchase or production may be sought through buying or making in large batches, which will in turn entail increased stock holding.
- In order to provide suitable levels of service, it may be appropriate to maintain warehouse stocks at particular locations (that is, 'location sensitive' uses of stock).
- It may simply be easier to manage operations if stock is held.

One technical point should be made here. The words 'buffer' and 'decoupling' are central to classical stock control theory. A comparison is often made to the use of a suspension system in a car to ensure a smooth ride for the car's occupants despite irregularities in the road surface. Thus, by analogy, a stock of materials absorbs demand or supply fluctuations in the short term. A number of 'organisational buffers' are relevant to Operations Managers, for instance demand fluctuations may also be more easily handled if we have spare productive capacity, ample support staff or a flexible manufacturing system.

By now you should have become suspicious of this line of argument. More stock and more buffering obviously leads to more expense. Thus our pursuit of short term convenience may lead to long-term unprofitability, or even a short-term cash flow crisis.

There is also a more subtle argument against casual buffering and excess stock holding. It can mask problems and remove the impetus for continual improvement. For example, consider the following example of problem visibility. If a machine breakdown would lead to a major stoppage in material flow then it is in our interest to maintain the machine properly and monitor its operating performance. Alternatively, if we keep plenty of work-in-progress then the opportunity cost of the breakdown may be minimal and we may not even bother to measure the cost of such an event or try to reduce its frequency. Even with the best intentions of efficient machine management we may be diverted to other more pressing issues, such as stock counts and preventing pilfering! Hence the use of ample stock buffers leads us towards lazy and ineffective management practices.

We may now begin to see why concepts such as Just-in-Time or 'stockless' production have attractions. They place a premium on effective general management of the workplace allied to a philosophy of continuous improvement but should not be seen as an alternative panacea to 'buffering'. There are a number of perfectly valid reasons for holding stock, provided such a strategy creates value for a customer (external or internal) and is economically sound. Retailing depends on precisely such a strategy and many service situations require accompanying material support. The existence of a strongly seasonal demand for a product may necessitate building up stock if productive capacity is fixed and must be utilised throughout the year (as seen in Chapter 8 when considering aggregate planning).

To explore stock holding strategies further we now turn to an examination of the costs associated with stock control systems.

# COSTS OF STOCK

Before working through the next section you might like to pause and see how many different types of cost you can associate with stock holding decision situations.

Roughly speaking there are costs associated with holding stock and with stock not being available. There are costs involved in obtaining stock and overall systems costs when stock must be controlled, that is counting, recording and so forth. More formally the following sub-sections describe the major costs categories with which we are concerned here.

## Cost of holding stock

There are a number of costs associated with the presence of stock, that is costs which would not be incurred if stock were absent. It should be noted that some of the following represent direct expenses while others are opportunity costs, for instance floor space is being used for storage while it might more profitably be used in some other way.

- Cost of capital – stock appears as an asset in a company's financial accounts and must therefore be balanced by capital in some form, which in turn involves possibly considerable cost directly related to the value of stock held.

- Storage, handling and insurance costs – the physical presence of stock entails the use of space and handling equipment.

- Administration and other systems costs – stock records must be maintained for accounting and operational management purposes.

- Deterioration and other losses – materials kept in stock may physically deteriorate or be damaged through handling, become superseded by alternative materials (stock obsolescence), may eventually not be required, become lost or may be stolen.

One point of particular interest is the way in which cost varies with quantity in stock and the time for which it is held. The cost of capital is directly dependent on the value of stock held and the rate at which this is charged is usually constant (for example 25 per cent of average stock value per annum) though this may hardly do justice to the marginal cost of capital for a company. This is not an issue we can explore in detail here beyond noting that financial controllers may have urgent needs to reduce stock holding on occasions, an action which may cause considerable problems for material planning and control systems. By comparison storage and administrative costs may have considerable fixed elements (for instance the cost of a specially designed warehouse or of a computer based stock control system). Whilst all costs are variable in the long term, the sunk cost of storage facilities may wrongly inhibit a drive for stock reduction. To make matters more complicated, obsolescence costs will depend on storage time whilst shrinkage (theft related) costs may well depend on stock visibility and ease of control by management.

The usual simplifying assumption is to set a standard annual rate of holding cost which is then multiplied by the average value of stock held to arrive at an annual cost of holding stock. Whilst useful for preliminary analysis, such simplifications should always be reviewed critically in any real management context. In particular such an analysis is likely to underplay the organisational implications of stock holding, such as a reduced urgency for continual improvement.

## Cost of obtaining stock

The costs of obtaining stock differ depending on the source. If stock is obtained from an outside supplier then one must consider the following:

- order processing costs
- handling and quality assurance costs on receipt of stock
- purchase cost, including quantity discounts if available
- transportation costs
- supplier relationship costs.

The first two of the above are likely to vary more with the number of orders placed than with the size of order. Purchase cost per unit may well depend on order size and is likely to include transportation. The final category is a fixed cost and includes, for example, the costs of setting up a supply contract and monitoring the performance of the supplier against such a contract.

In practice supply relationships vary greatly over a range of organisational contexts. A supplier to a major car manufacturer may be required to provide several deliveries of key components every working day in line with a tightly controlled long-term contract. Similarly, large suppliers to major retailers have established working relationships designed to minimise the above costs whilst more occasional supplies may be obtained on the basis of a single order from an approved supplier.

Perhaps the most extreme example of a supply contract is where the supplier is required to maintain stock on the premises of the customer, the latter being invoiced only on use of a stock item and, in addition, charging rental for storage space! Such an arrangement may minimise the non-purchase cost of obtaining stock from the customer's point of view but common sense tells us that the purchase cost must be greater in order to provide some profit margin for the supplier. The onus is, however, firmly placed on the ability of the supplier to manage stock holding in an economic manner, which will to some extent depend on the customer's willingness to give details of planned usage of the stock items in question. This example once again shows the advantages to be gained from co-operative rather than adversarial supply relationships.

Thus the costs of obtaining stock from an outside supplier are related to:

- frequency of order placing
- size of order
- administrative infrastructure.

The situation differs somewhat if stocks are replenished from an internal source, for instance an assembly and packing process producing finished goods. In this instance process economics must be balanced against stock holding costs. For example considerable economies of scale may be gained by running a process for a long time to produce one item but this will inevitably mean building up finished goods stocks of this item whilst requiring stocks of other items to be held to satisfy their demand when production capacity is unavailable. Thus stock holding costs will be traded off against savings in process set-up costs and reduced factory costs.

## Shortage and penalty costs

So far we have implicitly assumed that customer demand will be met. Alternatively we may fail in this regard, thus incurring penalty costs, or may even decide to backlog demand.

Penalty costs may be in the form of the draconian penalties which often accompany major supply contracts or be less tangible as when a customer seeks an alternative source of supply. The latter may, of course, be as damaging as the former. If we decide simply not to meet demand then customers may be able to go elsewhere, and may then stay with their new source of supply. Whether this is a viable strategy is an interesting commercial decision that most firms try hard to avoid!

A different situation arises when we are discussing raw material stocks and work-in-progress. Here the customer is our own production process and the shortage cost must be assessed internally in terms of process disruption, the costs of alternative supplies and eventual damage to customer relationships.

If we now make the optimistic assumption that we can reliably measure all the costs inherent in stock control situations, we must now address the issue of how we use such measurements as part of appropriate decision making and control systems.

## INVENTORY DECISION AND CONTROL SYSTEMS

We now turn to a more technical analysis of stock related decision making. The methods which we briefly introduce below have been known for a number of years and were, at one time, relied on excessively as the source of good management practice in stock control. The resulting formulae were blindly applied in the wrong situations or newer and ever more elaborate formulae were derived in pursuit of tiny cost advantages and little understanding of commercial opportunity. It needed the Japanese demonstration in the 1970s that production systems could be run with very little stock to awaken Western managers to the limitations of technique-driven stock control. Then things swung the other way and stock control mathematics was rejected as nonsense.

A more reasonable view is that such technical analysis is useful to clarify thought and as an aid to decision making in a range of appropriate situations. As with all areas of management, decision making cannot be reduced to mathematics but decision situations can be clarified by structured analysis.

## Independent demand inventory control

In the simple and introductory form of analysis given below we concentrate our attention on a point where stock of a particular item is to be kept. In computer based inventory systems we refer to an SKU (Stock Keeping Unit) as the basic unit of our analysis. We characterise this situation as an input–output model as shown in Figure 9.1.

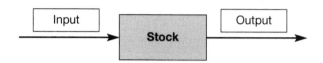

**Fig. 9.1 Stock as an input–output system**

We assume that the output is not to be controlled (that is we wish to meet the demand of an internal or external customer) but that it is possible to forecast the required output. We attempt to control the level of stock by controlling the input, in particular the size of input batch and the point at which we order an input batch. This latter point requires careful attention. Although we assume that the amount of input is within our control, it might be unwise also to assume that the exact timing of that input is always known with certainty. Delays may arise due to problems in the supply system. Hence we assume that a 'lead time of supply' exists between our ordering an input batch and it arriving and that this lead time may not be known with certainty.

The first step is to simplify things still further and introduce what is usually known as the 'EBQ formula'. This is done mainly to clarify fundamental concepts and lead us to a robust rule of thumb for input batch sizing. We begin by making a number of assumptions:

- constant and known output demand
- constant and known lead time of supply
- no stockouts allowed
- fixed costs and prices.

This situation may be illustrated by means of a 'stock–time' diagram as shown in Figure 9.2. The constant demand gives rise to a straight line stock depletion on the diagram which must, of course, be an approximation to any real situation. The constant lead time in conjunction with constant demand gives rise to the idealised situation where stock may be timed to fall to a zero value just as a new batch arrives. In general, stock–time diagrams are most useful devices which enable us to visualise key relationships in stock holding situations. A further assumption is that demand is 'independent', in contrast to the assumption of 'dependent demand' in MRPII systems (see Chapter 11).

We now introduce some notation to enable us to express the underlying relationships in this situation:

$D$ = demand rate (units per unit time)

$S$  = administration and other ordering costs per order placed (£ per order)

$C$ = unit purchase cost (£ per unit)

$i$  = inventory holding cost rate (per unit time).

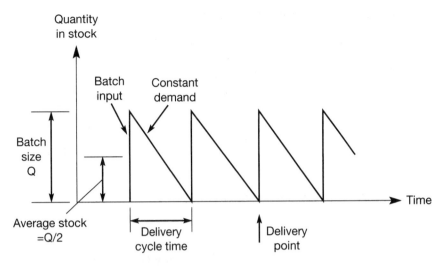

**Fig. 9.2 Stock–time diagram (EBQ)**

Thus, iC = inventory holding cost (£ per unit per unit time).

Typically the unit of time may be a year or a week as appropriate. We also introduce a decision variable, the batch size, which is of unknown value at present:

Q = batch size (units).

Thus we may use a little algebra to arrive at the following relationships:

Number of batches delivered in unit time = D/Q

(for instance if demand is 400 units per year and we order in batches of 100 then we need 400/100 = 4 deliveries per year)

Ordering cost per unit time = SD/Q

(Ordering cost per order multiplied by the number of orders placed in the time period)

Inventory holding cost per unit time = iCQ/2

(The average inventory is Q/2 (see Figure 9.2) and therefore the holding cost over the time period is the holding cost rate multiplied by the average amount in stock)

Total cost per unit time = TC = SD/Q + iCQ/2

(This is the ordering cost plus the holding cost. On some occasions we will also include the purchase cost, see example below)

An illustrative graph of total cost against the decision variable, batch size Q, is shown in Figure 9.3 in the context of a worked example. As can readily be seen, there is a batch size (which we term the 'Economic Batch Quantity') which has the lowest total cost. The value of this batch size can be obtained from the formula:

$$\text{Economic Batch Quantity (EBQ)} = Q_0 = \sqrt{\frac{2SD}{iC}}$$

Total Cost for EBQ = $\sqrt{2iCSD}$

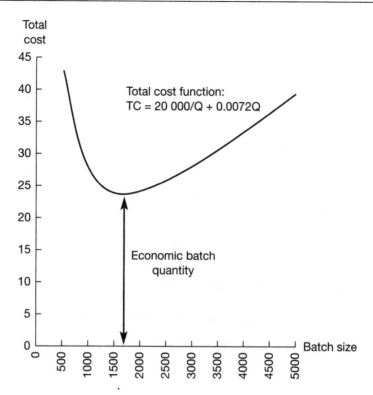

**Fig. 9.3 Cost function**

Thus on the basis of known and constant data we can find a value of batch size which balances ordering and holding costs to arrive at a minimum total cost.

(*Technical note:* The EBQ formula is arrived at by using the 'differential calculus'. You do not have to be able to do this to follow the argument given here but you will require a basic knowledge of this branch of mathematics if you wish to pursue such model building further. If you have studied calculus then, as you should know, you find the minimum cost by differentiating the total cost formula with respect to the variable Q and equating to zero. You should also check that this gives a minimum value by finding the second derivative and noting it to be positive at the optimum batch size.)

A simple example is now included to help you understand the details as well as the basic principles underlying this approach. Note that this example should be worked through in detail as it further develops the ideas in the text above.

## Batch sizing worked example

You have a contract to deliver items to a customer at a steady rate of 80 per day for the next year (assume five days per week and 50 weeks in the year). You buy the items from your usual supplier in batches of 1000 at a price of £2.40 per item. Delivery and handling costs are £50 per batch and the stock holding cost is 30 per cent of stock value per year.

*1. What is the average weekly cost of this arrangement?*

A convenient unit of time for this example is a week (an alternative unit would be a year). As stock related costs differ from week to week depending on the pattern of deliveries and payments we calculate the cost in a delivery cycle and average this over the week.

D = Demand per week = 400 units per week

S = Delivery related costs = £50 per delivery cycle

C = £2.40 per unit

i = 30 per unit of stock value per year

Thus the holding cost (assuming stock is valued at its purchase price) is 30 per cent of £2.40 per unit per year, that is:

iC = 30/100 × 2.40/50 = £0.0144 per unit per week

Current batch size Q = 1000

Hence the cycle time (time between deliveries) = Q/D = 1000/400 = 2.5 weeks

(we could have calculated the reciprocal of this quantity, number of batches delivered per week = D/Q = 0.4)

Ordering cost per cycle = S = £50

Ordering cost per week = 50/2.5 = £20 per week (= SD/Q)

Average stock held = Q/2 = 500 units

Holding cost per week = iCQ/2 = £0.0144 × 1000/2 = £7.2 per week

Purchase cost per cycle = £2.40 × 1000 = £2400

Purchase cost per week = £2400/2.5 = £960

Hence Total Cost per week (on average)

TC = 20 + 7.20 + 960 = £987.20 per week

(Note how the purchase cost dominates this sum. As the purchase price changes, however, at differing points in our calculation then its effect must be included.)

*2. An alternative supplier offers weekly delivery at the same price. Is this an attractive proposition?*

With weekly deliveries our ordering cost would increase from £20 per week to £50 per week whilst our holding cost would only reduce from £7.20 per week to £2.88. (Why?) Weekly purchase cost would remain constant. Therefore this is not a good idea.

(Note: How we can carry out a 'marginal' analysis for a small proposed change rather than repeating the whole calculation.)

*3. What is the economic batch size, delivery interval and weekly cost based on this information? Will it matter if we use a batch size which differs slightly from the economic batch size?*

We now assume that the batch size Q is a decision variable. Hence:

Number of deliveries per week = D/Q = 400/Q

Ordering cost per week = SD/Q = 50 × 400/Q = 20 000/Q

Holding cost per week = iCQ/2 = 0.0144 × Q/2 = 0.0072Q

Total cost per week = TC = 20 000/Q + 0.0072Q

(Note that we may safely ignore the purchase cost at this point as it does not directly affect the EBQ calculation. See Part 4 below however)

In Figure 9.3 we have a graph of the relationship between Q and TC. We can readily identify the EBQ and the minimum Total Cost but may also compute them from the formulae given earlier:

EBQ = square root (2 × 50 × 400/ 0.0144) = 1667 (to nearest whole number)

Delivery interval = 1667/400 = 4.2 weeks (approx.)

Minimum Total Cost = square root (2 × 0.0144 × 50 × 400) = £24 per week

This is an improvement on the weekly cost (not including purchase) given in part 1 of £27.20 per week.

If we look at Figure 9.3 we see that we may move a considerable distance from the optimal batch of 1667 without adding appreciably to the cost. The batch–cost curve has a flat bottom region and hence, in general, total cost is not sensitive to reasonably small variations in batch size. This is a very useful practical result.

*4. A different supplier offers batches of 10 000 at a lower price. What is the break-even price relative to optimal supply?*

Remember that optimal supply is a batch of 1667 with a total weekly cost (now including purchase cost at existing prices) of £24 + £960 = £985 per week

If we now assume Q = 10 000 (a 25 week supply) at a price £C per unit then:

Ordering cost per week = 50 x 400/10 000 = £2.00 per week

Holding cost per week = (0.3/50) × C × 10 000/2 = 30C

Purchase cost per week = (10 000/25)C = 400C

Total cost per week = 2 + 30C + 400C = 430C + 2

For break-even this must be the same as the previously calculated optimal cost, that is:

430C + 2 = 985 (£ per week)

Hence C = £2.286 per unit for break-even.

Thus apparently only a small price change (from £2.40 to under £2.286) would be necessary for a batch of 10 000 to be an economic proposition!

5. *In what ways are the above calculations unrealistic as a guide to inventory decision making?*

Quite simply, in concentrating on a small range of cost factors, they ignore the other factors mentioned earlier and the general environmental context. By fixing our stock holding over a 25 week period we tie up working capital, reduce purchasing flexibility (suppose a cheaper source is found), tie up warehouse space and ignore the greater likelihood of shrinkage and other losses. Of course if prices went up then a decision to buy a large batch would then seem a good idea but this is a separate issue.

Perhaps we could get the best of both worlds by negotiating a supply contract linked to current prices with a regular call-off of, say, 400 per week or even 50 per day. This might also be a better arrangement for the supplier if transport costs are low. If in addition we could insist on zero defects and suitably packaged units then perhaps we could reduce the ordering cost.

With imagination we might be able to improve this supply situation dramatically. The calculations given above do not tell us how many to order. They provide one important piece of analysis to add to a number of other considerations in making a suitable operating decision.

## Continuous review systems

The next major step in our analysis of independent demand inventory systems is to relax our assumption that demand is constant. This has two major implications in that we will now need a forecasting system to capture the essential features of demand (such as mean demand, trend, variability and seasonal fluctuations) and we also must accept that we may be wrong in our forecasts and may then run out of stock.

In Chapter 8 we introduced a basic forecasting system using simple exponential smoothing. For our illustrative purposes here we will assume there is no trend or seasonal variation to contend with, though it should be remembered that such features of a time series do commonly occur in practice. We will also assume that the lead time of supply remains constant.

One of the simplest systems used is the 'Continuous review system'. It is illustrated by means of the stock–time diagram in Figure 9.4. Here we see a more complex demand pattern producing an irregular depletion of stock. Eventually the stock line cuts the 'Reorder level' and a batch is ordered from the supplier. After a constant lead time this batch arrives, hopefully before stockout has occurred.

Once again we introduce some simple notation (using days as a unit of time for convenience):

ROL = re-order level (units)

L = lead time (assume constant) (days)

M = average demand over the lead time (units)

B = buffer stock (units)

Thus: ROL = M + B

The ROL is our decision variable in this case and M is the forecast demand produced by our forecasting system. You should note the word 'buffer' occurring once again but

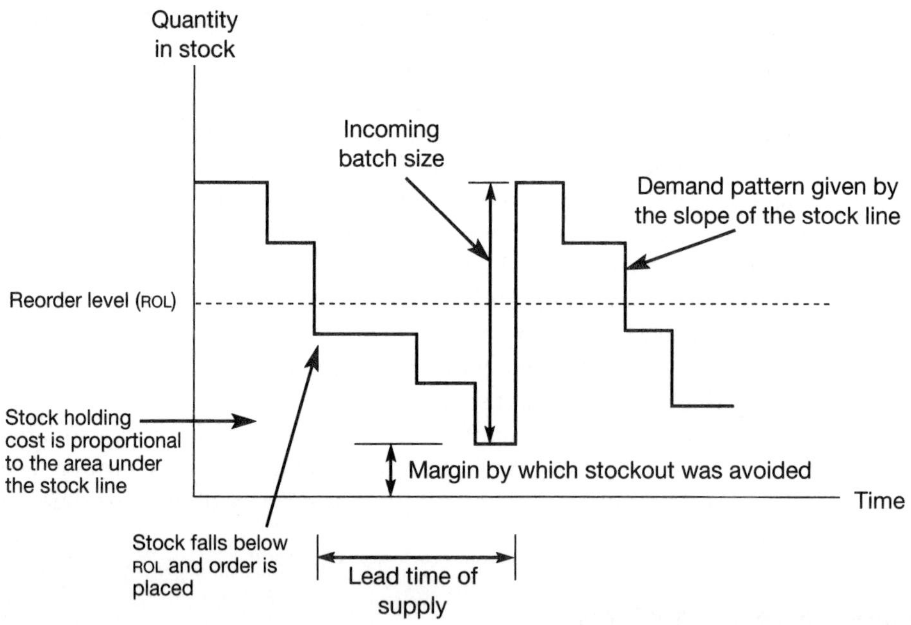

**Fig. 9.4 Stock–time diagram (ROL)**

with a more technical meaning in this instance. In this context, buffer stock (B) is the extra stock we hold to improve our chances of not running out during a delivery cycle.

This idea is worth exploring in more depth. We define 'service level' (in this case) as the probability of our being able to satisfy all the demand before the batch arrives in stock. If our ROL was set exactly at M then we would have a 50 per cent service level (technically this assumes that the average demand is the same as the median demand and we are ignoring the fact that the batch which cuts the ROL reduces stock to a point some way below the ROL – both points which should be addressed in a real system). We usually require a higher service level and hence need some extra buffer stock.

$$B = z\sigma \sqrt{L}$$

where  z = safety factor (2.33 for 99 per cent service level, see Table 9.1)
$\sigma$ = standard deviation of daily demand

**Table 9.1  Stock safety factors**

| Required % service level | Safety factor (Z) |
|:---:|:---:|
| 90 | 1.28 |
| 95 | 1.65 |
| 99 | 2.33 |
| 99.9 | 3.09 |

Our forecasting system will be capable of estimating the standard deviation of demand (a measure of the variability of demand usually assessed from the forecasting errors) and the service level is of our choosing. Safety factors for a range of service levels are given in Table 9.1. If you have done a course on Business Statistics you should recognise these as normal distribution ordinates, which shows us that yet another assumption is being made in this analysis.

**TASKS**

Table 9.2 (on p. 164) gives the past weekly demand for a key item of stock. The following information is also available:

Ordering cost, S = £150 per order
Purchase cost, C = £4.50 per unit
Inventory holding cost rate, I = 30 per cent per annum (assume 50 weeks in the year)

1. Use exponential smoothing to estimate average demand in future weeks.

2. Calculate the EBQ and total weekly cost in this situation.

3. An alternative supplier offers fixed batches of 5000 units at a purchase cost of £4.40 per unit. Is this an economic proposition?

4. What re-order level would you recommend for a 95 per cent service level and a supply lead time of two weeks? (Note: This requires you to estimate the standard deviation of demand. If you do not know how to do this, a rough estimate is given by calculating the mean absolute error of demand and multiplying the result by a factor of 1.2.)

## IMPLEMENTATION

Though most of this chapter has consisted of ideas and techniques, it would be quite wrong to think that if we get the mathematics right then a good stock control system will be easy to implement. Though we now have the advantage of powerful computer based stock control packages we must be careful to pick an appropriate one and must remember to take organisational factors into account. For example, computer based systems require good data sources and disciplined usage. These may be more evident in a large organisation with tightly rule based working practices than in the many organisations with a more casual and flexible approach.

In order to help structure a systems implementation project, or guide the continual improvement of an existing system, we include below some useful steps to take and questions to ask. These show quite clearly the complexity of introducing even limited change in a materials control system.

**Table 9.2 Demand data**

| Week number | Demand |
|:---:|:---:|
| 1 | 400 |
| 2 | 450 |
| 3 | 470 |
| 4 | 385 |
| 5 | 370 |
| 6 | 410 |
| 7 | 395 |
| 8 | 380 |
| 9 | 430 |
| 10 | 440 |
| 11 | 435 |
| 12 | 420 |

## Exploration and analysis of existing system

- Why is stock kept?
- What is the scope of the present system (for example, do we include work in progress, spare parts and so forth)?
- With what other systems does the stock control system interact?
- How *should* the present system operate? (What are the rules?)
- How *does* the present system operate in practice?
- Classify stock by value of annual usage to give ABC classification (see discussion of Pareto Analysis in Chapter 3). What other features of stock may be of importance? (For example, a raw material may be inexpensive but essential to a process.)
- Can we measure the performance of the present system in terms of existing objectives, for example:
  - What are the present stock holding costs?
  - What re-order levels are operating?
  - What are average stock levels in past year?
  - What is the frequency of stockouts?
  - What lead times have been observed?

The above might be summarised in terms of stock–time curve for each important item. This overall picture may then be related to objectives.

- What was the demand for each important item during the past year:
  - average demand
  - variability of demand
  - trends
  - seasonal variations.
- Identify critical points and bottlenecks in the existing system (for example, supplier problems, etc.).

## Objectives for proposed system

Possible objectives may be:

- consider stock as a profit centre and maximise profitability (very difficult in practice)
- minimise stock holding costs while maintaining a given level of service
- minimise capital invested in stock while maintaining a given level of service.

## System building

- Determine variables which need forecasting and set up systems of appropriate complexity (depending on classification). Variables may include demand, lead times, costs, prices. It may be possible to forecast for a group of items.
- Documentation system.
- Determine procedure for arriving at batch quantities (for example, EBQ).
- Determine procedure for arriving at reorder levels.
- Integrate with other systems.
- If necessary simulate the behaviour of the system or test by 'hind-casting' (i.e. using past data to test the effectiveness of a forecasting system).
- Determine what other actions, for example, rationalisation or variety reduction, may be appropriate.
- Monitor the performance of the new system with reference to objectives and revise as necessary.

**TASK**

If you are in a position to do so, choose a stock control situation and quickly work through the above checklist to show the potential complexity of decision making and control.

## FURTHER READING

Almost all comprehensive texts in Operations Management have chapters on forecasting systems and on independent demand stock control systems. To make further progress in this area requires an increasing use of mathematics and the research material can be highly technical. If you are very keen to develop this area (perhaps in conjunction with the material introduced in Chapter 11) see:

Vollman,T. E., Berry, W. L. and Whybark, D. C. (1992), *Manufacturing Planning and Control Systems* (3ed), Irwin, Homewood.

Silver, E. A. and Peterson, R. (1985), *Decision Systems for Inventory Management and Production Planning* (2ed), Wiley, New York.

# CHAPTER 10

# Managing Flows in Service Situations

The objective of this chapter is to extend our discussion of aggregate planning to service operations (note that Chapter 8, which introduced this area of work, was mainly concerned with manufacturing). This leads on to an exploration of the management of queues, a key issue in practical service management and important determinant of customer satisfaction.

## OBJECTIVES

This chapter:

- discusses issues of capacity management and aggregate planning in service situations
- illustrates aggregate planning in service operations through an extended case study
- outlines three approaches to the management of queues
- provides introductory worked examples relating to mathematical models of queuing situations.

## INTRODUCTION

We now return to the problems of capacity management and aggregate planning, but this time in the context of service operations. The need to match supply and demand in real time (that is, the impossibility of storing a personal service) makes this area of work in some ways conceptually simpler, though the resulting management problems are very real.

We begin with a consideration of capacity management in service contexts showing some of the strategies frequently adopted to vary capacity and manage demand. In terms of the latter, it should be noted that marketing and Operations Management are close partners in this regard. We then move on to a consideration of aggregate planning, mainly through a case exercise, 'The Windsor Hotel'. As well as giving you some exercise in solving the practical problems of service planning, this case emphasises the need to consider service operations in their environmental context. The management of the Windsor cannot reasonably plan their actions without considering the resort of Dunmouth and its other hotel provision.

Finally, we give some consideration to the management of queues. A well-developed area of operational research is the mathematical theory of queues and we show some simple ways in which results from queuing theory can be of practical use. There is, however, a more recent line of thought which suggests that the management of queuing psychology may be an area which will show some profit. For instance, the mathematics of queues will tell you how long you may have to wait but the psychology of queues tells the manager how to arrange things so that the waiting time seems less unpleasant!

In some ways, this attention to queue management seems to be an admission of failure. Surely queue avoidance through demand and capacity management has more to recommend it? Not all queues are visible, as statistics of waiting lists in the health services show only too well, and queues of all kinds may show not only some tactical problems in matching supply and demand but also fundamental problems regarding the allocation of resources in society. It would be over-optimistic, however, to think that we can plan the use of services so precisely that supply will always match demand and the service will also be economic to run. Queues of one type or another are the inevitable consequences of tactical mismatching but they can be managed in an attempt to minimise customer dissatisfaction.

## CAPACITY MANAGEMENT IN SERVICE SYSTEMS

As we discussed in Chapter 8, capacity management is particularly critical in service contexts as service cannot be stored. Unlike manufacturing, it requires the presence of the customer. Of course we may hold stocks of materials used in service delivery if this is an economic option. Also we may perform services for a client (for instance dry cleaning clothes) when time and customer participation may not be critical. We may even operate a booking system in an attempt to constrain the times when customers use the service on offer. Direct personal service, however, must be planned in such a way that supply is available when it is to be consumed, that is supply and demand must be continuously matched.

The presence of the customer has advantages and disadvantages. They may be persuaded to carry out some of the service themselves (as in a self-service retail context) or at least be actively involved. On the other hand there is often a degree of uncertainty in the arrival times of customers and in the time it takes to actually carry out the service function (the processing time).

Research has also shown that the relationship between perceived service quality, processing time and capacity is hard to quantify. A customer seeing available capacity (say, a number of unoccupied service assistants) may expect more attention and longer processing time in the delivery of a satisfactory service. On the other hand a customer may be appreciative of attentive service, though of short duration, if the service delivery system is obviously very busy.

A number of strategies are well known to service providers in this difficult game of balancing client needs and available capacity. The principal distinction is between strategies which seek to vary capacity and those which alter the pattern and timing of demand.

## Strategies to vary capacity:

- use flexible labour schedules (for instance through part-time staff)
- multiple uses of labour (when not serving, personnel will have other complementary tasks to perform)
- encourage customer participation (the effective customer provides some of the service capacity)
- share capacity with other providers (through sub-contracting; 'over-spill' arrangements for hotels; emergency services relying on neighbouring districts).

## Strategies for managing demand:

- moving existing demand to times with excess capacity through pricing and promotion
- developing new demand for times with excess capacity (new source of customers or new uses for the spare capacity)
- develop complementary services for customers at times of excess demand (for instance automatic service for routine bank transactions)
- customer appointment systems (though this leads to problems with 'no-shows' and overbooking)
- queuing (that is the physical backlogging of demand through an actual queue or the use of a waiting list).

It should be noted that most of these strategies require a careful thinking through of the relationship between the organisation as a whole and its customers. These are not narrow issues of operational tactics but involve marketing and other customer contact functions.

# AGGREGATE PLANNING IN A SERVICE CONTEXT

Service demand forecasting faces similar problems and uses similar techniques to manufacturing operations. Aggregate planning is in some ways simpler as issues of stocks are avoided, though backlogs may exist in the form of queues. There is an emphasis in service operations on flexibility, often through the use of labour, and the service industry in many ways relies on a pool of casual and part-time labour to solve many of its problems.

There still remains the problems of investment decision making and the forms of aggregate planning which lead to long-term contractual arrangements. This is illustrated in the case below. In some ways, the owners of the Windsor Hotel have little planning to do. The rooms exist, bookings are taken, staff are employed as necessary and at the end of the year the takings are added up to reveal if a profit has been made! To be more pro-active, the owners have to consider whether to refurbish the hotel, to take over the adjacent hotel or to enter into a deal with a coach operator. The first of these possibilities should affect demand, the second affects supply whilst the latter is concerned with regularity of demand over the year as a whole.

One of the major pre-occupations of many forms of service operations is yield management. An airline must decide in advance how many planes it will fly on what routes. Once this is decided then the operational and marketing problem is to maximise the revenue (or yield) from these flights which is not, of course, the same thing as filling the planes. Thus seats are sold at a variety of prices as part of various booking deals and the way this is to be done is a key part of aggregate planning.

In the hotel context shown below, the rooms exist but how should we attempt to fill them at differing times of the year? Let us now consider this case exercise in more detail.

## The Windsor Hotel – a case exercise

The Windsor Hotel is a long-established institution in Dunmouth currently managed by Karen and Steve Godden. Karen is the daughter of John Pierce, the owner of this and one other hotel in the town. In their mid-30s, the Goddens have been in hotel management for several years and are looking to develop the potential of the Windsor.

The prosperity of the south coast town of Dunmouth dates from the Regency period although the town itself has a longer history as a fishing village and minor port. Though a local centre of trade, with a well developed shopping precinct and nearby trading estate, the area by the sea front (a mile from the shopping centre) has been preserved as a traditional holiday resort, with a fine beach, promenades, gardens and a total lack of anything peculiar to the second half of the twentieth century. Despite the absence of arcade games and theme park paraphernalia, the resort is popular with families and young children although it must be said that the greatest degree of popularity is with older, reasonably affluent visitors. Several small hotels near the sea front have been converted into residential homes for the elderly.

A substantial amount of holiday accommodation remains, however, as summarised in Figure 10.1. The Windsor Hotel is medium sized and medium priced as shown in Figure 10.1 (the Windsor is the twenty-first hotel on the list and is shown in bold type). Unfortunately it is only modestly profitable and somewhat in need of refurbishment. In Figure 10.2 some statistics for the Hotel show its dependence on the summer holiday trade but with some out-of-season support. Guests to the hotel are almost exclusively on holiday rather than business. Out-of-season, much of the trade is based on weekend breaks and special deals for groups of visitors. Bookings by coach operators have not been actively encouraged in the past.

The Goddens are examining a variety of ways to exploit the substantial building and good position of the Windsor. One possibility is to encourage coach tour bookings. This would entail giving a discount of around 20 per cent on the rate which applied at a particular time of year (see Figure 10.2) but could ensure near 100 per cent occupancy from May to October. This added source of guests, allied with the high reputation of the restaurant and public areas of the Windsor, might increase demand way above capacity. In this case the Hotel might well lose some of its loyal long-term customers. Around 65 per cent of current bookings are made by customers who have stayed at the Hotel at some time in the previous two years.

| Ref. No. | Rating | Months Start | Open End | Rooms: Single | Double | Family | Summer Terms | Distance from sea |
|---|---|---|---|---|---|---|---|---|
| 1 | 4 | 1 | 12 | 13 | 39 | 9 | 620 | 0.3 |
| 2 | 4 | 1 | 12 | 8 | 43 | 6 | 570 | 0.1 |
| 3 | 3 | 1 | 12 | 11 | 23 | 4 | 510 | 0.1 |
| 4 | 3 | 4 | 10 | 8 | 32 | 13 | 445 | 0.5 |
| 5 | 3 | 1 | 12 | 6 | 49 | 7 | 440 | 0.1 |
| 6 | 3 | 1 | 12 | 9 | 25 | 4 | 410 | 0.5 |
| 7 | 3 | 3 | 10 | 0 | 7 | 1 | 350 | 5.0 |
| 8 | 3 | 3 | 10 | 5 | 26 | 5 | 330 | 1.5 |
| 9 | 3 | 2 | 12 | 22 | 46 | 7 | 310 | 0.1 |
| 10 | 3 | 1 | 12 | 2 | 14 | 3 | 310 | 10.0 |
| 11 | 2 | 3 | 11 | 1 | 17 | 2 | 350 | 1.0 |
| 12 | 2 | 2 | 12 | 1 | 14 | 1 | 330 | 4.0 |
| 13 | 2 | 3 | 11 | 5 | 16 | 3 | 320 | 2.0 |
| 14 | 2 | 3 | 10 | 2 | 12 | 2 | 300 | 0.5 |
| 15 | 2 | 3 | 11 | 1 | 11 | 3 | 300 | 2.0 |
| 16 | 2 | 1 | 12 | 2 | 16 | 0 | 290 | 3.0 |
| 17 | 2 | 1 | 12 | 4 | 13 | 4 | 280 | 0.3 |
| 18 | 2 | 1 | 12 | 3 | 29 | 10 | 270 | 0.1 |
| 19 | 2 | 3 | 11 | 8 | 18 | 8 | 270 | 0.1 |
| 20 | 2 | 3 | 11 | 4 | 19 | 5 | 260 | 0.1 |
| **21** | **2** | **1** | **12** | **6** | **26** | **5** | **260** | **0.3** |
| 22 | 2 | 1 | 12 | 5 | 9 | 2 | 250 | 10.0 |
| 23 | 2 | 3 | 11 | 0 | 15 | 2 | 240 | 2.5 |
| 24 | 1 | 2 | 11 | 0 | 18 | 1 | 210 | 2.0 |
| 25 | 1 | 2 | 11 | 1 | 6 | 2 | 200 | 5.0 |
| 26 | 1 | 1 | 12 | 2 | 5 | 1 | 190 | 2.0 |
| 27 | 1 | 1 | 12 | 0 | 7 | 0 | 180 | 2.0 |
| 28 | 1 | 1 | 12 | 0 | 7 | 0 | 160 | 2.0 |

**Rating** is Dunmouth Hotel Rating (similar to Stars rating)
**Summer Terms**    is summer weekly terms per person,
                    dinner bed and breakfast excluding VAT
                    Actual price depends on time of year and position of room in Hotel
**Distance from Sea**  is in miles (0.1 miles is on seafront)

Data relates to 1995

**Fig. 10.1 Hotels in Dunmouth**

Another possibility is an extensive refurbishment of the Hotel with the objective of increasing demand and allowing higher prices to be charged. Many other ideas have been suggested to increase demand, ranging from 'theme' weekends to installing an indoor pool and other leisure facilities (which would be expensive and marginally reduce the room capacity).

The most dramatic possibility is taking over the adjacent, smaller Highview Hotel (the seventeenth hotel in the list in Figure 10.1). Owned by an elderly relative of John Pierce, this Hotel would combine well with the Windsor, although extensive alterations and refurbishment would be necessary.

**Data for 1995**

| Month | Adult-weeks | Child-weeks | Typical adult rate/week | Total revenue |
|---|---|---|---|---|
| Jan | 56 | 5 | 160 | 9400 |
| Feb | 48 | 7 | 160 | 8300 |
| Mar | 79 | 8 | 160 | 13300 |
| Apr | 163 | 34 | 210 | 37800 |
| May | 191 | 10 | 210 | 41200 |
| Jun | 216 | 14 | 210 | 46800 |
| Jul | 225 | 26 | 260 | 61900 |
| Aug | 251 | 38 | 260 | 70200 |
| Sep | 230 | 18 | 210 | 50200 |
| Oct | 187 | 13 | 210 | 40600 |
| Nov | 81 | 4 | 160 | 13300 |
| Dec | 67 | 5 | 160 | 11100 |
| Xmas | 123 | 18 | 260 | 34300 |
| Total<br>% of max. | 1917<br>56.38% | 200<br>40.00% | | 438400<br>60.05% |

| | | | |
|---|---|---|---|
| Total Revenue = | | | 438400 |
| Adult Var. Cost = | 153360 | | |
| Child Var. Cost = | 16000 | | |
| Total Variable Cost = | | 169360 | |
| Fixed Cost = | | 240000 | |
| Total Cost = | | | 409360 |
| Annual Profit = | | | 29040 |

Note: An adult-week denotes one adult staying in the Hotel for one week

**Fig. 10.2  Windsor Hotel 1995**

Karen's father has a somewhat traditional view of the hotel trade in Dunmouth and is suspicious of any change which involves substantial expenditure or alterations to the character of the hotel. Profitability has been declining, however, and the future of the more marginal hotels in the town is in doubt.

For rough planning purposes, the annual fixed costs of running the Windsor (independent of the number of guests) will be around £260 000 in 1996 if no changes take place. Variable costs per guest per week are estimated at £80, that is cost estimates show no change from 1995 figures. Income per guest per week may be taken as 1995 terms plus 3 per cent. Assume that the Christmas/New Year period is two weeks and in addition each month is four weeks. This gives a 50 week year, an adequate approximation for this exercise.

The Windsor and Highview Hotels together might have a 1996 fixed cost of around twice that of the Windsor alone if some allowance for paying back the cost of alterations is made. Reasonable assumptions may be made for all other data, though such assumptions should be stated with justification.

**TASKS**

In order to provide a structured analysis of the Windsor Hotel case, it is recommended that the following tasks are attempted in the prescribed order. Tasks 1 and 2 are suitable for individual work but it is recommended that the remaining tasks are carried out through group activities as they involve creative thinking and value judgements.

### 1. Setting the scene

Based on Figure 10.1 and using graphical and numerical techniques as appropriate, summarise the basic facts relating to the provision of hotels in Dunmouth. In particular show how the Windsor Hotel fits into this general picture.

(This is a straightforward exercise in descriptive statistics and can lead to very attractive presentational materials if the graphics capabilities of a spreadsheet package are used. It demonstrates how important it is to operational planning and decision making to have a general picture of the environment of a system.)

### 2. The Windsor Hotel in 1996

Using the data in Figure 10.2 (making, and stating, appropriate assumptions as necessary) estimate how profitable the Windsor Hotel might be in 1996 if no changes are made. You should try to pinpoint as far as possible the major sources of contribution to fixed costs and profit. How sensitive is the final profit figure to changes in demand? (We have emphasised throughout the book the importance of linking operations with the general commercial objectives and performance of an organisation.)

### 3. The options for 1996

Produce a set of options for the Windsor Hotel in 1996 (and beyond) which appear to have a chance of improving the hotel's short-term and long-term profitability. (Your

▶

opportunity for group brainstorming, but remember that not all ideas are good ideas. After you have completed the free-flowing activity of idea generation you must come down to a short-list of the most likely ones for success. Each option should include details of pricing policy and necessary capital investments.)

**4. The plan for 1996**

Select one of your options for the Windsor Hotel in 1996 and carry out the following activities. At each stage you must be careful to list all the assumptions you make.

a) Produce a demand forecast for the Windsor Hotel in 1996.

b) Translate this forecast into an aggregate plan (using a table similar to that shown in Figure10.2)

c) Produce a profit forecast for 1996 based on the chosen option and plan. How sensitive is your profit estimate to changes in the 1996 forecast figures?

(If a number of groups are working on this case at the same time, then the final activity can lead to group presentations of the various plans.)

## MANAGING QUEUES

Few people enjoy queuing but it is a natural consequence of a short-term excess of demand over supply. In this section we will discuss the management of physical queues of people. Many material stock-holding situations may be formally modelled as queues but though the mathematics may be similar, the management issues vary from those explored here. Similarly we may think, for example, of patients spending months on hospital waiting lists as part of a queue but we would view this as an aggregate planning problem, that is a long-term mismatch in supply and demand.

We are here concerned with the many, everyday situations where people physically have to queue for a period of time in order to receive service. The quality of this queuing experience must be carefully managed as it obviously forms a key part of the customer's perception of quality as a whole. The queue itself also takes up space which may in itself represent an ineffective use of resources or an intrusion on other uses. We will consider the management of queues under the headings of physical organisation, psychology and the mathematical models which can be used to quantify some key aspects of queuing behaviour.

### The physical organisation of queues

If we have a situation where it is inevitable that customers may have to queue, we must make some physical provision for this and also organise the way in which the queue will work. Interestingly, the subsequent experience of queuing may well be affected by such considerations.

One point to note at the outset is that queuing behaviour appears to have considerable social differences between countries. In this section we are going to assume that organised behaviour is preferred to a general scrum and that patterns of behaviour we plan for will on the whole be observed.

The first point we should then note is the queuing discipline, that is should people be served in the order of their arrival (first come, first served) or should another priority system be used.

**TASKS**

1. List some queuing situations where first come, first served is the only acceptable discipline. How can this be arranged if a simple, physical queue is not possible due to lack of space?

2. Can you think of situations where first come, first served is neither reasonable nor desirable?

The most obvious queues where service follows the same order as arrivals occur in shops and other places where customers are perceived as equals in all ways including their needs. If space is restricted then some form of ticket system can be used to maintain an equitable order of service. This has the additional advantage of allowing customers to circulate and continue shopping, whilst awaiting specialist service.

The main shop-based exception may be when particular consideration is given, for instance, to elderly customers or those with special needs. This takes a more serious form in a hospital emergency unit when an early assessment of patient needs and the urgency of required treatment may lead to service being provided in a different order to arrivals.

The next issue of interest is the number of service points to be provided. This will of course change with demand but the possibility of multiple servers must be planned for. A key issue now is whether to use separate queues at each service point or one queue for them all. Currently common practice in supermarkets appears to be separate queues at checkouts whilst banks and post offices use a single queue feeding multiple service points.

**TASK**

What are the advantages and disadvantages of each of these arrangements?

The main advantages of the single queue from the customer's point of view is it reduces the queue switching which is necessary if one queue is held up because of the long service time required for a particular customer. In addition the single queue seems more equitable and, though obviously longer, is continually moving and hence some progress appears to be being made. From the point of view of management it concentrates the queue into a specific place rather than allowing what may be haphazard queues to stretch out from a variable number of locations. It is also easier to open new service positions and close existing ones when there is a common queue.

The disadvantage to all concerned is that it increases average queuing time. This is because of the time required for a customer to walk from the head of the queue to the vacant service position, a time which might, however, allow the server to complete paperwork and prepare for the next customer.

The next issue we might explore is the possibility of differentiating the arriving customers and handling them in differing ways. For instance we might be able to provide automated facilities which will be satisfactory for meeting some customers' needs whilst reserving personal service for those who need it and may be happier to queue for longer periods of time to receive it.

An interesting approach is to look at the economics of queue management from the service provider and the customers' points of view. The customer may well be willing to wait longer if the expected value to be received is higher but will be unwilling to wait for a marginal service. Management must bear this in mind but must also consider the relative economics of differing forms of provision. Automated service may be provided at lower variable cost but at higher fixed cost. Alternatively, the human server is expensive but can be diverted to other tasks when demand is low.

A final point to bear in mind is the physical attractiveness of the location in which queuing is to take place and the clarity of signs denoting what service is being offered. It is most unpleasant to queue for a period of time and then discover that you are in the wrong place!

## The psychology of queuing

If we accept that queues are inevitable, then it is interesting to look at them from the point of view of the customer. How does it feel to be in a queue? What can management do in order to make a period of waiting less unpleasant?

Possible answers to these questions were explored in a classic article on the 'Psychology of Queues' by Maister (see Further Reading). It is suggested that there are two basic laws of service management, one of which we have had cause to mention earlier:

**'Satisfaction equals perception minus expectation'**

and the other which, unfortunately, seems equally true:

**'It is hard to catch up after a poor start'**

The latter is particularly relevant to the manager of a queue as queuing is often the first activity of a customer receiving service! These pertinent pieces of advice have been expanded into a series of propositions about how it feels to be in a queue. These may be summarised into the following basic points. After reading each point, you should try to think of examples of ways it could be used to improve the total service package on offer:

- Waiting is less unpleasant if you are doing something or your attention is in some way occupied.
- Queuing before you have received any service attention is more unpleasant than waiting which occurs after service has commenced.
- A period of waiting seems longer if you are anxious or worried.
- Waiting is more unpleasant if you don't know how long you will have to wait or if the wait seems unfair (perhaps because another customer appears to have had a shorter wait).
- Waiting is less unpleasant if you know why you have to wait, for example if someone has explained the situation to you.
- You will be more inclined to wait longer for a service you value than for a less important one.
- Waiting by yourself is more boring than waiting as part of a group.

**TASK**

> As a manager of a popular restaurant, how can you placate customers who may have to queue for service at a busy period, say, at lunch time?

With skill and experience you may be able to design a package of attractions which greatly reduces the unpleasantness of queuing. Typical examples quoted in case studies include the following possibilities:

- Occupy waiting time in a positive way such as examining a restaurant menu, having a drink, filling in a form, playing an arcade game and so forth.
- Entertain the queue, educate it or make the queue part of the experience as, for example, in a theme park where queuing round a ride builds up a sense of expectation.
- Communicate continually with customers in a queue to assure them that appropriate service will soon be provided.
- Break the service up into small packages with occupied periods of waiting between each.

**TASK**

> Despite an appointment system, patients and their accompanying friends and family often have to wait for long periods in a hospital out-patients department. Could some of the above ideas be used appropriately in order to manage this situation better?

## Mathematical models of queues

However hard we may try to improve the experience of queuing, it is important that we have ways to predict how long customers are likely to have to wait in a given situation. This information may be useful in adjusting some parameters of the system to keep queues within reasonable bounds. A simple example to visualise is a supermarket where the number of checkout points in operation may be reviewed as the number of customers in the store varies.

With experience, we may well be able to do this by trial and error but when initially designing a service situation we will still have to set up the basic structure of facilities (for instance the maximum number of available checkout points). In such cases the mathematical theory of queues may be of value.

Queuing theory is part of a general set of models which analyse and predict the behaviour of a range of time-varying systems where stocks and flows interact. Such models are usually based on probability theory, that is some degree of uncertainty is assumed in our knowledge of the timings of particular movements through the system. With human queues the flows are of people arriving for service, moving through the system, receiving service and departing. The 'stocks' are people waiting at various points in the system.

(Note: Can you think of other operational systems which might be modelled as stochastic (that is, probabilistic and time dependent) processes? Hint: Think of stocks and flows!)

Unfortunately, the formulae used in queuing theory can appear to be very complex. Unless you are interested in such things and wish to consult the more advanced texts mentioned at the end of this chapter, you can use computer packages to carry out the necessary computations.

### Single server systems

In the section below we introduce a simple model in some detail, in order to give you some idea of the value of such models, and also mention briefly some further possible models in order to widen the approach. The basic model assumes that there is a single service point and queue (or waiting line) with a first-come, first-served (FCFS) service discipline. Arrivals into the service system (that is, to the far end of the queue) are assumed to be at random but with a fixed, average rate. Individual service times also vary randomly with a fixed, average rate which must be greater than the arrival rate or the queue would tend to increase without limit.

(Note: The precise details of these 'random processes' of arrival and service are contained in more advanced texts and are only an approximation to real human behaviour. People do not actually behave randomly but react to their surroundings in complex ways which we have little hope of predicting in detail but may roughly model as a totality.)

The formulae relating to this system are shown in Figure 10.3, using the standard notation to be found in almost all texts. It is essential that you work through some examples in order to familiarise yourself with this material.

Poisson distribution of arrival rate
First-come, First-served (FCFS)
One server with negative exponential service times distribution

$\lambda$ = Mean rate of arrivals
$\mu$ = Mean rate of service
$\rho$ = Traffic intensity = $\lambda/\mu$

Assume $\rho < 1$

| Probability of no customers in the system | $1 - \rho$ |
| --- | --- |
| Average number of customers in the queue | $\dfrac{\rho^2}{1-\rho}$ |
| Average number of customers in the system | $\dfrac{\rho}{1-\rho}$ |
| Average time a customer is in the queue | $\left(\dfrac{\rho}{1-\rho}\right)\dfrac{1}{\mu}$ |
| Average time a customer is in the system | $\left(\dfrac{1}{1-\rho}\right)\dfrac{1}{\mu}$ |

**Fig. 10.3 Queuing model M/M/1**

## Example 1

Using the notation of the single server model, the following are observed in a queuing situation:

Mean rate of arrivals, $\lambda$ = 10 people per hour

Mean rate of service, $\mu$ = 20 people per hour

Hence we can calculate the traffic intensity, $\rho = \lambda/\mu = 10/20 = 0.5$

(This is a ratio of flow rates and therefore has no units of measurement itself.)

Probability of there being no customers in the system (a new customer will arrive and be served immediately) = $1 - \rho = 1 - 0.5 = 0.5$; or, 50 per cent of new arrivals will be served as soon as they arrive.

$$\text{Average number of customers in the queue} = \frac{\rho^2}{1-\rho} = 0.25/0.5 = 0.5$$

$$\text{Average number of customers in the system} = \frac{\rho}{1-\rho} = 0.5/0.5 = 1$$

$$\text{Average time a customer is in the queue} = \left(\frac{\rho}{1-\rho}\right)\frac{1}{\mu} = (0.5/0.5)/20 \text{ hours} = 3 \text{ mins}$$

$$\text{Average time a customer is in the system} = \left(\frac{1}{1-\rho}\right)\frac{1}{\mu} = (1/0.5)/20 \text{ hours} = 6 \text{ mins}$$

In total this represents a reasonable queuing experience. Fifty per cent of new customers are served immediately and the average queuing time is only three minutes.

One important point to note here, however, is the danger of averages. Though the average queuing time may be only three minutes, how many customers may have to wait for, say, ten minutes? The more advanced texts on queuing theory can throw light on such problems, which might also be approached through the use of Simulation (see Further Reading).

## Example 2

Assuming a similar situation to that given above, let us assume that the system gets busier!

Mean rate of arrivals, $\lambda = 16$ people per hour

Mean rate of service, $\mu = 20$ people per hour

Hence, we can calculate the traffic intensity, $\rho = \lambda/\mu = 16/20 = 0.8$

The probability of there being no customers in the system (a new customer will arrive and be served immediately) $= 1 - \rho = 1 - 0.8 = 0.2$; so only 20 per cent of new arrivals will be served as soon as they arrive.

$$\text{Average number of customers in the system} = \frac{\rho^2}{1-\rho} = 0.64/0.2 = 3.2$$

$$\text{Average number of customers in the system} = \frac{\rho}{1-\rho} = 0.8/0.2 = 4$$

$$\text{Average time a customer is in the queue} = \left(\frac{\rho}{1-\rho}\right)\frac{1}{\mu} = (0.8/0.2)/20 \text{ hours} = 12 \text{ mins}$$

$$\text{Average time a customer is in the system} = \left(\frac{1}{1-\rho}\right)\frac{1}{\mu} = (1/0.2)/20 \text{ hours} = 15 \text{ mins}$$

Even the 'average behaviour' given above represents a considerable deterioration of the quality of customer experience.

## Example 3

*Compute the above statistics for arrival rates ranging from one person per hour to 19 people per hour (with service rate fixed at 20 people per hour) and draw appropriate graphs (with traffic intensity on the horizontal axis) to show how the service to the customer deteriorates as traffic intensity goes above 0.7 (roughly). What are the implications of this for Operations Management?*

### Multi-server systems

In many service situations we have the option of increasing the number of service points in operation, at a cost, and would therefore like to be able to make predictions of the result of this use of resources. The model given in Figure 10.4 is based on this situation and it will be noted that the resulting formulae appear considerably more complex. Fortunately, the basic interpretation of the model is quite similar to that for single service systems.

Poisson distribution of arrival rate
First-come, First-served (FCFS)
$c$ independent servers with negative exponential service times distribution

$\lambda$ = Mean rate of arrivals
$\mu$ = Mean rate of service
$\rho$ = Traffic intensity = $\lambda/\mu$

Assume $\rho < c$

| | |
|---|---|
| Probability of no customers in the system | $P_0 = \left\{ \sum_{n=0}^{c-1} \frac{\rho^n}{n!} + \frac{\rho^c}{c! \, (1 - \rho/c)} \right\}^{-1}$ |
| Average number of customers in the queue | $L_q = \frac{\rho^{c+1}}{(c - 1)! \, (c - \rho)^2} P_0$ |
| Average number of customers in the system | $L_s = L_q + \rho$ |
| Average time a customer is in the queue | $W_q = \frac{L_q}{\lambda}$ |
| Average time a customer is in the system | $W_s = W_q + \frac{1}{\mu}$ |

**Fig. 10.4 Queuing model M/M/c**

Note: The standard formulae given in Figure 10.4 necessarily use a more advanced notation which may be unfamiliar to you. If so, you may wish simply to note the results.

## Example 4

Using the basic data in Example 2, we now open a second service channel. Thus:

$\lambda$ = 16 people per hour

$\mu$ = 20 people per hour

$\rho$ = 0.8

$c$ = 2

The most difficult part of the calculation is the following:

Probability of no customers in the system =

$$P_0 = \left\{ \sum_{n=0}^{c-1} \frac{\rho^n}{n!} + \frac{\rho^c}{c! \, (1 - \rho/c)} \right\}^{-1}$$

$$P_0 = \left\{ \sum_{n=0}^{n=1} \frac{0.8^n}{n!} + \frac{0.8^2}{2! \, (1 - 0.8/2)} \right\}^{-1} = \{1 + 0.8 + 0.64/1.2\}^{-1} = 0.42857$$

Average number of customers in the queue:

$$L_q = \frac{\rho^{c+1}}{(c-1)! \, (c-\rho)^2} \, P_0$$

$$L_q = \frac{0.8^3}{1! \, (2 - 0.8)^2} \, 0.42857 = 0.15238$$

Average number of customers in the system $L_s = L_q + \rho = 0.15238 + 0.8 = 0.95238$

Average time a customer is in the queue $W_q = \frac{L_q}{\lambda} = 0.15238/16$ hours = 0.57 mins

This represents a very considerable improvement on the 'single server' average queuing time of 12 minutes.

Average time a customer is in the system $W_s = W_q + \frac{1}{\mu} = 0.57 + 3 = 3.57$ minutes

## Example 5

If you are confident in carrying out the above calculations, then you should experiment with differing numbers of servers and flow rates, preferably using a spreadsheet or a programmable calculator to ease the burden of arithmetic.

**FURTHER READING**

Morris (1993) provides a suitable reference for the descriptive statistics necessary for a preliminary analysis of the Windsor Hotel case. Lovelock (1992) (pp. 176 to 187) gives an excellent article on the management of queues, including comments on Maister's model.

Technical details of the mathematics of queuing is in Taha (1992), including a discussion of Simulation modelling. Hall (1993) includes a computer package which provides answers to queuing problems as well as other material covered in this book.

Hall, O. P. (1993), *Computer Models for Operations Management* (2ed), Addison-Wesley, Reading.

Lovelock, C. H. (1992), *Managing Services* (2ed), Prentice-Hall, New York.

Morris, C. (1993), *Quantitative Approaches in Business Studies*, Pitman, London.

Taha, H. A. (1992), *Operations Research* (5ed), Macmillan, New York.

# CHAPTER 11

# Planning and Controlling Material Flows

**The objective of this chapter is to describe the dominant methods by which material flows are planned and controlled in a manufacturing context. This leads inevitably to a consideration of computer based planning techniques as well as the Just-in-Time philosophy of manufacturing management.**

## OBJECTIVES

**This chapter:**

- **introduces general concepts of supply chain management in a manufacturing context**
- **describes manufacturing resource planning**
- **explores the world of Just-in-Time manufacturing, including ways in which its main ideas can be incorporated into computer based approaches.**

**The numerical details of the above techniques are not described in detail in this text but may be found in other Operations Management and engineering texts. The emphasis here is on the underlying management principles of manufacturing management decision making and control.**

## INTRODUCTION

In previous chapters we have considered a number of issues connected with the management of material flows. In particular, Chapters 8 and 9 analysed problems of forecasting, aggregate planning and inventory control. Less obviously, the earlier discussions on such topics as process choice, technology and the management of quality addressed issues which in practice are central to the effective management of material flows. Line manufacturing, for example, assumes a fairly straightforward approach to layout and material flows whilst batch processing can result in very complex flows between machining centres. Similarly, it should be obvious that variable quality, possibly with materials being returned to earlier work stations for rework and rectification, can lead to a very confused and complex pattern of flows.

This chapter is concerned with planning and controlling flows rather than with issues of layout and the physical movement of materials. The latter is assumed to be an engineering matter since decisions are largely dependent on technical issues to be judged by specialists. This is in contrast to Chapter 10, relating to flows of people, where layout and physical movement are of more direct concern to Operational Managers.

To the outsider, technical issues of material transformation, physical movement and quality must appear to be the key factors in successfully managing production systems. Of course these matters are of importance in systems design and must be subject to continual monitoring and improvement. The issue which can, however, cause massive problems to an organisation, or be an important source of competitive edge, is the planning and subsequent control of flows. Part of the reason for difficulties in this area of work is the essentially integrative nature of such planning. One may be able to consider a machining or quality problem in isolation but the management of flows is mainly about co-ordination, possibly involving many outside companies. Planning and control are ongoing activities and have a direct impact on the customer. Finally, it does not appear possible to arrive at a definitive system which can be used to handle all flow decision making. Though this has been attempted (mainly through the use of MRP II – see below) it appears that the problem is simply too large and complex. Indeed systems such as JIT (also see below) explicitly recognise the need for continual human problem solving and innovation.

Planning and control must be carried out with respect to differing time scales and in differing degrees of detail. This is true whether we are talking about financial planning, human resource management or any other aspect of work. Long term issues of aggregate planning and capacity management have been introduced earlier but in this chapter we are concerned with medium and short term plans, right down to the level of what parts are machined on a particular day and when an actual customer will get the goods they have been promised. This represents the everyday work of many staff in the operations function and, like quality management, should be an area in which any Operations Manager is comfortable in their knowledge and have practical experience of delivery. Shopfloor control and inter-organisational logistics represent the sharp end of manufacturing operations.

# SUPPLY CHAIN MANAGEMENT

The recognition that issues of material flow should be considered holistically has been growing for a number of years. This has led to a number of conceptual approaches with varying degrees of success.

### Purchasing management

In a very traditional organisation, many different staff may purchase materials with resulting poor control of cost and confused relationships with suppliers. An obvious solution is the centralisation of purchasing as a separate function with professionally trained staff. As the proportion of product cost devoted to bought-in components and materials grows, there is an inescapable logic to the idea that the relationship with material suppliers must be as carefully managed as internal production operations.

The power and profit potential of the purchasing function in retailing can be seen as an example of the value of this approach.

### Materials management

For a number of years, organisations have experimented with the idea of similarly centralising the management of material flows within the organisation. The result has been the methodologies described later in this chapter.

### Physical distribution management

Moving from the supply side of the organisation (or 'upstream' if one prefers the river analogy) to the 'downstream' relationship with customers, the physical movement, transportation and warehousing of goods is an obvious area of activity to be seen as a whole, though whether it is part of the 'operations' or 'marketing' functions is often not clear. Once again, retailing provides an example of the potential value of good management in this area of work.

It should be clear to the reader that each of the three functions mentioned above may have problems at the boundaries with the others. Purchasing managers will see the materials manager as an internal customer but may well argue that economies may accrue to the organisation as a whole if they can influence production schedules rather than simply meet them. Indeed, in a highly technological organisation, the supply function can be a key source of innovation through searching the market for new components and sources of supply. Thus, a reactive role in merely meeting schedules may be a poor way to exploit the purchasing power of an organisation.

Similarly, the interface between production and market distribution can be uncomfortable with the two even working to different, possibly irreconcilable, schedules reflecting the tensions between what customers have been promised and what can be delivered. The key issues here are ease and readiness of communication, the regular flow of information and the pattern of organisational responsibilities for day-to-day decision making and control. There appears to be a growing case for even more integration!

## Logistics and supply chain management

Why do we not consider the entire flow of materials in an integrated fashion? This is common in retailing, under the heading of merchandising, when the lack of direct 'production' and the need to provide an often daily flow from producer to customer makes this a natural concept. In manufacturing the situation is far more complex. The 'logistics' concept is used in a number of ways from the management of transportation to the management of everything in a supply chain. The 'supply chain' concept is no less ambitious and refers unambiguously to the co-ordination of supply from as far upstream to as far downstream as the organisation can reasonably exercise control. Indeed, if an organisation considers itself expert at supply chain management, it need hardly bother with actually making things but may earn its money largely through such co-ordination. This is an extreme situation but it appears that maintaining ownership over core and highly profitable activities (such as design, marketing and some production) whilst managing all other activities as an external supply chain can be a very satisfactory strategy, incorporating a flexible attitude to capacity management.

Discussions of this type often lead to the highlighting of the benefits of ever increasing integration. It must be recognised that extremely effective information and management systems must be in place for such integration to work. Great strain is also placed on managers in such situations, particularly as crises occur. The organisational structure may well have to be redesigned, as with project management (see Chapter 6) although the result may not be the same. In this context it is interesting to compare this thrust towards supply chain integration with the methodology of Business Process Re-engineering. The latter may be a useful way of implementing the former but both may well have to be preceded by 'Business Re-engineering' where the fundamental structures, values and practices of an organisation are called into question.

**TASK**  If possible, consider your own organisation and the extent to which the 'supply chain' concept is in operation. Is your company's way of handling the total flow of materials effective?

## PRODUCTION MANAGEMENT SYSTEMS

We now move away from our strategic overview to a consideration of the particular methods which have been tried and tested as approaches to the management of material flows in a manufacturing context.

Some of the key approaches are shown in Figure 11.1. Scientific stock control was discussed in Chapter 9. It will be remembered that it was based on a 'disaggregation'

| SSC | MRP |
|---|---|
| Scientific Stock Control | MRP II Manufacturing Resource Planning |
| JIT | OPT |
| Just-In-Time | Optimised Production Technology |

**Fig. 11.1  Production management systems**

approach whereby each stock holding point was considered separately. This led to an easier analysis, suitable in the pre-computer age from which this approach dates, and also led us to consider some fundamental points about the balance of costs which are important in any approach.

The other three approaches shown in Figure 11.1 are discussed in separate sections below though it must be emphasised that the actual systems implemented in a given production context may be a mixture of all these approaches tailored to the specific context to be managed. Thus, an organisation may decide to use MRPII as a general planning framework; OPT to isolate bottlenecks and arrive at medium term plans; JIT as a means of shopfloor control away from the bottlenecks; and SSC to control raw material stocks from less reliable suppliers!

Let us ignore this complexity for the moment, however, and concentrate on the fundamental principles underlying the remaining three approaches.

## MANUFACTURING RESOURCE PLANNING

The idea that one should try to plan all the stocks and flows of materials in a manufacturing system as part of one big exercise is not new and, indeed, is really quite obvious. Attempts have been made throughout the century to do exactly that but have always resulted in partial approaches and useful rules of thumb simply because the total management problem is too difficult for a manual system.

Let us carry out a 'thought experiment' to see if we can specify a material flow control system. This will give us the opportunity to clarify our thoughts. At any point in this discussion you might like to stop and attempt to fill in the next stage before reading the text.

First, we must have good sources of data on projected customer demands. Knowledge of demand ultimately drives the system but unfortunately we may have to use a mixture of actual orders and forecasts based on past demands for specific product lines (note how we cannot now forecast in aggregate monetary terms – we are planning the production of actual items). We will, of course, have considerable problems with forecasting the demand for new products and declining ones, particularly if decline quickly follows growth as in the fashion goods trade.

Let us assume that we can arrive at an agreed list of demands for given products at specific points of time in the future, a database we will refer to as the 'Master Production Schedule' (MPS). It is obviously important that this database is agreed between production and marketing. Naturally, we will have less confidence in the reliability of the MPS as it extends further into the future.

Secondly, we must have a good knowledge of the internal production characteristics of our factory in terms of production capabilities (What can be done?) and capacity (How much can be made at specific points of time?). This must also include product characteristics, process times, routes and so forth. We must also be aware of new products and changes to existing products.

We will refer to the collection of data referring to product manufacturing details as the 'Bill of Materials' (BOM). This is usually organised hierarchically (for example, to make a table you need, amongst other things, four legs; each leg requires a variety of materials; each of these in turn requires ... ). The BOM also includes lead times for each stage of operation (for example, how long it takes to assemble a table, or batch of tables, from its parts).

We then require information on the characteristics of material suppliers, particularly the volumes which can be supplied and associated lead times (that is the time between placing an order and the actual receipt of the goods). Finally, we require up-to-date information on the current state of material stocks whether held in store or currently in-process (the Inventory File).

This is a demanding specification of information, much of which is continually changing. Firms which attempt to implement central computerised planning may fail at this first hurdle of data gathering or may attempt to run such systems with inadequate information.

This is a useful point at which to introduce a central issue in the design of planning systems, namely the extent to which such systems are robust in the face of data inaccuracies. We would like to design a system with a considerable degree of robustness but a central problem with highly integrated material planning systems is that a small mistake or inaccuracy in, for example, the availability of one component may hold up a large order and totally destroy our plans and schedules for the near future. Of course there are other problems which may also affect our schedules, such as poor quality and machine breakdowns as well as customers changing their minds.

Thus, we must find ways of making our manufacturing systems robust not only in the face of data inaccuracy but other disruptive features. We might do this through the use of a variety of buffers such as holding stocks, spare capacity or building some allowance into our time estimates. It should be obvious, however, that there are considerable costs involved in building what might be seen as 'waste' into our systems. Such an approach may also lead to a careless attitude on the part of staff to controlling such buffers. It is often easier to work in a buffered environment where your mistakes and inefficiencies are masked.

We might also attempt to make our manufacturing systems more flexible to give us room for manoeuvre when problems occur, such as switching to another machine or material supplier. Ironically, the more flexible a system is then the more decisions we have to make in its management and this in turn entails more information.

Assuming that we can manage to put together such information, presumably in the form of computerised databases, how do we link them to produce an effective planning and control system. One attempt is shown in Figure 11.2 which shows a very basic Materials Requirements Planning (MRP) system:

- Known orders and demand forecasts come together to form the MPS (which must be an agreed document to which the whole organisation can work).

- The MPS, BOM and Inventory File are now analysed through a process called 'netting and offsetting' to produce a detailed plan of what needs to be done on the factory floor (including timings) and what needs to be ordered from suppliers (again with timings).

- Actual work is now controlled against the plan in order to produce the goods, with replanning as necessary as demand and other factors change. The Inventory File is updated as goods are made or received.

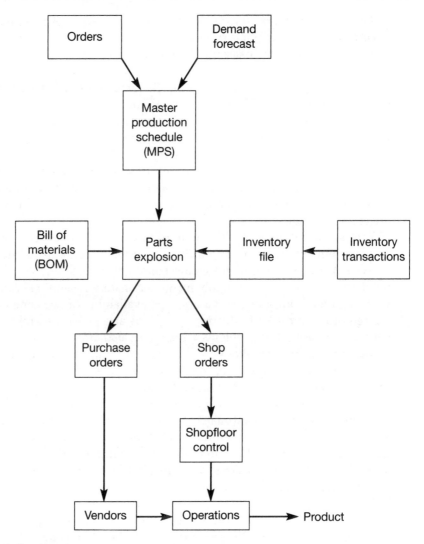

**Fig. 11.2 Basic MRP**

This sounds very straightforward at first but a number of problems have to be considered:

- The MPS includes 'known orders', but these presumably have been agreed through a process of order promising whereby sales staff tell a customer when a product can be made and delivered. This in turn requires a knowledge of current schedules and thus a continual cycle of planning and replanning is necessary. At worst this can become unstable but, in practice, some robust ways of giving reasonable dates based on rough schedules can be found.

- The individual manufacturing lead times (from the BOM and suppliers) may accumulate to a total lead time which is unacceptable to customers and is noncompetitive. In this case we must either find ways of reducing lead times or must either manufacture to a forecast (thus holding finished goods stocks against projected demand) or hold stocks of partly finished goods. Once again this introduces an additional cost into the system but this can be managed through holding minimal stocks of fairly common parts which can be quickly converted into the specific goods required.

- This form of planning and control is usually associated with batch production and it may not be economic to manufacture items in the exact batch sizes required by the customers. For a variety of technical reasons we may wish to manufacture in fixed batches. This once again is likely to lead to additional stock holding. A further and very important implication is that manufacturing lead times are likely to be dependent on batch sizes – at the simplest level, it takes longer to make a large batch and you will have longer to wait to make batch X if the preceding batch Y is also large.

- Continuing our consideration of lead times, we may ask why a lead time takes a specific value? In part it will depend on the processing time for the batch but it is likely also to include a large waiting time allowance as the batch waits for a machine, or the appropriate labour, to become free. Yet the actual waiting time must itself depend on schedules and we appear once again to have a circular line of reasoning – schedules depend on lead times which themselves depend on schedules! This point is directly addressed by OPT (see below).

- Even if we manage to work our way down the MRP process to a set of plans for shopfloor action we may then hit a massive problem. We have managed to conduct this whole discussion with little mention of capacity. It is quite likely that we simply do not have sufficient capacity (or the right kinds of available processing capacity) to make the schedules work. We must include at an earlier point in our planning some way of assessing capacity, but how do we do this until we actually know the schedules?

- It is difficult to know the effects that problems, changes and the other 'random shocks' which are commonplace in manufacturing will have on the final systems. Will the schedules be robust to such changes or will we be in the unacceptable situation of continually having to change our stated plans, which is unlikely to lead to a good relationship with our suppliers and customers.

- Finally the MPS (as well as the BOM) is continually changing through product design and our wish to meet customer needs. Indeed, the whole point of MRP, is to provide a planning vehicle for managing a continually changing pattern of demand. How often should we replan? Is it not possible that each stage of our replanning will introduce such drastic changes into our schedules that the whole exercise is largely meaningless?

It should be obvious from this set of potential problems (which is by no means exhaustive) that the simple MRP system of our 'thought experiment' must be considerably adapted or it simply will not work. There is no one simple way of doing this that will work for all situations. The problem really is very complex and difficult (although a massive amount of work has been done in an attempt to make centralised computer-based planning work) for reasons which should be obvious from our earlier discussion of supply chain management. This may be a difficult task but the rewards are also potentially great.

In Figure 11.3 we show some of the ways in which MRP can be enhanced to improve its performance. It must be said, however, that some of the problems to be overcome are very fundamental. The major change shown is the introduction of various forms of capacity check. Thus aggregate planning (see Chapter 8) provides a long-term framework for the amount of work which can be carried out at different points of time. Rough-cut Capacity Planning is meant to provide an immediate check on the likely feasibility of the MPS before the full 'parts explosion' is carried out. A variety of capacity planning methods (finite capacity schedulers) can be used at a later stage in order to fine-tune plans and schedules. In addition, it is essential that a formal 'Change Control' system be introduced for the Bill of Materials, particularly as frequent product changes are pursued by many organisations as the path to competitiveness.

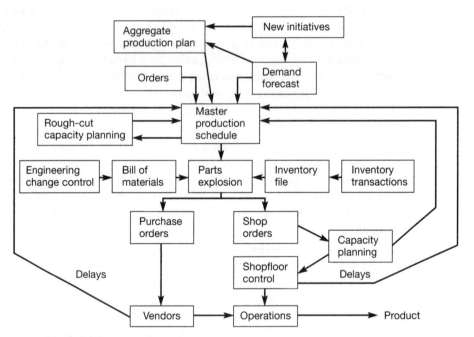

**Fig. 11.3 Closed loop MRP**

Finite capacity scheduling is a challenge in itself. Even if we are satisfied that sufficient capacity exists we still have a considerable technical problem in allocating that capacity to production activities in a way which minimises costs and meets customer delivery deadlines on a day-by-day basis. Though a number of manual techniques exist to handle such problems the interested reader is best advised to explore the relevant computer based packages. In the absence of these, considerable progress can be made and learning achieved through experimentation in the use of spreadsheets and relational database management systems for this and other aspects of MRP technique.

In spite of the problems evident from attempts to make integrated material flow systems, the advantages to be gained are so considerable that even higher degrees of integration are attempted. MRPII (Manufacturing Resource Planning) links the above with other commercial and engineering design systems as part of a move towards Computer Integrated Manufacturing (CIM).

# JUST-IN-TIME MANUFACTURING

The complexities of MRP can be very frustrating and lead one to ask a rather obvious question: 'Is it possible to develop a simple system for the control of material flows which avoids these difficulties without the extensive use of buffer stocks?'

Engineers at the Japanese car manufacturer Toyota faced a similar problem in the early 1960s when growing demand and a shortage of finance for raw materials forced them to rethink how production could be made more effective and economical.

Once again, let us engage in a 'thought experiment', this time with the objective of uncovering the barriers to stockless production. The first step is to ask what production control mechanism might lead to manufacturing with minimum stocks. This leads directly to the idea of 'pull scheduling'.

In one sense all production is based on the pull of demand from the customer but this is handled in different ways. Within MRP, the various 'pulls' of individual customers' orders and forecasts are combined into a schedule which is used to plan production. Goods are then 'pushed' through the supply chain by a series of decisions and actions with the intention of being available when the schedule states that they should be. As we saw in the previous section, this may well lead to stockholding at various points in the chain, even if the schedule remains valid.

An alternative approach is to wait until a demand actually occurs and then to directly supply to meet this demand. The idea is that the customer tells the provider that something is required and each operation up the chain makes similar demands on its suppliers. Eventually, raw materials are provided and pass downstream through the chain, with various operations being carried out on them, until the finished product reaches the customer. This avoids stockholding and also ensures that the customer, eventually, receives the product requested. There is obviously a similarity with service situations and job shop manufacture where the customer triggers the action.

The drawbacks to this scenario should be clear – the customer has to wait the full supply lead-time before the goods are received and we have once again assumed infinite capacity as the process in question may be occupied in fulfilling other demands. Of course, if we have overcapacity or the customer will accept a queuing situation then the latter point may be met. The earlier point does seem to present considerable problems.

Let us work a little harder at trying to make a 'pull' situation work. Consider a comparison with retailing where the customer will accept a limited choice of goods (relative to the totality of all goods that could have been provided) but also expects to pick them from the supermarket shelf. Here some stock has to be held but could we keep this to a minimum? Could we arrange for reductions in shelf stock to trigger replenishment immediately from the supply chain?

This requires good communication along the supply chain and the possibility of fast and economic response. Back in a factory context, let us assume that customer demand draws from a small finished goods stock but that a signal (the Japanese word 'Kanban' is usually used here) is sent upstream to the next process in the line requesting more stock. The process commences production which means it draws on its own stocks of raw materials and must then also issue appropriate Kanbans for replenishment. This continues up the line and on into suppliers (if they are contracted for JIT supply) or to raw material stocks which are managed in more conventional ways. The rule usually adopted is that production (or movement) of goods is only allowed on receipt of a Kanban and only in the quantity specified. Items are neither made nor moved down the chain without the authorisation of a Kanban and thus stocks are not allowed to build up beyond a level set by the physical number of Kanbans in circulation.

Though logically elegant, this arrangement does give the picture of idle workstations waiting for something to happen, with occasional frenzied activity. Also one must ask what is likely to be the effect of process breakdowns, quality problems, temporary labour shortages and so forth. The originators of this concept were so intent on achieving the benefits of stockless production that they worked hard to solve these problems. The resulting methodology was eventually disseminated to the West in the 1980s under the title of Just-in-Time (JIT) production and the following paragraphs follow a fairly standard description. (See Further Reading at the end of the chapter for the origins of the ideas and sources of further material; this is an area where it is wise to read widely to gain a full appreciation of the ideas involved.)

JIT manufacture is best seen as an ideal towards which a company may travel, though never finally arrive. The goal is sometimes stated as the elimination of waste, but in this context 'waste' has a very broad meaning. It includes stockholding, poor quality, delays due to machine breakdowns; in fact any non-value-adding activity. The elimination of waste is to be achieved through the development of the human resources in an organisation, both in terms of their skills and their creativity. The result is intended to be a conceptually simple material control process based on pull scheduling but built on the integrated effort of everyone in the organisation to achieve an environment in which JIT is possible.

This latter point is best shown through the use of the 'Stage 1–Stage 2' model of JIT implementation. The Stage 1 activities prepare the ground without actually introducing pull scheduling. Without them, pull scheduling simply will not work as we showed in the description above. The Stage 1 activities typically are the following:

- Focusing on the most important products and the key resources which are required to make them and organising the production environment in the most appropriate way, for instance through a concern for machine layout and material flow. A typical JIT layout will emphasise individual lines for products or families of similar products with workstations (often involving small machines) close together to minimise the distances to be travelled by materials.

- For the chosen products, great care will be taken in design (for instance to use common parts and ensure ease of manufacture).

- Quality control is paramount in such systems with an emphasis on Statistical Process Control.

- Machine maintenance will be carefully planned to avoid any disruption to planned production time through breakdowns or routine maintenance.

- Set-up reduction is a key engineering technique in JIT implementation because the 'small batch' system to be introduced will require extreme machine flexibility in terms of frequent and quick changeovers between products.

- Issues of training and education must also be addressed and staff must be prepared for new working disciplines, although the changes listed above will provide a good introduction to what is likely to happen next. Training should also be aimed at multi-skilling the workforce and improving flexibility. The most difficult parts of this may involve changes of status and patterns of reward for production workers, particularly if this entails a move away from individual bonus systems towards group bonuses.

Implementation of Stage 1 techniques will entail some expenditure but the general advantages gained, though not as dramatic as those to be sought through pull scheduling, should still cover costs and lead to a far simpler, cleaner and more effective working environment. It may even be argued that the above could be effective when linked with almost any production control methodology. In many ways they simply represent good production management practice.

Stage 2 JIT is far more ambitious and cannot be sensibly attempted unless Stage 1 advantages have been achieved. It consists of the following:

- Ensuring that all aspects of production management and control are visible. This notion leads to the display of quality information, schedules, progress, productivity and any other key aspect of work performance. If anything goes wrong or has the potential to go wrong then it must be noted immediately and acted upon. The reason for visibility is to promote quick remedial action and to allow for a very 'hands-on' form of management and shopfloor control.

- Involvement of people in problem solving and enforced improvement. At its best, this leads to empowerment of the workforce, engineers and technical staff not only to solve current problems but also to continually set new challenges (for instance, to achieve a given result with less resource, at less cost or in less time). It can only be carried out with a well-informed and highly motivated group who also have the knowledge and skills to effect improvements. This may well require considerable changes in the attitude of management as well as shopfloor staff.

- Pull scheduling of small batches should now be possible as the main barriers have been removed. The workplace should have the flexibility to respond quickly to changes in customer demand and work should flow very quickly through the factory thus removing the principal objection to pull scheduling, that is, that it results in long lead-times. One interesting point to make is that this form of production is based on a virtuous circle: good quality management helps pull scheduling, which leads to a fast throughput of goods, which makes quality problems immediately visible, which facilitates good quality management, and so forth!

- Supplier JIT can now be seen as a future goal as in-factory JIT provides a good base for involving and educating suppliers.

This form of manufacture has had a large effect, particularly in industries which are mainly concerned with high volume assembly (cars and electronics). In effect, although originating in an attempt to improve batch manufacturing, it appears to be a more responsive and adaptable form of mass production and can lead to decisive competitive advantage. One cannot be sure as to the extent to which a full-blown form of JIT has been developed outside a narrow range of frequently quoted manufacturers, but the underlying ideas have had a considerable effect. Even if a company only takes onboard the ethos of good housekeeping, quality and worker involvement it will have gone some way towards improvement and the further steps of set-up reduction and performance visibility will eventually be less difficult to achieve.

The drawbacks of JIT are the long implementation times and the lack of an explicit long and medium term planning framework. This latter point is addressed by JIT manufacturers through the development of computer based planning and commercial systems. In fact some see JIT and MRP as complementary in many situations, the former addressing issues of shopfloor control and the latter providing a customer interface and platform for planning.

## OPTIMISED PRODUCTION TECHNOLOGY

The final method to be examined is an attempt to gain the advantages of JIT and of computer based planning without the drawback of a long development period. It is based on the original work of E. M. Goldratt and has been developed into a comprehensive treatment involving planning systems, general production management and accounting systems for the workplace.

The key concept is the notion of a bottleneck. This is a capacity constraint which restricts the actual throughput of goods to the customer and hence acts as a restraint on the revenue potential of the organisation. It is argued that the flow through bottlenecks should be maximised by taking all reasonable, cost-effective measures and that schedules should be organised with this in mind.

The heart of the OPT system is a computer package which identifies bottlenecks. These may change with differing product mixes and volumes and hence their identification is dependent on a Master Production Schedule, as with MRP. Detailed work schedules are then derived for all activities which influence the flow through the bottlenecks. It is considered reasonable that a large batch form of production may be preferred at a bottleneck even though this may lead to the build up of some stocks in the system. When a resource centre, however, is not a bottleneck, nor affects one, then small batch, JIT-style approaches are more useful as the need is now to keep stocks down rather than increase the flow rate.

This approach, which differentiates parts of a system depending on their effect on constraining final throughput, is both sensible and should be a guiding principle in any form of production planning. The strength of OPT is the determined way in which this line of logic is pushed through to its conclusion. It avoids the illogicality of predetermined lead-times (in OPT lead-times are determined by the schedule and not vice versa) and allows for a sensible approach to batch sizing. Its basic approach is that of a finite capacity scheduling package but with the added attractions of sound advice and rules of thumb on the basics of production management.

The software is highly complex and expensive, though its use may still be profitable for large organisations. There is, of course, no reason why other finite capacity scheduling packages may not be used as alternatives, though a less sophisticated organisation may be wary of such a technical solution being applied to a central business process.

## SUMMARY AND CONCLUSIONS

The above methods provide a formidable array of tools to handle material flow situations in manufacturing. They also show the tight links which exist with other areas of concern for the Operations Manager. It is perhaps surprising, therefore, that the planning and control of flows remains a problematic area. The point, that must be realised, of course, is that we are addressing a central concern which is highly integrated and highly competitive. Whatever levels of performance are achieved by one company in terms of order promising, delivery performance and cost effectiveness are then merely a challenge to all the others to emulate or exceed. The target is therefore always moving and systems must be continually improving in order to keep up.

This leads us finally to consider the implementation and continual improvement of planning and control systems. As we summarise in Figure 11.4, stock control systems, although usually computerised are not always systematically reviewed and improved, except perhaps as new software becomes available. In fact, stock control systems are now likely to be parts of larger packages, modules to be added on as need arises. Therefore it is ever more important to review the performance of such systems regularly and to have an accepted procedure for introducing modifications and improvements. It may not be effective to leave such reviews to information managers (with little direct contact with material flow) or to finance managers (with a possibly one-sided view of the cost implications of holding stock).

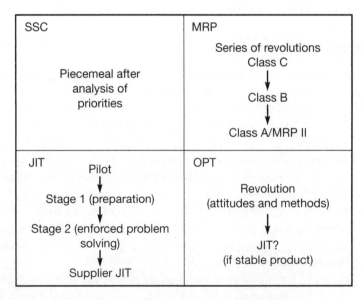

**Fig. 11.4 Implementation of production management systems**

Just-in-time management has the great advantage of having a built in review mechanism. It explicitly sees performance as relating to a moving target, indeed the movements in the target are often generated internally. The problem with this approach may be perceived to be its slow and gradual nature. Once again this has advantages in securing the commitment of all involved but the final timescale may simply be too long. Of course it is possible to import new techniques and ways of working from other organisations. The Japanese transplant factories in the UK have the advantage of incorporating the years of learning carried out by the parent factories in Japan. This form of 'organisational learning' (see Chapter 4) is crucial to strategic improvement and can to a limited extent be 'bought-in'.

MRP and OPT are computer based methodologies, the principles of which each can be used in any context to throw light on problems of work and to improve working practices. There is, however, an extent to which their introduction involves a revolution in systems, attitudes and methods of working. This can lead to very considerable problems as has been extensively documented in the case of MRP. Both can be implemented to a greater or lesser extent in a given manufacturing context and MRP at least can be progressed to MRP II and wider levels of systems integration. In both cases there is a danger that the system and its implementation project are 'owned' by middle managers and technical staff without the broad levels of commitment of workers.

If these systems are now to be integrated with broader commercial systems and communication networks to form the basis for supply chain management, then the commitment and involvement of almost all functions in an organisation becomes essential. This is a very major strategic issue involving large expenditure in pursuit of high potential gains.

As a final point one should note the very real difficulties of financially justifying the investment costs of such systems changes. It is possible that both likely costs and potential benefits will be underestimated in such an analysis thus making justification and project cost control difficult.

## FURTHER READING

For comprehensive details of all the areas of work mentioned above see Vollman et al. (1992). Good general background is contained in Browne et al. (1988). JIT is specifically addressed in Bicheno (1991) (a comprehensive statement of the 2 stage model). The novel written by Goldratt and Cox (1992) provides a gentle introduction to the ideas underlying OPT. Schonberger (1986) and Womack et al. (1990) give valuable case study background on the potential of JIT and similar methodologies.

Bicheno, J. (1991), *Cause and Effect JIT*, PICSIE Books, Buckingham.

Browne, J., Harhen, J. and Shivnan, J. (1988), *Production Management Systems*, Addison Wesley, Wokingham.

Goldratt, E. M. and Cox, J. (1992), *The Goal*, Gower, Aldershot.

Schonberger, R. J. (1986), *World Class Manufacturing*, Free Press, New York.

Vollman, T. E., Berry, W. L. and Whybark, D. C. (1992), *Manufacturing Planning and Control Systems* (3ed), Irwin, Homewood.

Womack, J. P., Jones, D. T. and Roos, D. (1990), *The Machine that Changed the World*, Rawson Associates, New York.

# CHAPTER 12

# Strategic Issues

In this final chapter we draw together some of the major themes in the book in a strategic context. We also look forward to areas of work, such as strategic management, which play an important part in the later stages of business and management courses.

## OBJECTIVES

This chapter:

- describes some of the main strands in operations strategy, thus providing a link with future studies in corporate strategy
- discusses some issues in productivity, learning and flexibility, each being major sources of competitive advantage for an organisation
- briefly introduces some of the key ideas that link operations with the important emerging area of environmental management.

## INTRODUCTION

In this chapter we draw together some of the strands of thinking from the previous chapters by asking fundamental questions regarding key issues in the design of operational systems. This leads on to a discussion of the issues of productivity, learning and flexibility in order to show how these concepts are central to systems design.

We then look briefly at the impact of current ideas on environmental management on operations. This gives us the opportunity to gain a fresh perspective whilst at the same time emphasising the strategic assumptions underlying any set of operational decisions. There is not one comprehensive and correct prescription for managing operations. The fundamental aims, policies and values of the organisation provide a context which radically affects operational strategies within a given economic and competitive setting.

The first section in the chapter therefore introduces some of the issues in operations strategy. This is intended to provide a link between the long-term management of an organisation as a whole and its operational systems and policies.

## OPERATIONS STRATEGY

Operational decisions often have long-term consequences. Investments in sites, buildings, retail outlets, warehouses, plant and equipment are obviously major commitments and may bind a company into following a given developmental path for many years into the future. Similarly investments in people, training, knowledge acquisition and planning and control systems may commit a company to considerable ongoing expenditure. Such decisions must be made in full knowledge of the strategic direction an organisation wishes to follow.

Under the general umbrella of corporate policy, a key linkage must be made between operations strategies and marketing strategies. Assuming an organisation is market led, the marketing function has an obvious responsibility in anticipating future markets and liaising with other functions in setting out the intended products and services for those markets. It also has a key role in planning volumes and timings of product and service offerings in various markets. Such planning must relate to operational capacity and capability. In a manufacturing context one must be able actually to make what is required in sufficient volumes at the right times for market plans to be realised.

A number of methodologies exist for expressing this strategic relationship between operations and marketing. One key contribution (Hill 1985) emphasises the importance of developing a profile of operational characteristics (for example, process choice, manufacturing methods and control systems) which matches the life cycles of products and the decision making priorities of customers. For example, with a new product, a customer may make a purchase decision on the basis of design, performance and availability with less emphasis on price. Thus the manufacturer must make sure that delivery promises are kept and products do actually work!

For a mature product in a competitive market, the customer may simply not be interested in any offering which falls below a basic threshold level of quality, performance, design and so forth (referred to as 'qualifying criteria'). The purchase decision may then be made on the basis of price and service (the 'order winning' criteria). This places great stress on the manufacturer to achieve consistent output at low cost, which fortunately may be quite possible as the manufacturer should be a long way along the learning curve. Things may, however, be difficult for a new entrant to that market unless some new product design or form of production technology can be found.

**TASK**

Consider a service system, for instance a private health care organisation. Describe some typical characteristics of the market served by such an organisation and use these to profile the operational capabilities which the organisation must be able to provide.

(Hint: Consider a small organisation with a well-defined market niche, for example one providing services for the elderly or for individuals with a particular form of illness or disability. This will make it easier to list the necessary operational capabilities required.)

# THE KEY OPERATIONAL DECISIONS

In most operational situations we do not have the advantage of starting with a clean slate. Previous management has left us with factories, shops, warehouses, a workforce and customers. We might wish to change some or all of these things, and indeed we may do exactly that, but the history of the organisation acts as a constraint.

Let us suppose, however, we are in a position to set up operations in a 'greenfield' situation. What should we do? What plant should we buy? How much labour? etc. Perhaps it would be better if we take a step back and ask the more basic question: *'What decisions must we make?'*

Let us simplify this further in three ways. First of all we assume that a well-defined corporate and marketing strategy exist for the organisation. Then we divide our decision making into two distinct, though connected, areas: process design and infrastructure design. For simplicity we will initially consider only the decisions involved in setting up a manufacturing plant.

## Process design

By process design we are referring to the decisions which relate to the direct transformation of materials into finished goods. Starting with a specification of what the customer wants we must decide:

- how, in general terms, the required goods are to be made (the materials and process which are likely to be involved)
- how much of this activity we wish to carry out ourselves (do we wish to make everything from the most basic raw materials or do we buy in components and assemble them)
- process specifications for the work we are to do ourselves and material specifications for bought in parts
- basic issues of process choice (batch or line) and the required flexibility of processes
- the actual transformational process, with particular attention to the mix of labour and equipment
- the equipment to be used and the skills required of the workforce
- the capacity of the process
- the location of the process and associated warehousing
- the physical organisation of the process, including layout and materials movement.

## Infrastructure design

A transformational process will not work in isolation. It must have a context, in this instance defined by answers to the following questions:

- *What is the link with product design? How are new designs and modifications to existing products brought into regular production?*

- *How is quality controlled and improved?*
- *How is the flow of materials planned and controlled?*
- *What information systems (manual and computer based) are necessary to support production and provide interfaces with other functions?*
- *How are the equipment and buildings to be maintained?*
- *How are human resource needs to be met? (For example, from motivation and reward to training and welfare, not forgetting safety?)*

This may be an exhausting list (though by no means exhaustive). Perhaps you might like to try to develop something similar for service operations and office operations. Remember that in a service context one has many of the characteristics of manufacturing but with the added concern of the presence of the customer.

**TASKS**

1. Starting with the lists above, outline in general the decisions necessary to set up a service facility paying particular attention to the extra features relevant to customer presence. (Hint: Look again at the discussion of Service Quality in Chapter 2 and Service Process Choice in Chapter 1.)

2. Choose a particular example (for instance a new theatre) and look at the decisions to be made.

3. Carry out a similar exercise in an office management context, preferably after observing activities in an actual office.

Of course, in most situations we come across we do not have a free hand to design and change as we see fit. We start with existing facilities and, thus, a number of choices have been made for us. We might then ask the following questions:

- How well is the existing process performing compared with similar processes in other organisations or parts of our organisation? (We benchmark the process.)
- What would we have done if starting from scratch? Could we have done better?
- What freedom do we have to change things and how does this relate to parts of the process which are not performing as well as they might?
- Do we have the authority and power to make changes? Can we influence decision making sufficiently to make appropriate changes?

Now if the process is performing well and we can't think of anything we would have done better or alternatively we don't think we have the freedom or power to change things then perhaps we have no alternative but to get on with managing the process to the best of our ability. On the other hand this is hardly a creative approach! Perhaps we should look harder at the possibilities for improvement and look more widely at methods employed by other organisations.

# PRODUCTIVITY, LEARNING AND FLEXIBILITY

The above three aspects of operational systems are often discussed as separate entities and yet they are obviously linked if we are thinking strategically.

Productivity is concerned with the effectiveness with which inputs are transformed into outputs. It is a term also used by economists and engineers and although an apparently straightforward concept it is actually quite hard to measure productivity in a practical context.

Learning relates to the changing relationship between input and output as a system is used over a period of time and experience is gained. Thus, whilst productivity relates to points in time, learning is concerned with changes and improvements over time.

Flexibility addresses the key managerial issue of whether a system can adapt to changing needs. This, once again, is a more subtle point than one might at first expect. One form of required adaptation is the ability to do something new. Another refers to the speed with which a system can move from doing one thing to doing another, even if it has had experience of the latter in the past.

Let us examine the issues surrounding productivity in more detail before making further general points regarding the inter-relationships between these concepts.

## Productivity

Though we could leave this as a general and vague notion for discussion, there are obvious advantages if we can find ways to measure productivity. Remembering that productivity is concerned with the relationship between inputs and outputs, we might proceed as follows.

If we are using one performance related input to produce a single output, then a simple ratio of the two might indicate productivity. For example if we are using labour to attach components to a printed circuit board, then if we observe that 100 hours of labour are required to make 50 boards then equivalent measures of productivity are:

one hour of labour produces 0.5 boards (a 'single factor productivity' measure)

two hours of labour are needed to make one board (a 'technology coefficient')

Notice that we have not, as yet, concerned ourselves with the materials required in this context. If some wastage in materials is observed, then we will note that the yield is less than 100 per cent. Similarly, we have not concerned ourselves with machinery and the use of other fixed assets. We are assuming that sufficient supplies of these are available. Finally, if asked the question whether the same source of labour could make other products we might reply that this is a separate productivity question.

Thus if we are prepared to make a number of simplifying assumptions then we can use single factor productivity measures. This is an important point as multiple factor productivity measures (where the performance of a system is dependent on several performance related inputs) are far more difficult to define and interpret. This is partly due to the fact that different inputs may be measured in different ways and have different (possibly varying) prices attached to them. In the Further Reading at the end of the chapter we provide references relating to this problem.

Returning to our single factor case, we have arrived at a measurement which seems quite concrete and reliable – one hour of labour makes 0.5 boards. Perhaps this is a positive achievement compared to last month when one hour of labour made 0.4 boards. Productivity has gone up by 25 per cent! Has the labour force worked 25 per cent harder? This may be true but we should stop at this point and consider other reasons why this apparent productivity increase has occurred:

- the specification for the board has changed and it is now easier to make
- different components are being used (possibly fewer but more expensive integrated components)
- new technology has been introduced to make the work easier and faster
- in the previous month, there was a shortage of materials or of orders and the workforce were not making these boards for part of the time or perhaps working slowly compared with the current rush for output volumes
- last month the product was new and the workforce had to learn how best to do the job
- more experienced workers (with higher rates of pay) are now being used on this production line
- last month only 200 boards were made in a 'job-shop' context whilst this month a production line has been set up to make 1000 boards
- current high productivity is being obtained at the expense of reduced yield or poor product quality
- last month frequent set-ups were required as work changed between a variety of jobs whilst this month the work schedules allowed larger batches to be made.

Any experienced production manager could extend this list of alternative reasons for apparent productivity changes. It merely illustrates the difference between measuring something and tying down cause and effect relationships. We might see this as a reason for setting up ever more comprehensive measurement systems in order to isolate the causes of productivity changes. An alternative approach is to set up simple financial measures, preferably related to the financial performance measures of the organisation as a whole, and to assume that managers who are close to the job can find practical reasons for changes in these financial measures and take appropriate actions.

Whatever approach is taken it is obvious that:

- productivity is important
- productivity must be managed continually
- measuring productivity and productivity changes is important as the basis of a monitoring and control system for productivity
- productivity is affected by many factors, even if our measurements concentrate on a small number of factors
- the cause and effect relationships between the factors are hard to untangle and continually change over time.

It is, therefore, easy to see why successful manufacturers, such as the Japanese car and electronic goods makers in the past decades, have paid such an obsessive interest in the management and improvement of shopfloor productivity. Much of the emphasis on 'quality management' is concerned as much with productivity improvement as with improving the quality of goods received by the customer. In fact the customer gains in two ways by such efforts – product quality goes up and prices come down (as high volume and productivity brings down costs).

Office productivity, relating to information processing, is subject to much the same concerns as manufacturing and modern computing systems emphasise productivity improvements through high performance hardware and software and greater inter-connectivity between systems and users. The service industries, as usual, are more problematic. Whilst technology may often be used to increase the productivity of mass service delivery, other forms of service often have a far more subtle relationship between outputs and inputs, the latter depending partly on the customer in any case. Indeed service productivity may often be sought through arranging for the customer to do more of the work!

## Learning and flexibility

The idea of quantifying learning in a productive system and arriving at a learning curve has been well known to engineers for some time and strategic learning is a key component in some theories of corporate planning. Empirical studies of learning curves often show dramatic improvements in productivity over time and these may translate into genuine strategic competitive advantage. Whereas the productivity improvements resulting from the use of line and repetitive manufacture to achieve high volumes are referred to as 'economies of scale', the learning curve shows a 'dynamic' scale economy whereby volume of manufacture provides the basis for learning and makes the effort involved in detailed and meticulous improvement pro-grammes worthwhile.

Thus manufacturing a fairly standard item in very high volumes gives two very substantial advantages to the producer – the ability to gain economies of scale through the use of a dedicated, highly engineered plant and the opportunity to learn and to refine manufacturing methods and processes over time. This form of manufacture was well understood by Ford in the early part of the twentieth century. Its disadvantages are also well known. Other firms may be able to duplicate such methods, thus giving rise to fierce competition, and the customer may require greater variety and innovation in the goods they receive.

Many of the recent advances in engineering have been aimed at developing manu-facturing systems which will allow for flexibility in production at low cost whilst maintaining quality. Other advances have targeted the effective development of new products and their translation into full production. Thus both major issues are being addressed – the ability to make new products and also to change over from making one product to another.

There is far more to flexibility in operational systems, however, than the direct man-agement of machine-based processes. We must also be able to maintain flexibility in our relationships with suppliers, with labour, in developing new control systems and in our relationship with the organisation as a whole. Technology continually provides us with possibilities for improved systems but their implementation can have widespread consequences. An interesting example is provided by computer integrated manufacturing which not only offers advantages in operational planning and control, but improved links with other commercial systems.

It should always be remembered that flexible and responsive operations, whether in the manufacturing or service sectors, may fail to promote high organisational performance if other commercial systems are not in tune with them. In this context it becomes obvious why recent methods such as business process re-engineering address organisational processes as a whole with little respect for functional boundaries. The issues then become ones of strategy and organisational design, an appropriate emphasis with which to leave this discussion.

## ENVIRONMENTAL MANAGEMENT AND OPERATIONS

An area of considerable concern to modern management as well as the general public is the effects that organisations have on the environment. Here we are not using the word environment in its systems context, meaning anything outside a system or organisation, but in its more everyday, 'green' sense. Organisations are often felt to have a harmful effect on the natural and social environments through their usage of natural resources and their production of waste. It is often the day-to-day operations of an organisation which appear most culpable in this context, though product design and misuse can be equally to blame.

Therefore green issues are of concern to the Operations Manager. This obviously relates to manufacturing, though service industries, such as tourist industries, may similarly affect the environment. Most of the literature and the principal causes of public outrage, however, seem to relate to manufacturing and the transportation of materials (such as oil and chemicals) and thus we will concentrate on this in the following discussion.

A useful first step, however, is away from the direct operational issues and towards the fundamental objectives of organisations and their recognition of the rights of various stakeholders. A useful device for structuring our thought is the following hierarchy of organisational objectives:

- cost minimisation
- short-term profit maximisation
- long-term profit maximisation and strategic innovation
- planning for uncertainty and risk
- holistic management.

It is argued in the literature that organisations differ dramatically in their underlying value systems which gives rise to fundamental differences in stated objectives. If the goal is cost minimisation or short-term profit maximisation then it is unlikely that constructive, environmental action will be taken. If, however, one sees the future of an organisation as a long-term venture then innovation and risk management become important. Holistic management is a term sometimes used when an organisation is to be seen as a constructive part of the environment.

This latter point may be related to the difficult concept of sustainability. Sustainable development has been defined as:

**...development which meets the needs of the present generation without compromising the ability of future generations to meet their own needs.** (Turner et al. 1994)

On the one hand this is a very laudable aim and the holistic organisation might even aim to improve the position for future generations. It might equally be argued, however, that any use of non-renewable natural resources inevitably compromises sustainability as do forms of pollution whose effects persist over time. This whole area is, not surprisingly, one of vigorous debate by economists and other scientists.

Whilst traditional business literature refers to the foremost objective of an organisation as generating wealth for its shareholders, another approach uses the language of 'stakeholders'. These are individuals and other organisations which have a valid interest in the future of a firm and include customers, employees, insurers and the community at large as well as more obvious providers of finance. Now one may argue that having an eye to the well-being of stakeholders will, in the long-term, generate wealth for shareholders and hence there is no contradiction here. This is, of course, linked with future vision and long-term objectives. The cost minimiser may in practice take actions which benefit some stakeholders but is likely to do other things which act against the interests of others.

Of course, some might argue that this is an ethical rather than a practical debate. Interestingly this argument can be used both by the supporters of a broad or a narrow view of stakeholder concerns. The danger for the Operations Manager is that unresolved strategic tensions exist within an organisation and that public anger is aimed at those involved in day-to-day management.

Since environmental policy and management are long-term issues, there is a danger that nothing will be done about them unless there is an emergency or unless legislation is brought in to curb undesirable practices. Specialists in promoting good environmental practice therefore emphasise three important factors. The first is the need for a company to have a genuine environmental policy in order to focus action and free resources. Fortunately such a policy can also be used in a public relations context which may prove attractive for senior management anxious not to appear to be wasting money!

The second good practice is to institute various systematic forms of environmental review which not only bring environmental issues to light but also measure the risks involved. The final point made is that good systems are not only environmentally friendly but also cost effective; a simple example would be energy conservation.

Environmental reviews will naturally cover many aspects of operations as well as product design. Typical targets will include the sourcing of energy and materials, effectiveness of processes, waste management, transport, packaging and issues relating to health and safety. Waste management in itself is a large area of concern with ramifications going far beyond waste disposal and towards product and process design.

A useful review methodology is product life-cycle assessment, sometimes called 'cradle to grave' assessment. As we mentioned in Chapter 2, the Taguchi approach to quality costing reflects the view that when designing products we should take a very long-term perspective and examine all issues from the extraction of the raw materials used to make the product to its eventual disposal at the end of its useful life. Naturally this has many implications for the design of manufacturing and service operations. It should, however, be noted that no matter how clear and attractive the concept, life-cycle assessment may be very hard to carry out due to the large number of areas of impact a major product, such as a car, may have on the environment.

## FURTHER READING

It is particularly valuable to study operations strategy at the same time as taking a course in corporate strategy. This gives one the opportunity to see clearly the relationships between them. One of the earliest texts in the USA on manufacturing strategy was Hayes and Wheelwright (1984) which was soon followed in the UK by Hill (1985). Both texts are valuable for the serious student of operations strategy (although they refer exclusively to manufacturing) and the latter provides a good description of process profiling. Garvin (1992) contains a large number of mainly manufacturing case studies which are of particular value in bringing the subject of operations strategy to life for the reader.

Service operations strategy is harder to pin down but Lovelock (1992) provides a useful set of readings and cases. A general picture is painted in Harrison (1993), which includes further discussion on productivity and flexibility. Slack et al. (1995) includes much discussion on flexibility as well as extensive discussion and cases on strategic issues in operations.

Much of the material in Welford and Gouldson (1993) relates environmental concerns to operations. The accompanying case book on environmental management (Welford (1994)) contains much material of interest, for example the analysis of life-cycle environmental management at Volkswagen Audi. Also of interest is the introductory examination of fundamental economic concerns in Turner et al. (1994), with particular reference to the issue of sustainability.

Garvin, D. A. (1992), *Operations Strategy: Text and Cases*, Prentice Hall, New York.

Harrison, M. R. (1993), *Operations Management Strategy*, Pitman, London.

Hayes, R. H. and Wheelwright, S. C. (1984), *Restoring our Competitive Edge*, Wiley, New York.

Hill, T. (1985), *Manufacturing Strategy*, Macmillan, London.

Lovelock, C. H. (1992), *Managing Services*, Prentice Hall, New York.

Slack, N., Chambers, S., Harland, C., Harrison, A. and Johnston, R. (1995), *Operations Management*, Pitman, London.

Turner, R. K., Pearce, D. and Bateman, I. (1994), *Environmental Economics*, Harvester Wheatsheaf, New York.

Welford, R. (1994), *Cases in Environmental Management and Business Strategy*, Pitman, London.

Welford, R. and Gouldson, A. (1993), *Environmental Management and Business Strategy*, Pitman, London.

# Terms Used in Operations Management

In describing operations we have to be clear how certain key words are used. In the following sections we set out some of the central terms and explain why these are important in describing operational situations.

## Process

The idea of an operational process is of particular importance. A process is a set of tasks or activities which transform some input into a desired output. The output is intended to satisfy the needs of a customer.

## Customer

A customer may be external to our organisation or our operating unit (which is the everyday use of the word) or may be internal to our organisation. A customer has requirements which we have agreed to meet.

This simple idea is somewhat complicated when the customer has an active role in the operational process, for instance in a self-service supermarket. In the extreme case an internal customer may be part of a broader process, for instance in a production line the next person down the line from ourselves is in some sense our customer. This latter case is somewhat confusing (though important in discussions of Total Quality Management) and should be treated with care.

## Transformations

The main transformations with which we shall be concerned are those involving materials, people and information.

## Material Transformations

These may involve cutting, shaping, chemical reactions, assembling, moving, inspecting and so forth. For simplicity we refer to them in total as factory operations. They involve a variety of inputs (materials, people, technology, knowledge, capital, etc.) but the outputs are essentially material in form. An interesting variant on this theme is storage and warehousing which is essentially about the location, security and availability of materials. We will include this under 'factory' operations although it is a key feature of the retail trade.

## People Transformations

Where the objective is in some way to transform the customer we refer to this as service operations. This may possibly involve physical change, say in a hospital, or the moving of a customer to a new location (transport) or some change in their knowledge or behaviour. The key feature is, however, the participation of the customer and their personal transformation.

## Information Transformations

In modern organisations, much attention is given to data and information management through the use of computers and communication links. Such activity is not only central in facilitating factory and service operations it must also be considered as a legitimate transformational activity in providing something of value to internal and external customers. Thus we refer to office operations to cover information transformations (data capture, processing, communicating and presenting).

## Manufacturing and Service Industries

It would be quite wrong to assume that service industries are identical with service operations and 'people' transformations. Both manufacturing and service organisations (in the private and public sectors) use all three types of transformation to a greater or lesser degree. Naturally a manufacturing company will give great attention to its material transformations but its competitive edge may be provided by improved service or better use of information technology.

This rather obvious point appears to have escaped some of the early writers on production operations but is a central feature of modern thinking in this area. To be knowledgeable about Operations Management you must be concerned with all three types of transformation and the particular problems of their management.

## Infrastucture

Though processes are at the centre of our discussion, we must not ignore the infrastructure that supports the operation of these processes. By infrastructure we mean the activities in the organisation which are not actually part of the processes under consideration but which contribute to their success.

If we consider a travel agency and concentrate our attention on the process of serving the external customer then it is immediately obvious that the following, amongst other things, are important:

- a physical environment (building) which is properly maintained
- staff support in the form of training, welfare services, wage payment and so forth
- technology to facilitate holiday enquiries and bookings
- financial services.

Similarly if we consider a manufacturing company, actual production will be supported by design, engineering, maintenance, cost accounting and many other functions.

Thus, the infrastructure supports the processes we are concerned with. Of course we may adopt a different focus and concern ourselves with these supporting processes themselves. Thus we examine training as a service operation with an internal customer base which includes production workers. This change of focus can be very beneficial when analysing operations provided we make it clear at every stage which set of activities we are referring to as the process (our central concern at that time) and which are the infrastructure which supports the process.

### Environment

We adopt here the normal terminology of systems theory in which the environment is everything outside the system under consideration but relevant to its performance. There may be some confusion when environmental (or 'green') issues are being discussed (as in Chapter 12) but it is useful to have a general definition including a wider set of influences.

Classifications of the environment are common in books on strategic management where environmental analysis is a major concern. Typical are considerations of the economic, social, institutional and technological environments. These are often linked to consumer and raw material markets, though the labour market must not be omitted from consideration. Social considerations (including demography and regional working culture) obviously affect the availability and characteristics of production and service staff as well as managers.

Some books refer to the internal environment, in much the same way as we have used the more positively supporting term 'infrastructure'. To complicate matters further, some social scientists use the word infrastructure to refer to parts of the environment (for example, roads). Therefore you can see why it is important that we define how the terms are to be used in Operations Management. In short:

- processes transform and must be operationally managed
- the infrastructure supports and must be managed as part of the same organisation
- the environment provides a context, including external customers, and though we may exert influence it is outside our control.

## LIST OF ACRONYMS AND ABBREVIATIONS

| | |
|---|---|
| ACWP | Actual Cost of Work Performed |
| AMT | Advanced Manufacturing Technology |
| AoA | Activity on Arrow (diagram in project management) |
| BCWP | Budgeted Cost of Work Performed |
| BCWS | Budgeted Cost of Work Scheduled |
| BEP | Break Even Point |
| BOM | Bill of Materials |
| BPR | Business Process Re-engineering |
| BS EN ISO 9000 | International standard for quality management systems |
| CAD | Computer Aided Design |

| | |
|---|---|
| CADCAM | Computer Aided Design and Manufacturing |
| CAM | Computer Aided Manufacture |
| CIB | Computer Integrated Business |
| CIM | Computer Integrated Manufacturing |
| CNC | Computer Numerically Controlled |
| CPA | Critical Path Analysis |
| CPI | Cost Performance Index |
| DCF | Discounted Cash Flow |
| EBQ | Economic Batch Quantity (in stock control) |
| EDI | Electronic Data Interchange |
| EET | Earliest Event Time (in project management) |
| EF | Earliest Finish (in project management) |
| ES | Earliest Start (in project management) |
| FC | Fixed Cost |
| FCFS | First Come First Served (in queuing theory) |
| FMS | Flexible Manufacturing Systems |
| HRM | Human Resource Management |
| IT | Information Technology |
| JIT | Just in Time (management) |
| LET | Latest Event Time (in project management) |
| LF | Latest Finish (in project management) |
| LP | Linear Programming |
| LS | Latest Start (in project management) |
| MPS | Master Production Schedule |
| MRP | Material Requirements Planning |
| MRPII | Manufacturing Resource Planning |
| NPV | Net Present Value |
| OC | Operating Characteristic (curve) |
| O&M | Organisation and Methods |
| OPT | Optimised Production Technology |
| OR | Operational Research |
| PERT | Programme Evaluation and Review |
| QFD | Quality Function Deployment |
| ROL | Reorder Level (in stock control) |
| SERVQUAL | Service Quality (model) |
| SKU | Stock Keeping Unit |
| SPC | Statistical Process Control |
| SPI | Schedule Performance Index |
| SPU | Standard Production Unit |
| SQC | Statistical Quality Control |
| SSC | Scientific Stock Control |
| TPM | Total Productive Maintenance |
| TQM | Total Quality Management |
| VC | Variable Cost |
| WBS | Work Breakdown Structure |

# INDEX